Power Relations and Judicial Corruption in the Islamic Republic of Iran

This book is part of the Peter Lang Regional Studies list.
Every volume is peer reviewed and meets
the highest quality standards for content and production.

PETER LANG
New York • Bern • Berlin
Brussels • Vienna • Oxford • Warsaw

Mehdi Khosravi

Power Relations and Judicial Corruption in the Islamic Republic of Iran

PETER LANG
New York • Bern • Berlin
Brussels • Vienna • Oxford • Warsaw

Library of Congress Cataloging-in-Publication Data

Names: Khosravi, Mehdi, author.
Title: Power relations and judicial corruption in the Islamic Republic of Iran / Mehdi Khosravi.
Description: New York: Peter Lang, 2021.
Includes bibliographical references.
Identifiers: LCCN 2020038774 (print) | LCCN 2020038775 (ebook)
ISBN 978-1-4331-8211-2 (hardback) | ISBN 978-1-4331-8210-5 (ebook pdf)
ISBN 978-1-4331-7338-7 (epub) | ISBN 978-1-4331-7339-4 (mobi)
Subjects: LCSH: Judicial corruption—Iran. | Criminal justice, Administration of—Iran—History. | Corruption--Law and legislation—Iran. | Rule of law—Iran. | Criminal justice, Administration of (Islamic law) | Judges (Islamic law)
Classification: LCC KMH4513 .K46 2021 (print) | LCC KMH4513 (ebook) | DDC 345.55/0124—dc23
LC record available at https://lccn.loc.gov/2020038774
LC ebook record available at https://lccn.loc.gov/2020038775
DOI 10.3726/b17700

Bibliographic information published by **Die Deutsche Nationalbibliothek**.
Die Deutsche Nationalbibliothek lists this publication in the "Deutsche Nationalbibliografie"; detailed bibliographic data are available on the Internet at http://dnb.d-nb.de/.

80 Broad Street, 5th floor, New York, NY 10004
www.peterlang.com

to Navid Fazel

Contents

1	Introduction	1
	Overview	1
	Introduction to This Study	3
	Introduction to an Independent Judiciary	4
	Judicial Corruption Is a Social Evil	5
	Corruption in the Judiciary in Iran Today	6
	About This Research	7
2	Literature Review	15
	Understanding Corruption	16
	Reducing Corruption and Its Obstacles	29
	Literature Review – Judicial Corruption	33
	Reviewing Previous Research on Judicial Corruption in Iran	50
3	The Complex Structure of the Iranian Judiciary	61
	History of the Criminal Justice System in Iran	61
	The Current Structure of the Judiciary in the Islamic Republic of Iran	72
	Charts	75

Definition of the Judge and the Judiciary 76
Examining Anti-Corruption Laws in Iran 79
The Role of the Judiciary in the Massacre of Political Prisoners in the 1980s 81
The Evil Judges 82
The Committee of Inquiry of the Islamic Consultative Assembly 83

4 Research Methodology 87
Research Approach 87
Data Collection 89
Awareness and Ethical Framework 92
Coding and Content Analysis 94

5 Data Analysis 97
Introducing Interviewees 97
Data Analysis 99

6 Comparison and Assessment 141
Shortcomings and Advantages of Comparative Approaches 141
Comparative Approach (Iran, England and Wales) 142
Comparison of Iran and China's Judiciary Systems 143
Assessing the Judiciary Based on International Transparency Standards 146

7 Conclusion 153
Summary of Findings 153
Examination of Corruption in the Judicial System 155
Future: Improving Conditions in the Judiciary 170

Appendix 177
Bibliography 243

Figures

Figure 2.1	Representation of the concepts from Routine Activity Theory	26
Figure 2.2	Fraud triangle	28
Figure 3.1	Structure of the Iranian judiciary	75
Figure 3.2	Structure of the Iranian judiciary (Provincial courts)	76
Figure 5.1	Text Cloud	138
Figure 6.1	The rule of law index (Iran and China)	145
Figure 7.1	Formation and increase in judicial corruption in Iran	166
Figure 7.2	Reproduction of judicial corruption in Iran	168
Figure 7.3	The spread of corruption from the judiciary to other sectors	171

1 Introduction

Overview

White collar crimes such as corruption and fraud could have severe consequences in society. Damage from the international financial crisis in 2008–2009 was over eleven thousand billion dollars, which has had an adverse effect on the world's economy. One of the main factors of this crisis was fraud and corruption in the process of loan applications in the United States (Button & Tunely, 2016). What is astonishing is that even in developed countries, necessary attention is not given to this issue. Most politicians do not dedicate enough budget and facilities to this very sensitive matter. For instance in the UK, politicians attempt to allocate more police resources to other crimes such as knife crime, and not as much to fraud or corruption (Levi, 2003).

In recent years, though Iranian citizens and the media hold more debates about corruption among executives and senior authorities in power, they have not spent much time on its outcomes or the roots of corruption.

It is worth noting that corruption comes in different forms, with consequences varying from case to case. Some do more harm and damage compared to other forms. For example, corruption in banks can cause the destruction of the economy, whereas corruption affecting environments could carry more adverse social consequences (Klitgaard, 1998). Negative consequences of corruption on society are far beyond the exchanging of a sum of money to do an illegal job, or the seizing of money or goods in a manner unlawful by a member of the community. As the findings of this study indicate, corruption has calamitous consequences on society, which can endanger society's security in the long run. It can infringe on human rights, cause a declining economy, and devalue the rule of law and overall interfere with the healthy progress of society, which could result in poverty. Quoting from James Wolfensohn, World Bank CEO, corruption is the most significant barrier in society:

> We need to deal with the cancer of corruption. In country after country, it is the people who are demanding action on this issue. They know that corruption diverts resources from the poor to the rich, increases the cost of running businesses, distorts public expenditures, and deters foreign investors. They also know that it erodes the constituency for aid programs and humanitarian relief. And we all know that it is a major barrier to sound and equitable development. (WB Group, 1996)

Any type of corruption can be dangerous; however, based on this specific study, the most detrimental form is judicial corruption. This could affect society in a range of different ways, leading to a gradual ruination of a country.

The aim of this study is to examine the extent of judicial corruption in Iran. Living in the UK for a long while facilitated me with opportunities to embark on making comparisons between Britain and other countries. Great Britain was the birthplace of industrial revolution; hence, it has played a significant role in shaping the modern world. While studying and comparing the two countries, on average the UK possesses a healthy judicial system, free from corruption, or at least with minimal corruption. This judicial system has led to the formation of a robust democracy with little aggression while the power from the monarchy has slowly shifted to government departments.

This difference is more tangible when during the Constitutional Revolution of Iran (1905–1911), activists asked the Shah to build a Judiciary, whereas in the UK, over the course of many years, the system of justice had itself become one of the effective tools to create political accountability.

Comparison between the judicial system of Iran and the English courts has furnished me with a better understanding of the failings and strengths of the judiciary. For example, at first it was strange for me to comprehend why barristers do not shake hands with one another in the UK.

Why there is a need for analysing judicial corruption in Iran? There exists a wide and long-standing system of judiciary in the Islamic Republic of Iran. We must first understand and familiarise ourselves with this judiciary system to recognise corruption within it.

The constitution of the Islamic Republic of Iran has fundamental faults which do not recognise individual rights and freedoms. On the other hand, the corrupt judicial system cannot and does not have the capacity to defend such fundamental rights. In most cases citizens are unable to lodge claims for contravention of their rights in judicial courts. This has a noticeable effect on every single citizen's life in Iran.

The most influential tool in every society to combat corruption is the judicial system. Now if the judicial system itself is affected by a high level of corruption, then there will no longer be an effective system in place to fight corruption in society. Ultimately, corruption could spread like an epidemic throughout the government. In other words, the best way to fight corruption in government would be to have an independent judiciary, but if the judiciary itself is diagnosed with such corruption, not only would the judiciary be in a weaker position to fight corruption, it can become a source to promote and reproduce corruption in both society and the government.

The importance of understanding judicial corruption is appreciated more when the judiciary (as the most significant factor in anti-corruption campaigns) is turned into an agent that reproduces corruption. In effect, instead of being a tool for resolving major problems in society, it places itself at the heart of problems, and eventually turns into a solid barricade for combating corruption.

Consequences of corruption in any judicial system are far more than the exchanging of bribes or enhancing the personal interests of judges or any officer, and it will be demonstrated in this study that such corruption will intervene in most aspects of society.

Introduction to This Study

A few matters worth considering about the judicial system in the Islamic Republic of Iran:

The most important characteristic of any judicial system is its impartiality and independence.

In liberal democracies, the definition of judiciary is accompanied with impartiality and a transparent system. However, this has become complicated in the Constitution of the Islamic Republic of Iran, and the judiciary is no longer impartial or transparent. For demonstration purposes see below:

1. The Human Rights Committee of the United Nations has officially announced Iran's judicial system to have fundamental problems from the roots (Al Hussein, 2016, September 13).
2. According to what is reported by the media, the Intelligence Deputy of the judiciary in Iran has been arrested for a series of allegations involving participation in bribery, embezzlement, unlawful possession of properties and extortion (Saham, 2015, August 22). What is astonishing is that one of the most significant roles of this person is to cooperate with the country's law enforcement to fight against corruption in the judicial system.

Introduction to an Independent Judiciary

We should first establish a definition for a transparent and corruption free judiciary before elaborating further on other aspects of the judicial system in the Islamic Republic of Iran. A non-corrupt judiciary should have the following characteristics:

1. Independence with having checks and balances in place.
2. Immunity of judges and independence from any external or internal influences.
3. Impartiality and non-interference of personal opinions or ideologies.
4. Equality of all citizens in the judicial system.
5. Competency of judges in terms of legal knowledge.
6. Having independent disciplinary courts and a regulatory body in place, which can oversee transparency and counter corruption.
7. The judges being answerable to the disciplinary courts.
8. Transparency in judges' actions and the judiciary; publishing annual budgets; allocation of decent salaries for the judges; and publication of all verdicts and judgement of judges in the public domain.
9. It should also be mandatory for all judges to publish their reasonings in reaching decisions and determinations.

The United Nations General Assembly Resolution 40/32 of 29th of November 1985 identifies the independent judiciary in accordance with a need for justice as the prerequisite for achieving international co-operation in promoting and encouraging respect for human rights and fundamental freedoms without any discrimination. The resolution explicitly urges the states to respect and observe the independence of the judiciary. Article 2 of the resolution also clearly emphasises the cardinal importance of the independence of the courts and explains this trait of the judicial system as the following:

The judiciary shall decide matters before them impartially, on the basis of facts and in accordance with the law, without any restrictions, improper influences, inducements, pressures, threats, or interferences – direct or indirect – from any quarter or for any reason.

From what can be gathered, impartiality and independence are two very important features in a judicial system. As you will see further in this study the absence of such features has led to serious judicial corruption.

Judicial Corruption Is a Social Evil

In Chapter 2, we will be discussing the relationship of trust between the public sphere and the courts. If citizens respect the courts, they still respect the law even if other branches of government fail. However, if citizens lose their respect for the courts, then law and order will vanish. It is obvious that judges' independence has an immense degree of importance in shaping and creating order in society. This means whenever citizens have any civil or criminal claims they are reassured of a just and impartial system to uphold justice.

La Porta, De Silanes, Eleches and Sheleifer (2004) analysed judicial independence with political freedoms and the development of a country. They analysed diverse information between seventy countries in the world, and have concluded that judicial independence directly impacts people's enjoyment of fundamental freedoms on the one hand, and economic growth on the other.

The independent judiciary is the essential factor for good governance. If one evaluates good governance, as Kaufmann and Kraay put it, one will see that the rule of law and control of corruption are the two principles of good governance. Hence, good governance and an independent judiciary are interwoven. The rule of law can not only prevent corruption, it also promotes good governance in the country. In effect, judicial corruption is directly and deeply interlinked with these two features:

1. The effect of judicial corruption on the rule of law:

Judicial corruption will cause an undermining of the rule of law in any society. The danger of this fact is very extensive. According to Knaul, a United Nations reporter on this issue, corruption in the judiciary, be it limited or extensive, will make the rule of law questionable and the inability of the judicial system to protect human rights will be manifest (Knaul, 2012).

2. Linkage between judicial corruption and controlling other corruptions:

In any country, the practical and most effective tool to control and combat corruption would be the judicial system (Rose-Ackerman, 1999). When there is widespread corruption throughout the judiciary, there will be no system to prevent occurrence of other types of corruption.

Therefore, corruption in the judiciary damages the rule of law and by doing so undermines good governance. Other aspects of good governance will also be affected by judicial corruption, which will be elaborated on later in this study.

It must also be noted that the rule of law cannot be formed properly without a transparent, impartial, and reasonable judicial system. Indeed, the rule of law is directly associated with freedom and plays a substantial role in shaping justice as fairness. In the absence of the rule of law, no freedom can be guaranteed; hence, there will be potential dangers and threats to such freedoms.

Corruption in the Judiciary in Iran Today

After the 1979 Islamic Revolution in Iran, a new judiciary system was installed to carry out the justice duties; however as it appears, there has not been much success in this goal. One will note the following:

1. No rule of law exists in place. A study carried out in relation to the rule of law in Iran has shown there is no solid rule of law with no fair and independent justice system (Cress, Kent & Nayyeri, 2014).
2. Corruption in the economy and in official organisations have disabled practical management of the country. One of the main duties of any judicial system is to fight corruption among various official organs. It must be said the judiciary in Iran has been unsuccessful in achieving this purpose. Iran's ranking in Transparency International's annual corruption report is 136 among 180 countries surveyed (Transparency International, 2014)

3. The most imperative tool to contend with corruption in every country is to have an independent and crystal-clear judiciary. Not only is such a system non-existent in Iran, the extensive corruption in the country has impaired the rule of law as well.

About This Research

Questions about the Research

This study evidently poses a question as to the widespread judicial corruption in the Islamic Republic of Iran and asks what factors have been engaged in the creation of such corruptions, and furthermore, what is their impact on the routine running of society. This study investigates the root causes of such corruption and how it can be curtailed. For this purpose, the role of bribery and services gained in return will be investigated. Some light will also be shed on how the justice system is diluted by senior judicial officials, both financially and non-financially. In addition, the relationship between judicial corruption and the lack of independence in the judiciary will also be investigated.

The following questions will be taken into consideration:

- What is the extent of judicial corruption in Iran today?
- What types of corruption exist in the said judiciary?
- Is there any alternative to counter such corruption?
- How is this corruption cultivated and developed? And is the judiciary in Iran a source of nurture for such corruption?
- How far has this corruption had an impact on society?
- Does this corruption cause further corruption in any other parts of society?
- What are the possible remedies?

The Process of Study

The following methods are used for the purposes of this study:

1. Firstly, the definition of corruption is explained in general terms, and secondly, the definition of judicial corruption will be looked at in depth.
2. The rule law and norms concerning judicial corruption in the Islamic Republic of Iran are reviewed.

3. The history of the judiciary in Iran today and the underlying rules for fighting corruption are analysed.
4. The current situation of the judiciary in Iran is evaluated against international standards.
5. Finally, the impact of such corruption on Iranian society and its impact on a wider spectrum will be examined.

The Need for This Study

The author has been unable to find any academic research in Persian or in English about judicial corruption in the Islamic Republic of Iran.

Prohibition on the freedom of information, absence of accurate and credible sources, and the apprehension of witnesses to carry out such research in the academic world are contributory factors in undertaking this study. The following points make the purpose of this study more important:

1. Awareness of the public on the consequences of such corruptions, which could have a direct influence on reducing the level of corruption.
2. It should not be ignored that the impacts of corruption and its consequences mostly affect the poorest and most vulnerable parts of society.
3. Access to fair trial is the basic human right of every citizen in a democratic society. However, a corrupt judicial system will inevitably cause infringement of such human rights, and will directly affect the rule of law in its radius. This will cause rampant corruption to spread through different parts of the government.
4. Corruption in the long term reduces political legitimacy, undermines economic productivity, and creates inequality in society.
5. Various studies have shown that when corruption is so widespread in an organised manner in a country, making efforts to reconstruct the economy or the administrative system will not produce effective results. The liberation of an economy will only cause the formation and development of corruption, mostly in sectors where legislative activities have previously taken place.
6. In a study carried out by Feld and Voigt (2002), it is concluded that economic development and an independent judicial system are interwoven. This raises the question; can we argue that judicial corruption itself is defined by a lack of independence? Hence it is necessary to have a full scientific review of corruption in the judiciary in Iran.

This research will also have the following positive outcomes:

1. In case of democratic changes in Iran, this research will facilitate recognising injustice or recovery from it, and reach a robust national reconciliation.
2. The results of this research will lay down the necessary system of an independent and just system with transparency in the future.
3. This corrupt judicial system could be noted as an important barrier for forming a democratic regime in Iran. Hence becoming familiar with such corruption could be considered as the first step to achieve democracy.
4. Judicial corruption will cause loss of faith and trust from investors, which will encompass a lack of public trust and a sense of belonging of citizens to society. Identifying such corruptions and successive efforts to reduce corruption will eventually lead to a healthier and more prosperous economy, and more benefits for the citizens.
5. There are millions of pending legal cases in Iranian courts, which indicates that a large population of the citizens have daily involvement with judicial corruption.

Terminologies

The World Bank defines corruption as the abuse of public office for private gain (World Bank, 1997). Transparency International stipulates corruption is defined as the misuse of power based on trust endowed on a person. This corruption may not only be of a financial nature, but also in return for other gains or to receive higher rankings in politics or job promotions. Hence judicial corruption is of a type that any person could damage the independence of the courts in whatever shape or form (Transparency International, 2020).

The following definition for judicial corruption is concluded by this study:

It is a judicial corruption whenever a person involved in any parts of a judicial system misuses his entrusted powers or discretions and undermines the independence of courts (either by actions or inactions) to:

1. Secure private gain for himself.
2. To achieve a sense of group interest.

This corruption can happen at any of the following stages:

1. Investigation process

2. Process of individual cases
3. Courts' judgements and determinations
4. Enforcing judgements
5. The process of Appeal.

The reason for dedicating time to elaborate on a specific definition of judicial corruption is because it differs from any other corruptions taking place in any other sectors of the government, because: (i) due to the principle of separation of powers, efforts have always been made to have an independent system of judiciary; and (ii) the judges by default have a wide discretion.

The Hypothesis

With reference to the findings mentioned earlier, the existence of judicial corruption in the Islamic Republic of Iran will be hypothesised as follows:

1. Corruption does exist in Iran's judiciary and to a large extent.
2. Impartiality of the courts becomes questionable when there is high inclination to payments of bribes.
3. Due to the prevalence of judicial corruption in Iran, there is a general belief that courts' decisions or determinations can be bought.
4. Low salaries can be a good reason for the continuous recurrence of corruption; however, it is not the main factor for such corruptions to exist. On the contrary, what strengthens corruption is mentalities that do not consider such corruptions as immoral, and the lack of credibility this gives the judicial system, and the nonexistence of independent disciplinary court and regulatory bodies. Also lack of efficient laws to fight corruption have all been contributory factors for its propagation.
5. Lack of transparency in selecting judges as well as the process of sentencing and issuing judgements have provided a good platform for the spread of this corruption.
   There is a closed circle ruling the Iranian judicial system, and it will not permit people who are not corrupt to receive any promotion.
6. There is no independent disciplinary court with transparency to combat corruption in the judiciary in Iran.
7. This corruption causes the reproduction of corruption in other parts of government.

Methodology

This research study is interdisciplinary, and legal and sociological aspects in relation to corruption are assessed. Despite clear and evident existence of judicial corruption in Iran, this subject is still one of the areas that carries perplexity.

Conducting a survey in Iran is an almost impossible chore; hence, a quantitative approach will not be as practical as a qualitative approach.

For the purposes of information gathering, a semi structured interview has been adopted. In undertaking qualitative approaches, there exists various ways, for which a qualitative content analysis has been taken.

Data Collection

To acquire primary data, several human rights lawyers in Iran, whose names should not be released for security reasons, have approached some of their clients, and asked them for permission to be interviewed. Undertaking such deep interviews with these citizens has provided the researcher with the opportunity to evaluate corruption in the judiciary in Iran. Also, some Iranians living abroad have made it possible to have access to their personal experiences with the corrupt judicial system in Iran.

It is worth noting that every one of these individuals has expressed diverse points of view about their dealings with the judicial system. Overall, this will assist us in having a better comprehension of what exactly goes on in this system and in a more tangible manner.

A Qualitative Approach

In carrying out the research, a qualitative approach has been followed, which has predominantly been based on interviewing ordinary citizens.

1. Due to security reasons for those individuals residing in Iran, none of the citizens' voices have been recorded or any video clips made. The individual names are also anonymous. However extensive notes have been made to satisfy the purpose of this research.
2. It is important to note some of the individuals have been selected particularly for this purpose. This means, these witnesses have been carefully selected based on their very close dealings and experiences with the judiciary in Iran. This approach is called Purposive Sampling.

3. Every witness, or interviewee, is from a different city in Iran with their own individual case.

A Comparative Study

Comparative studies in criminology is the basis for learning from others and their policies; in fact, it is learning about other countries' faults and success stories.

Therefore, the judicial system in the Islamic Republic of Iran will be compared to the system in Britain as well as some developing countries' judicial systems, such as China, through this study. This will enable us to highlight existing flaws in those systems in order to identify failings in the Iranian judicial system.

What is necessary to understand is the definition of the rule of law to recognise judicial corruption. Without a doubt, English Law has created a platform for the proliferation of the rule of law. The English judicial system is considered to be transparent; hence, efforts are made to have a comparative study between existing corruption in the English and Iranian judicial systems. This will better introduce the phenomenon of corruption in both systems to the reader.

Research Ethics

This study will avoid any pre judgemental attitudes in the development of the arguments. Though corruption in the judicial system in the Islamic Republic of Iran is quite evident, strict endeavours are made to have a neutral and unbiased perspective throughout this study.

References

Al Hussein, Z. (2016, September 13). *Ravand Ghazei dar iran moshkel darad.* [Iranian judiciary has fundamental problems], Retrieved from: http://www.radiofarda.com/a/b5_human_rights_council_open_geneva_zeid_raad_alhussein_iran/27984270.html

Button, M., & Tunley, M. (2016). *Criminal Activity in the Financial Sector*, The Security Handbook Volume 2. Can be retrieved at: https://goo.gl/NAcFt8

Cress, R., Kent, C., & Nayyeri, M. (2014). *Rule of Law in Iran. University of Essex.* Retrieved from: https://www.essex.ac.uk/hri/documents/rule-of-law-in-iran.pdf (accessed 31-03-2016).

Feld, P., & Voigt, S. (2002). *Economic Growth and Judicial Independence: Cross Country Evidence Using a New Set of Indicators.* Germany: University of Marburg.

Kaufmann, D., Aart, K., & Lobatón, P. (1999). *Governance Matters.* World Bank. Retrieved from: https://goo.gl/h3Fs7V; (accessed 31-03-2016).

Kaufmann, D., & Kraay, A. (2008). *Governance Indicators: Where Are We, Where Should We Be Going?* Oxford University Press. doi:10.1093/wbro/lkm012.

Kaufmann, D., Kraay, A., & Mastruzzi, M. (2006). *Measuring Corruption: Myths and Realities.* Washington, DC: The World Bank.

Kaufmann, D., Kraay, A., & Mastruzzi, M. (2009). *Governance Matters VIII.* Washington, DC: The World Bank Development Research Group Macroeconomics and Growth Team.

Kaufmann, D., Kraay, A., & Mastruzzi, M. (2010). *The Worldwide Governance Indicators: Methodology and Analytical Issues.* World Bank Policy Research Working Paper No. 5430.

Kaufmann, D., Kraay, A., & Zoido-Lobato′n, P. (1999). *Aggregating Governance Indicators.* Policy Research Working Paper 2195. Washington, DC: World Bank.

Klitgaard, R. (1998). Combating corruption. *UN Chronicle, 35*(1), 90.

Knaul, G. (2012). Report from *The United Nations Special Rapporteur on the independence of judges and lawyers.* Retrieved from: available at: http://www.ohchr.org/EN/NewsEvents/Pages/DisplayNews.aspx?NewsID=12692&LangID=E#sthash.198TkyID.dpuf (accessed 31-03-2016).

La Porta, R., De Silanes, L., Eleches, C., & Sheleifer, A. (2004). Judicial checks and balances. *Journal of Political Economy, 112*(2): 445–470. https://doi.org/10.1086/381480.

Levi, M. (2003). The Roskill Fraud Commission revisited: An assessment. *Journal of Financial Crime, 1*, 38.

Rose-Ackerman, S. (1999). *Corruption and Government: Causes, Consequences and Reform.* Cambridge, UK: Cambridge University Press.

Saham, N. (2015, August 22). *Bazdasht moaven ghoveh ghazeio for rape* [Deputy of Iranian judiciary was arrested for rape]. AlArabia. Dubai. Retrieved from http://goo.gl/PpUuVo

Transparency International. (2014). *Corruption Perceptions Index 2014.* Retrieved March 1, 2017, from https://www.transparency.org/cpi2014/results

World Bank. (1997). *Combat Corruption.* Poverty Reduction and Economic Management, Helping Countries, Washington, DC.

2

Literature Review

Judicial corruption is like an iceberg. Since people for several reasons, such as threat to their lives, do not report it, the real volume of this phenomenon is not revealed. This is the situation in certain developing countries where a lack of democracy, transparency, the absence of free media, and the clientelist state prevent the disclosure of corruption. The 2019 Global Corruption Barometer by Transparency International reported that in some jurisdictions, 8% of the people who had been in contact with the courts reported that they had paid a bribe to receive a positive judgement.

In this chapter, first a general introduction to existing literature on corruption, the rule of law and good governance will be discussed in order to highlight possible areas of contribution for this thesis. Then, theories frequently used for describing corruption will be presented.

It must be noted that corruption in the judicial system is a complex phenomenon with multiple aspects affecting it. To identify them, this subject must be viewed from various angles. For this reason, the section relating to reviewed research is longer than is common, and necessary efforts have been made to analyse the subject of judicial corruption from different perspectives.

It is also noteworthy that the identification and scientific analysis of white-collar crime is not an easy task. Newburn (2013) argues that white-collar crimes have not received enough attention for the following reasons: (i) media attention to these crimes is different from conventional crime, because these crimes are "less prominent" and there is less space devoted to white-collar crimes; (ii) due to the nature of this type of crime, conducting scientific research and data collection in this field is not so easy, and usually criminologists in this field do not have the expertise (i.e. understanding of the financial sector). Furthermore, Newburn refers to another body of research, and argues that the commodification of knowledge has reduced the willingness of criminology to challenge authority (Tombs and Whyte, 2007, cited by Newburn, 2013).

Judicial corruption is one of the most complex criminal phenomena. To study this invisible crime, one requires special expertise, and must be familiar with the legal culture of the society as well as have an understanding of corruption as delinquency.

In this chapter, there will be a general analysis of corruption and attention will then be devoted to judicial corruption, judicial independence, the rule of law, and good governance.

Understanding Corruption

Definition of Corruption

There exists no agreed-upon definition for corruption (Hough, 2013; Brook et al., 2013, Ibrahim, 1997). For this reason, we must first try to define it in order to investigate its causes and determine how it must be cured. Since corruption in Iran today is influenced by Islamic ideas and interpretations, the definition of this invisible social criminal phenomena also requires specific investigation and analysis.

Considering that corruption is normally motivated by greed, and is often associated with bribery, it must be defined economically. From this perspective, corruption is defined as "a situation where the benefit (to a corrupt agent) of acting against the expectation of a principal, outweighs the cost, or where public goods, services or office is sold for personal gain". *Political Science* describes corruption "as a symptom of more deeply rooted problems in the society's structure related in particular to the means of attaining and maintaining power and the weak or non-existent safeguards against its abuse". Legal scholars define corruption as "the deviation (for private gains) from binding rules, the arbitrary exercise of discretionary powers and the illegitimate use of public resources". And finally, sociologists tend to define corruption as "a social relationship represented in the violation of socially accepted norms of duty and welfare" (Shihata, 1997, pp. 453–458).

In general, corruption is a distortion in behaviour. Wilson (1968) described corruption as a phenomenon where someone, to achieve personal gain, demonstrates behaviour that we don't expect (considering his job title). The World Bank Group analyses the disproportionate impact of corruption on the poor and most vulnerable, identifying increasing costs and reducing access to services, including health, education, and justice. Think, for example, of the effect of counterfeit drugs or vaccines on the health outcomes of children and the life-long impacts that may have on them (WB Group, 2019). The World Bank's General Counsel has long described corruption as:

> Corruption occurs when a function, whether official or private, requires the allocation of benefits or the provision of a good or service . . . In all cases, a position of trust is being exploited to realize private gains beyond what the position holder is entitled to. Attempts to influence the position holder, through the payment of bribes or an exchange of benefits or favours, in order to receive a special gain or treatment not available to others is also a form of corruption, even if the gain involved is not illicit under applicable law. (1997, p. 20)

Corruption can be categorised in accordance with its nature in various contexts. The following provides a short typology of corruption.

The Agency Model of Corruption

Rose-Ackerman identifies this social evil as the "misuse of power for private gains" (1999, p. 26). She further emphasises that the meaning of misuse must be carefully defined (2004). Some researchers have focused on the relationship between the principal, agent, and client. For example, from Klitgaard:

> Corruption may be represented as following a formula: C = M + D – A. Corruption equals monopoly plus discretion minus accountability. Whether the activity is public, private, or non-profit, one will tend to find corruption when an organization or person has monopoly power over a good or service, has the discretion to decide who will receive it and how much that person will get, and is not accountable. (1998, p.4)

In the above scenario, corruption occurs when the agent misuses or abuses the trust of the principal for his own private gain. The situation for the formation of corruption occurs as long as the agent holds certain discretion.

In this theory, corruption occurs when the delinquent has discretionary power. There must be some kind of economic rent linked to this discretionary power, and the delinquent must believe it is unlikely for law enforcement to persecute him (low level of deterrent).

Institutional Corruption

Traditionally, corruption is defined as the misuse of power for private gains, especially when this behaviour violates "the rules of the game" (Situngkir, 2001, p.5). This traditional view approaches corruption on the micro level and sees corruption as an act done by an individual, and tries to analyse it on the level of individuals. The traditional definition of corruption is focused on breaking the common norms or rule of the game. As Huntington (1989) claims: when an official attempts to achieve private gain, and his behaviour deviates from common norms, that behaviour is corruption. However, sometimes corruption happens at the macro level. Obviously, this kind of corruption is far more complex from micro-level corruption. Sometimes, one cannot identify a delinquent who receives or pays bribes. However, that corruption still harms society. Take the example of judges who form their judgement based on their ideology – in this case nobody pays or receives any bribe; however, we can still identify corruption in that judicial system. Simply, traditional concepts of corruption cannot explain this kind of corruption.

For Thompson, institutional corruption undermines the rules of a legitimate process and takes place when "an institution or its officials receive a benefit that is directly useful to performing an institutional purpose, and systematically provides a service to the benefactor under conditions that tend to undermine procedures that support the primary purposes of the institution." (2013, p. 3)

In his seminal article entitled "Institutional Corruption", Lessing traces the causes of this category of corruption in the systemic structure of societies:

> Institutional corruption manifests where there is a systematic and strategic influence which is legal, or even currently ethical, that undermines the institution's effectiveness by diverting it from its purpose, weakening its ability to achieve its purpose, including, to the extent relevant to its purpose, weakening either the public trust in the institution or the institution's inherent trustworthiness. (2013, p. 2)

In order to understand institutional corruption, attention must be paid to the meaning of institution. Scott describes institutions as established practices, and defines them as "cognitive, normative, and regulative structures and activities that provide stability and meaning to social behaviour" (1995, p. 33). Therefore, individuals reproduce institutions (by repeating them).

An individual may follow institutional codes involuntarily and continually use those codes. If a corrupt practice becomes a code, then decent souls can harm society by repeating that code, and a bad thing can come from good people.

Corruption as an Informal Social Contract

Traditionally, scholars model corruption as a delinquency or illicit behaviour when an agent misuses his entrusted power while he is acting on behalf of a principal (Rose-Ackerman, 1999; Klitgaard, 1988). When the agent is an elected official, who has been elected by citizens, ordinary citizens can hold him accountable through the electoral mechanism, and they can discipline elected officials via subsequent voting. However, the empirical evidence linking the level of democratic accountability to corruption shows that there is a weak relationship between democratic accountability and corruption (Teorell, 2007).

Teorell argues that corruption is not a problem of accountability, but generated by "an informal social contract" (2007, p. 10). He insists that in that informal social contract, some principals (voters) may accept some level of corruption, and he tries to analyse "corruption as an institution in itself" (p. 10). If a researcher models corruption as an institution, then it is possible to understand the causes and consequences of corruption in a different perspective. He believed the reason behind corruption could be the existence of an informal social contract, especially in regions where corruption is prevalent (p.11).

Typology of Corruption

Scholars have outlined different types of corruption as Bribery, Embezzlement, Fraud, Extortion, and Favouritism (Brooks et al., 2013). One of the researchers of the World Bank tried to categorise corruption into several categories, and he described each category, which helps us to have a better understanding of the concept of corruption. He divided corruption and characterised it as following:

1. Petty Corruption: Petty corruption is also called bureaucratic corruption, which is a single incident during which an employee abuses his position for private gain, that can include immense sums of public property.
2. Grand Corruption: Shah defined this type of corruption as "The theft or misuse of vast amounts of public resources by state officials—usually

members of, or people associated with, the political or administrative elite—constitutes grand corruption." (2006, p. 235)

3. Patronage/ Paternalism Corruption: Under this type of corruption an individual uses his given rights and trust for providing services to others from the same group as himself. They could belong to the same ethnic background or political or social groups, or have the same culture or regional operations in common (2006).

A report from the United Nations pointed out that in petty corruption the person defies the rules, where the corruption itself is against government rules and requests. On the contrary, with grand corruption, individuals are high ranking in government and use governmental structure to their advantage, for example, when a Member of Parliament abuses his assigned powers in making the rules and uses them in reinstating those rules that favour his personal benefits (United Nations Office on Drugs and Crime, 2004).

Measuring Corruption

The purpose of this study is to understand the extent of judicial corruption; therefore, it is important to analyse whether corruption can be quantified. Corruption occurs in private (away from the public eye) and it is not easy to detect it; therefore, researchers face difficulty in measuring corruption. This has created a widespread myth that corruption cannot be quantified.

Kaufmann, Kraay and Mastruzzi (2006) argued that corruption can in fact be measured (i.e. the scope of corruption in a particular case, in a specific project, can be measured). Other researchers believe corruption can be quantified either directly or indirectly, although the accuracy of their findings can cause slight hesitation (Brook et al., 2013).

Contributory Factors to the Creation of Corruption in Society

Creation of corruption can be analysed from several different viewpoints. Sometimes, the delinquent attempts to achieve personal gain, and it is the main factor contributing to the formation of corruption. Sutherland was one of the first people to address this issue in his annual speech (1940) and divided the then current theories that outlined factors affecting white collar crimes, namely that it was due to either a person being poor and in need of money to survive, or that a person has been influenced by mental illness. He believes this viewpoint to be shallow and falls short of reality (Sutherland, 1940). To understand the phenomenon of corruption, one must examine factors such as culture, religion, governmental structure, and the welfare of society, including:

1. Perception in society: Perception of the existence of corruption in society can be a factor in corruption occurring. Fehr, Ernst, and Urs Fischbacher (2005) claimed if ordinary people have the perception that corruption and tax evasion are widespread, then the likelihood that they will do the same will increase.
2. Religion: La Porta, Florencio Lopez-de-Silanes, Shleifer and Vishny (1997) suggested that societies with more dominant hierarchical religions have greater corruption. The findings of Paldam (2001) also verify the above finding. He is further of the opinion that in societies where the main religions consist of Islam, Buddhism, and Hinduism, there exists more corruption.
3. Democracy: It seems corruption affects both democratic and non-democratic countries; however, one can argue that corruption should be lower in democratic countries because in these countries there is free media and other methods for checks and balances which could decrease levels of corruption. Rose-Ackreman (2001) believed that corruption cannot be quantified against democracy in a country; there is however a great chance of reducing corruption in the long run after democracy has been accepted as the norm for a long period of time in a country. Montinola and Jackman (2002) compared autocratic regimes and medium-democratic regimes, and made the claim that moderate levels of democracy do not decrease corruption. Lambsdorff (2007) also maintained that eventually, where there is democracy in a country then corruption will be reduced; however, he pointed out that societies that are only moderately democratic may experience more corruption than totalitarian countries, but that ultimately there will be a reduction in corruption levels after a proper democratic society has been formed. He refers to an important issue of the relation between hierarchical structure in society and corruption, and pointed out that hierarchical structure is a contributory factor in increasing corruption.
4. Women's status in society: Swamy, Knack, Lee, and Azfar (2001) studied the relation between gender and corruption. Their findings show that there is a direct link between women in parliament (and other managerial roles) and the reduction of corruption in society.

5. Other factors: What should not be overlooked is that the religion and culture of a society are not the only components in the formation of corruption. There are other factors which must be investigated too. Sullivan and Shkolikov (2004) outlined the following as contributory factors to the formation of corruption:
   - Lack of distinct and proper laws and the lack of stability of these laws.
   - Lack of transparency and accountability.
   - Politicians being in receipt of donations for elective campaigns and their political activities.
   - Low wages of employees in the public or private sector.
   - Unfair and arbitrary enforcement of the laws.
   - Little punishment or lack of investigation over corrupt individuals.

Lambsdorff (2005) outlined seven other contributory factors for the creation of corruption: (i) Government Size and Decentralisation, (ii) Institutional Quality, (iii) Levels of Competition, (iv) Salaries in the Public Sector, (v) Press Freedom and the Judiciary, (vi) Democracy and the Political System, (vii) Culture.

Theories of Corruption

Social Control Theory. The philosopher of natural law, Thomas Hobbes, is the architect of the social contract theory. Having been deeply concerned with the problems of his time, that is, dispute between the church and the state, on the one hand, and quarrel between the king and the parliament, on the other, Hobbes tried to pull his society up from anarchy and civil war. For him, as it is also evident in today's life, sedition and civil war are the causes of disorder and anarchy. Therefore, the urgent need of a society in chaos is to bring the social order back to the routine life of people. Civil peace and social order/unity are best achieved by the establishment of a commonwealth (civil society) through social contract. In *Leviathan* (1651), named after a word derived from the Hebrew Bible for a "sea monster", he introduced social contract as the ideal solution against disorder and civil war, He stated that without a social contract, life will be miserable (Hobbes, 2001, p. 162).

In spite of the imperatives of the state of nature that requires man to struggle for power for security, man is inclined to peace. Indeed, the passions that incline men to peace are to avoid the fear of violent death. This requires people to cooperate with others for peace if others seek the same thing. To achieve this purpose, people surrender their absolute freedom in return for security against the state of war of all against all. Here is where the social contract is created. A social contract is convened through the rational choice of free people.

Hirschi presents the same idea as "social control theory" in a modern form in 1969 in his book: *Causes of Delinquency*, and his social control theory is considered as the validated explanation of criminal and delinquent behaviour. In his book, Hirschi tried to explain delinquent behaviour from a different view; instead of asking why criminals commit a crime, he posed a different question: "Why don't we do it?" (Hirschi, 1934, p. 34). He explains that there is more evidence reflecting the second question which further facilitates answers.

Hirschi believed individuals with a strong social bond are less willing to accept the risks and consequences of criminal behaviour (in comparison with individuals with a weaker bond), for the following reasons:

1. Individuals with strong social bonds are more sensitive to the opinion of others; therefore, they are emotionally attached to other members of the society.
2. Individuals with strong social bonds try to achieve better status in society; therefore, they will have to experience phases such as seeking education and then securing a career for themselves with the gradual progression one will make in their careers. Now if individuals commit crime then, obviously, they risk everything, and all of their dreams might perish.
3. Individuals with strong social bonds spend most of their time on conventional activities, they have involvement in schooling or work, etc., and have less time for delinquency.
4. Individuals with strong social bonds believe in the moral validity of the norms and law in their society; therefore, it is less likely for these people to commit crime.

Self-Control. The general theory of crime, also known as self-control theory, developed by Gottfredson and Hirschi, pays particular attention to internalised control, and argues that crime is a means to obtain immediate gratification. Self-control theory suggests that low self-control is the main factor for criminal behaviour, and to understand the crime, this theory focuses on development in childhood via effective parenting (Siegel and McCormick, 2006).

Based on this theory, most people are after their own interests and create enjoyment for themselves while trying to stay away from any pain or trouble (Newman, 2013). Under these circumstances the consequences of crime become a handy tool to encourage people to not only try to maximise their enjoyment but also to minimise their estimated pain.

Differential Association Theory. Sutherland (1947) formed the notion that crime is learned by interacting with other individuals who find lawbreaking tolerable, and this interaction causes the transfer of criminogenic behaviours and attitudes. Differential association theory describes how association with delinquent behaviour can lead to one's own delinquent behaviour. This theory tries to explain that delinquent behaviour is learned through social interaction with others (Hoffmann, 2002).

Sutherland and Cressey (1978) assert the theory that crime is a kind of deviance that the criminal learns, and they argued that this criminal behaviour is learned in interaction with others. When a person is placed in a circle of individuals where deviance is spoken about in a positive and approved manner, they go on to pick up the same attitudes despite the fact that such behaviour is not approved of by ordinary and reasonable people. In this situation, that deviance begins to be considered a common norm, which can influence the mental perception of the individual.

Newburn (2013) analysed Sutherland's theory, and explained that in Sutherland's point of view, the learning process includes:

1. Learning different methods to committing a crime, where it can be complicated at times.
2. Justifications and motivations behind committing such crimes.

This researcher reminds us that although Sutherland's theory has not been used in recent years for white collar crimes, this phenomenon (social learning), which Sutherland brings into focus, can help the researcher understand white collar crimes such as corruption (Newburn, 2013). He insists that Differential Association Theory is an efficient tool with which to study the working environment.

Sutherland's theory has significance in analysing corruption, particularly where he emphasises crimes being learnt in groups, where group members have close relations with one another (i.e. the workplace). In fact, Sutherland believes these groups create criminal behaviour. This is a crucial point when evaluating this theory in relation to judicial corruption. The question to ask is whether judges and the court personnel learn corruption from one another or not. Sutherland's understanding and his focus on concepts of Differential Association Theory has drawn certain criticism, as based on this perspective, the role of society and organisational structures which helped the creation of corruption have been overlooked.

Some criticisers have rightly noted that white collar criminals, in their ordinary lives, do not commit any crimes. So why should being placed in an organisation and being under certain circumstances bring about a temptation or a tendency to commit a crime?

Routine Activity Theory. What is paramount for a criminal is having the opportunity to commit a wrongdoing. Clark and Mayhew (1989) have analysed suicide rates in Britain. In the 1970s there was a hazardous gas that had been used in the past for cooking or heating purposes (it was called Town Gas). This was replaced in homes by natural gas, so people with suicidal thoughts no longer could use the former gas. According to their surveys there was a drastic drop in suicide attempts, and many of those who would have desired to harm themselves did not even consider any other methods to self-harm. They stipulated that if the existence of an opportunity to commit a suicide has an important role, then the existence of opportunity is an important factor for committing crimes.

Like the majority of crime, corruption is opportunistic too. One should pay particular attention to "opportunity" while studying any corruption. The Routine Activity Theory (which is an opportunity focused theory) is a suitable tool in explaining white-collar crime including corruption (Koppen, De Poot, & Blokland, 2010).

Now let's look at ordinary activities. Formulated by Cohen and Felson (1979), the Routine Activity Theory asserts that offenders commit crime because they take up opportunities for offending that arise while undertaking their regular activities, therefore a crime occurs when three elements come together in time: (1) a motivated offender, (2) a suitable target, and (3) an absent capable guardian. This theory argues that a lack of any one of these could prevent a criminal event. Yar describes the theory:

> Thus, at a general level, the theory requires that targets, offenders and guardians be located in particular places, that measurable relations of spatial proximity and distance pertain between those targets and potential offenders, and that social activities be temporally ordered according to rhythms such that each of these agents is either typically present or absent at particular times. (Yar, 2005, p.410)

In fact, this theory focuses on the criminal event, and asserts that criminals come into contact with suitable targets because of their daily activities; therefore, this theory pays particular attention to the opportunity. Cohen et al. (1981) assert that any article that is more visible, accessible, or proximate to criminals was more likely to be victimised. This theory argues that for preventing crime, one should focus on reducing opportunities for crime (Figure 2.1).

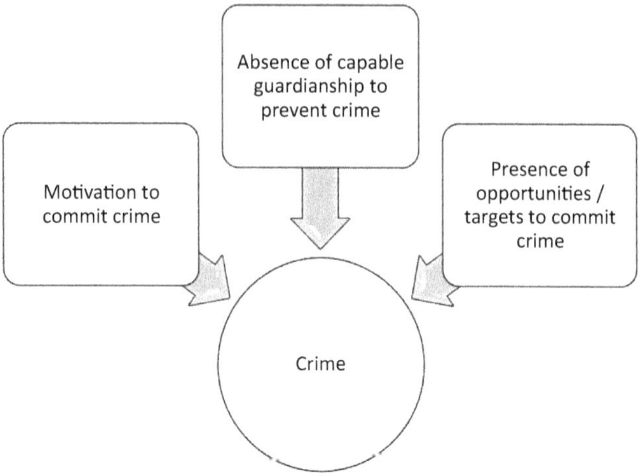

Figure 2.1: Representation of the concepts from Routine Activity Theory. Source: Adapted from "*Social Change and Crime Rate Trends: A Routine Activity Approach.*" By Cohen, L., Felson, M. (1979), American Sociological Review.

Rationalisation: A Platform for the Promotion of Corruption. The idea of rationalisation tries to explain how some people believe they are morally upright, but commit unethical acts such as corruption. And how do these people defend themselves from this troubling fact (being corrupt)? Rationalisation is a defence mechanism that protects the ego of these kinds of people (Zyglidopoulos, Fleming & Rothenberg, 2009). These scholars suggested that a combination of opportunity, pressure, and rationalisation will lead to corrupt acts. Not only does this rationalisation help the corrupt person to commit crime, but it also will assist him to use it as a weapon to convey a more convincing argument for breaking the norms of society again. Brytting, Minogue, and Morino asserted that perpetrators create rationalisation and will try to trivialise fraud and corruption, and they might not be fully conscious that those rationalisations are untrue; indeed criminals sometimes change the name of their deviated behaviour from corruption or fraud to "common practice" or "tricks of the trade" (2011, p. 59).

Such a rationalisation helps criminals justify their deviated behaviours, and assists them to commit the crime without remorse or feelings of guilt. This also helps them justify their behaviour in front of others. Scholars believe that the rationalisations are "mental strategies that allow employees (and others around them) to view their corrupt activities as justified" (Anand, Ashforth, & Joshi, 2004, p. 39). In fact, the corrupt criminal does not view themself as a corrupt person, and will attempt to employ rationalisation tactics, and justify their deviated behaviour as normal business activities. Anand further elaborates how such criminals justify their wrongdoings by believing what they have done is not wrong, or that they are themselves part of a system and that their wrongdoings are justifiable being in such situations in a wider society. They will adopt different rationalisations, and try to justify their crime by arguing that they have no other choice, that their action is a victimless crime, or that they tried to achieve higher-order value.

Why is justification needed? A person desires to justify his criminal acts, because he is looking for a means to enable himself to look in the mirror and yet feel good about himself. When a person is corrupt, and looks in the mirror, he would not feel very good at all and will seek to justify his wrongful actions. He will try to justify his corrupt actions by reasoning, for example, that what he is going to do or has done will not harm anyone, that everyone does it, and that it is his ultimate right to do it too.

Scholars have analysed cases relating to corruption and have concluded they all share one thing is common; those individuals who have committed corruption are the most trusted in an organisation, to an extent they help charities, or they care for their seniors such as parents and their colleagues; therefore, there will not be any room for suspicions to arise.

Newburn (2013) explains that the concept of rationalisation allows us to realise how some individuals appear to be law abiding, but deviate from moral and just behaviour. This also enables us to see how some people can temporarily overlook the norms of their society and commit corruption. Cressey (1973) argued a person can commit fraud if only he can justify his act in his mind. Although Cressey did not directly address the issue of corruption, his expertise is mainly in fraud, where admittedly there are differences. His argument will help us to understand better how corruption is formed. He believes for fraud to take place there must exist three elements:

1. Opportunity factor. He believes for a crime to take place there must exist an opportunity and a situation so the act can take place. For instance, it would be enough for the individual to believe there are no risks or dangers in terms of legal action or a whistle blower.
2. The wrongdoers need. The person must need such money. Of course, everyone's needs are characterised by several social factors.
3. The act can be justified. What is more important is how well the individual can justify his action.

Based on the above argument, Cressey created the fraud triangle as the following (Figure 2.2):

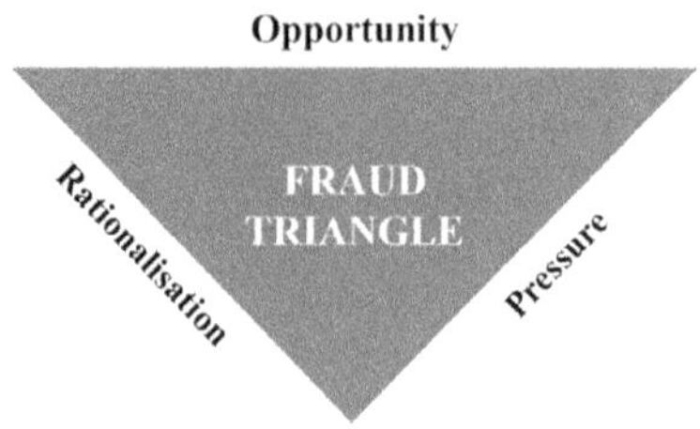

Figure 2.2: Fraud triangle. Source: Adapted from "Other people's money: a study in the social psychology of embezzlement" by Cressey. D. (1953), *Free Press, Glencoe*

Connections between Corruption and Power. To make a thorough examination of judicial corruption, we must understand how judges act after arriving at the position of judgement. Brytting, Minogue, and Morino (2011) argue that when someone is assigned power, they pay less attention to the viewpoints of others, or how other people feel or think. This itself could be a reason for that individual to become isolated and distant from the norms of their society. That person then becomes more passive about these norms or what the majority of the population agree to be ethically acceptable behaviour or approaches. On the other hand, this could lead to a person thinking they belong to a superior category in society; therefore, their expectations and living standards will increase accordingly and they will become eager to achieve more to favour their increased personal interests. This can simply be the underlying structure for corruption to form. Furthermore, these scholars suggest that the person who has reached the position of power attempts to act similarly to their peers in power.

Theories on Formation of Corruption – Organisational Culture Theories. Organisational culture theories are among the most suitable theories for understanding judicial corruption; therefore, this theory will be reviewed briefly. According to De Graaf (2007), organisational culture theories argue that a certain culture or a certain group culture will lead to the creation of a certain mental state, which leads to corrupt behaviour. That culture will lead an innocent character to act corruptly; in other words, corruption is contagious. De Graaf, then, relied on Punch's view when he described corruption within police departments:

> If we scan these activities then it is plain that we are no longer dealing with individuals seeking solely personal gain but with group behaviour rooted in

> established arrangements and/or extreme practices that have to be located within the structures and culture of police work and the police organization. The implication is that in tackling corruption and other forms of police deviance, it is vital to focus on group dynamics, the escalation from minor to serious deviance, and on the negative elements in the police culture. (2000, p. 34 and p.317)

The theory of organisational culture argues that when corruption is widely distributed among the majority, it would be very hard not to become corrupted. Proponents of this theory look at corruption in a sense, and in their view, common corruption is the cause of forming more corruptions and its prolonged existence. In such a situation, if one does not behave like the others and does not become corrupt, then it appears he has betrayed the others (Punch, 2000). Caiden and Dwivedi (2001) as well as Klitgaard (1998) in his book *Control of Corruption* expressed the same view.

Surviving Corruption in Organisations. When a new member joins an organisation, one expects that the new member, who is not part of that corruption, should endeavour to preclude continuous corruption, while in practice it is not the same thing. Scholars argue, if corruption exists in an organisation, when a new member joins that organisation, at first, they may be overwhelmed by the volume of corruption, hence they may be encouraged to leave their job and that organisation. This raises an opportunity for other members who are involved in corrupt activities to attract only individuals who would not be affected by their morality and are happy to join in (Anand et al., 2005).

Reducing Corruption and Its Obstacles

Mechanisms of Reducing Corruption

De Graaf (2007) asserted that different theories for countering corruption may seem promising; however, in practice they are not efficient. Klitgaard (1988) developed a formula which is devised to measure and better understand the concept of corruption:

C=M+D -A

"Corruption equals monopoly plus discretion minus accountability" (p. 75). Klitgaard argued that the existence of corruption is related to the official's discretion at his disposal; in other terms, how broadly he can act freely without being supervised or held accountable.

In the public sector (in any society) one of the most important factors for fighting corruption is how willing politicians are to combat corruption. Caiden,

Dwivedi, and Jabbra (2001) argued that there have been various theories developed to combat corruption; however, none of them will succeed in achieving results independently. They assert that success in fighting corruption is dependent on willingness among politicians to fight corruption. Hough (2013) asserts that a successful fight against corruption requires distinct policies, governmental determination, perseverance, and adherence to those policies in the long run. Unsurprisingly, Ackerman (n.d.) suggested that many governmental reforms for countering corruption are inefficient.

Bracking (2007), however, has taken a different approach from economists' points of view which only try to reduce motivational factors and increase the risk of getting caught to combat corruption. He asserts that that view is simplistic and will produce a flawed policy to counter corruption; he suggests that anti-corruption policy should be adopted based on political backgrounds and the social background of the society in question. A general policy cannot be a successful policy. He suggests that to create a counter corruption policy, one needs to pay particular attention to "social and political context, rather than be taken off the shelf in a 'one size fits no-one' approach" (p. 70).

Suggestions from Webster (2007) provide us with a rough idea about different means to reduce corruption, including:

1. Freedom of press (to expose corruption).
2. Existence of laws which guarantee access to information to the citizens (Freedom of information).
3. Transparent protocols underlying all acceptable behaviours, defining corruption, and announcing that every corrupt and fraudulent act will not be tolerated (Zero Tolerance Policy).
4. The lack of immunity from prosecution and discipline for corrupt individuals.
5. Long imprisonment for people who commit corruption.

Culture in a Society Is an Important Tool or Barrier to Combat Corruption

Twenty years ago, this author witnessed how Turkish immigration officers on the border between Iran and Turkey asked for bribes. In exchange for Turkey's entry stamps they would take bribes from those who were allegedly not legally allowed to enter, and they, quite shamelessly, demanded that bribe in front of everyone. From the perspective of individuals present in that office, including the briber, immigration officers, and other passengers (visitors), such a situation was not strange. Now compare the above example with an imaginary situation in the UK where if an immigration officer attempted to receive a bribe from any visitor. In this scenario, both the briber and the bribe receiver would face severe punishments, and one can imagine other visitors would react and object. Apart from the fact that the law prohibits bribes in both countries, another important factor contributes to such corruption, and that is the culture which governs in the society. On the border between Iran and Turkey, none of the people in that office object to bribery (even those witnessing it), but in the UK, this is a very shameful act. The above example gives way to the concept that a society's culture can raise a barrier against corruption.

The most important obstacle to the fight against corruption is the complexity of this phenomenon and its relation to the culture of the society. Balogun (2003) asserted that if the citizens of the society, whether they are in power or an ordinary citizen, do not see corruption as immoral or bad, or feel that they will not be able to react to corruption, then any anti-corruption campaign will be condemned to failure beforehand. He believes that public integrity is like a seed. Whether we will see the formation of a society without corruption or not is dependent on the culture of the society. He also points out that the most efficient way to fight corruption is to educate the public and change the behaviour and personality of the people. Unsurprisingly, combating corruption is not a simple task because it is not easy to impress on the culture (De Graaf, 2007).

The importance of culture in shaping or preventing the occurrence of corruption is so high that Caiden and Dwivedi (2001) claim that no law, regulation, or threats can force government officials to behave in a way that is ethical, unless they work with their conscience to serve others in the public sector, and are also accountable for their own actions. Otherwise, the formation of an ethically orientated government is unlikely.

Widespread Corruption Is Aggressive

Thoumi (1987) investigated the implications of the growth of the underground economy, and asserted that white collar crimes are part of this underground economy. He goes on to argue that when there is widespread corruption and dishonesty in a society, it will be costly to behave and act honestly. He rightly argued that an individual can act honestly in one environment (where there is no widespread dishonesty); however, the same individual will act dishonestly in another environment (where dishonesty is widespread). Hence, when the same individual lives in an environment (where dishonesty is widespread) then "he becomes more apt to behave in dishonest fashion" (p. 44). He then argues in the long run, values in society will change which will have two important impacts: firstly, respect for the law will become costly and the costs for such legalities will increase; secondly, getting involved in and attempts to engage in criminal acts becomes more acceptable. It means the level of corruption will increase, and society will have more tolerance for corruption. Thoumi (1987) suggests in this situation, society will enter and remain in an "illegality and dishonesty trap" (p. 45).

In fact, the greater the expansion of corruption, the more costly being clean can become. Over a period, even innocent people will be influenced by the majority; hence, it is likely they will act corruptly too. This is where the society gets stuck in an unethical trap, for which escaping from such behaviours would be difficult.

It is noteworthy that judicial corruption will contribute to the creation of this trap more than any other kind of corruption. Scholars assert that if the existence of corruption damages public opinion and trust in the judiciary, then public trust in other sectors will be damaged too, and corruption will spread easily (Buscaglia & Dakolias, 1999).

How to Penalise Corrupt Acts?

Scholars believe that criminals see penalties as a form of cost (Becker and Stigler, 1974). Some scholars have tried to look at corruption as a financial transaction. For example, if a judge undermines due process without receiving any money (e.g. to protect the interests of a third party), and if we accept that there are no monetary exchanges between the judge and receiver of the services, still that judge commits corruption and this phenomenon can be considered as a financial transaction and as such can be analysed.

For fighting against corruption, some scholars focus on transaction costs. Coase (1937) created Transaction Costs, and he noted that in any financial transaction, a number of transaction costs are involved, including that of finding a buyer or seller, the communication and exchange of information, and reaching an agreement and enforcing it. Dahlstrom and Nygaard (1999) categorise three types of transaction costs: bargaining, monitoring, and maladaptation costs.

Lambsdorff (2002) investigated the impact of transaction costs on corruption, and stated that there will be secrecy and limited transparency in participation in any corrupt agreement; hence, the Transaction Costs of a corrupt agreement will increase dramatically because of the need to conceal the agreement. He outlined the following reasons: (i) parties in a corrupt agreement are vulnerable to each other (each party has placed himself at the mercy of the other), (ii) enforcing the agreement for each party will be costly and a strategy must be developed, (iii) the process of gathering the necessary information about the agreement will be costly, (iv) even after the exchange of services and return, parties in corrupt deals will be engaged in an agreement, because each party can harm the other and, for example, attempt extortion (i.e. threaten to expose them). He suggested that in certain conditions, penalising the individual alone can stabilise the corrupt agreement. Lambsdorff concluded that to combat corruption, one should focus on destabilising corrupt agreements.

Lambsdorff and Neil (2007) noted that the payer or the receiver of the bribe cannot use legal means to record the agreement or use any usual system to enforce their agreement. In fact both offenders may cross each other during this financial transaction; hence, giving legal immunity or a reduction can encourage one party (receiver or payer) to force the other side to fulfil its obligations. However, imposing unequal punishments on offenders can be helpful in combating corruption. These scholars provide the following recommendations for drafting punishment laws for perpetrators and bribery:

1. Government employees negotiating and agreeing to receive bribes should not be punished unless they actually receive a bribe,
2. Bribers should face punishment if they offer to pay bribes or make promises to pay bribes.
3. A lighter punishment can only be considered if bribers voluntarily report the crime they have committed themselves.
4. A lighter punishment of government employees can be considered only if they voluntarily report receiving bribes to the authorities responsible.

Literature Review – Judicial Corruption

Corruption in the judicial system is a complex phenomenon and can be examined from a variety of dimensions. In the following, judicial corruption will be reviewed in its various aspects.

Essential Traits for a Non-corrupt Judiciary

Judicial corruption has not received enough attention, maybe because there is less judicial corruption in democratic countries; and for undemocratic countries the main concern with the judicial branch was with the independence of the judiciary. Mayne (former assistant to the UN Special Rapporteur on the Independence of Judges and Lawyers) argued that most international standards focus on the impartiality of the judiciary system and the absence of political influence. However, the issue of judicial corruption has attracted less attention. He noted that the reason for this was that the international community's attention was focused on the independence of the judiciary in undemocratic societies and less concerned with the issue of the accountability of the judiciary systems. He then argued that The Bangalore Principles of Judicial Conduct (2002) were developed based on six integral components: independence, impartiality, integrity, equality, propriety, and competence and diligence. He rightly asserted that to achieve integrity and propriety, judges or court staff must avoid any corruption (Mayne, 2007), and these fundamental components will encompass staying away from corruption. In the following section, we will review these qualities.

Essential Qualities – Impartiality of the Judge. The Oxford English Dictionary (1989) defines the term "partial" as "unduly favouring one party or side in a suit or controversy, or one set or class of persons rather than another; prejudiced; biased; interested; unfair" (p. 265). That same source defines impartiality as not being partial, to not favour one party more than another, and avoiding being biased, unfair, or unjust.

A judge can be considered impartial if they have no bias, animosity, or sympathy towards either of the parties (Alsheban, 2017). Judicial impartiality can be undermined if the judge has a personal interest in the case outcome (e.g. by accepting a bribe), if the judge has relational interests in the case outcome (e.g. if the judge has pre-existing relationship with one party), if the judge has political interests in the case outcome, or if the judge has personal biases for or against case participants (Geyh, 2014b). The Bangalore Principles of Judicial Conduct (2002) asserted that Judicial impartiality is essential to the proper discharge of the judicial office, and claimed: "A judge shall perform his or her judicial duties without favour, bias or prejudice."

The European Court of Human Rights suggested two requirements for the impartiality of the judge: objective impartiality and subjective impartiality and argued that "a subjective approach, that is endeavouring to ascertain the personal conviction of a given judge in a given case, and an objective approach, that is determining whether he offered guarantees sufficient to exclude any legitimate doubt in this respect" (judgement of first January 1982, PIERSACK v. BELGIUM).

Essential Qualities – Judicial Independence. Researchers suggest that there is an inverse relationship between judicial independence and human rights violations and assert that to promote human rights, it is necessary to strive for independence of the judiciary. The question is, what is the definition of judicial independence? Does this independence mean a lack of oversight on the judiciary? What is the relationship between judicial independence and corruption?

Unfortunately, there is no common approved definition for judicial independence. Ginsburg (2002) claimed, judicial independence is like the concept of freedom, everyone is asking for it, but nobody knows what it means. Robertson (2014) defined judicial independence as enabling judges to follow their conscience and the justice of the case, and to be safe from any pressures from any source of state power and influence. The Bangalore Principles defines judicial independence as: "A judge shall exercise the judicial function independently on the basis of the judge's assessment of the facts and in accordance with a conscientious understanding of the law, free of any extraneous influences, inducements, pressures, threats or interference, direct or indirect, from any quarter or for any reason" (The Bangalore Principles of Judicial Conduct, 2002). They also insist that judges must be free from inappropriate connections from the executive and legislative branches of government.

Researchers suggest that a lack of independence of the court will contribute to the creation of judicial corruption (Mayne, 2007), and it seems to be true that corruption can be understood as the influence of an external factor on the court, and consequently the lack of court independence. If we consider this definition, even paying bribes or the imposition of influences can be considered as external factors on the court which undermine judicial independency. Pasquino (2003) reviewed the history of judicial independence and claimed that judicial independence has always been a means of achieving impartiality of the court, and this independence should be defined in a way that ultimately leads to the following:

1. Judge's impartiality in the proceeding.
2. Putting the judges in a position to be free from pressure from any power outside of the court.
3. Avoidance of bias in the courts.
4. Pasquino's viewpoints, with consideration for other researcher's views in this respect, will be examined in the following.

Essential Qualities – The Independence of the Judiciary (internal and external). Modona (2012) categorised judicial independence in two categories:

1. External Independence. This type of independence will make the judiciary immune to any external and political pressures. To achieve this type of independence, there should be a separation of powers, plus transparency in the manner of electing judges and job promotion.
2. Internal independence. This is the immunity of the judges from pressures within the judicial system and from colleagues and managers of the judiciary. The process of assigning cases to judges is very important and should be protected from any influence. Modona asserted that a chief of a corrupt judicial system can become a gateway and a means of exerting pressure from other areas of government on the Courts.

Essential Qualities – Personal Independence. In order to achieve judicial independence, the judge needs to issue a ruling only in accordance with the law, and, during the issuance of his judgement, he should be immune from any influence, either political or governmental, or personal ideologies.

Judges will enjoy personal independence if they are able to act completely impartially and in accordance with the facts in the case, the existing laws and procedures, and are immune from pressure or influence of powers outside the Courts (Melton & Ginsburg, 2014). The factors which can undermine independence of a judge can be very wide. For example, scholars emphasise that a judge should, in order to be truly independent, remove themselves from the ideological clause they have in mind and not allow personal opinions to affect their work (Chemerinsky, 1989).

Melton and Ginsburg (2014) rightly argue that judicial independence is "an important component in many definitions of judicial quality" (p. 190), and outlines six elements for judicial independence, including:

1. Existence of constitutional provisions on judicial independence.
2. Ensuring lifetime appointments for judges to strengthen independence.
3. Judicial appointments should be transparent and free from any political pressures.
4. Judges must be secure from any threat of removal, and the removal procedure must be clear and transparent.
5. Limiting removal conditions.
6. Judges' salaries must be protected from reduction.

Essential Qualities – Organisational independence. It is worth mentioning that without the independence of the judicial branch from other parts of the government, principally the personal independence of the judges will no longer have any meaning (Hughes, 2000). In the next section, the doctrine of separation of power will be reviewed.

Essential Qualities – Separation of Powers. A distinct definition of the organisational independence of the courts can be seen in the doctrine of separation of powers. The roots and history of this theory are in Aristotle's book, *Politics.* Centuries later in 1689, John Locke in his book *Two Treatises of Government* referred to the separation of executive and legislative powers, and although Locke argued that legislative power must have ultimate authority (Paragraph 143), he did not mention anything about judicial power; in fact, he saw the judiciary as an institution, not a separate body with power. In 1748, it was Montesquieu, who emphasised the fact that courts should be independent. In his book, *The Spirit of the Laws,* Montesquieu developed Locke's statement, and argued that the judiciary, executive, and legislative functions of the government must be allocated to different bodies to restrain each from undermining political liberty. He further argued that if the Courts were to act under the authority of the legislature, then judges would become legislators, and they could do whatever they wished. On the other hand, if the judiciary operated under the authority of the executive branch, then the executive branch may misuse the Court. Montesquieu expressed that if the executive and the legislative bodies assemble in one institution, this new body will restrict freedom; and if the judicial body is not separated from the other two bodies, they will restrict freedom too (Montesquieu, 1949).

Judicial independence is best explained by James Madison, one of the Founding Fathers of the United States, who in *The Federalist 47* argued that the combination of legislative and executive power in a centre of power is a form of tyranny. It is of less importance if this centre of power consists of a single person or a group of individuals. Even in this regard, it does not matter that these power holders have gained power by popular votes, etc. the accumulation of power in this way is tyranny (Madison, 1788, February 1). It should be noted that Madison believed that power has an "encroaching nature" and in *The Federalist 48,* he asserted that the power should be effectively restrained from passing assigned limits (Madison, 1788, February 1, 1st paragraph).

Essential Qualities – Checks and Balances. The doctrine of the separation of power tries to prevent any concentration of power; however, as Vile (1998) argued, this theory does not indicate how to restrain a branch which is trying to exercise its power improperly, or trying to accumulate power. Hence, to maintain the separation of power, checks and balances must exist and "each branch was given the power to exercise a degree of direct control over the others by authorizing it to play a part, although only a limited part, in the exercise of others' functions" (p. 20).

The accountability of the judicial system is closely related to the independence of this branch. The question is how it can be ensured that an institution monitors the work of the judiciary without misusing such supervisory powers for exerting pressure on the judiciary – especially when this pressure can undermine the independence of the judiciary and create judicial corruption (e.g. not abusing given powers or forcing the court to adjourn a case). On the other hand, the transfer of indefinite independence to the judiciary also causes corruption if this institute is not accountable in any way.

In order to ensure that each branch of government is accountable, some scholars have proposed a doctrine of checks and balances. Based on this doctrine, each of these three branches functions in a completely independent manner, but the other two powers also have limited powers and can limit other bodies if they see any wrongdoing or abuse of power. James Madison in *Federalist 47* argued that it is necessary to protect and preserve liberty so that these three main parts of power remain separate and distinct (Madison, 1788, February 1). Following the adoption of the US Constitution, some criticised the views expressed and believed that the separation of powers had not been respected. For example, the presidency has the right to veto laws passed by Congress and can influence the process of the ratification of laws. James Madison responds to the question with some innovative analysis. In *Federalist 47* he argued that Montesquieu was never of the belief that the three powers should not have control over one another; instead he believes if a power of an institution becomes superior to another, then the political liberty is undermined, and there is no evidence that suggests Montesquieu had any intentions to make absolute separation between these powers from one another. Furthermore, in *Federalist 51*, he argued that the best way to cope with the slight accumulation of power in a single power is to empower other branches with some authority in the constitution and enable them to counter any attempts to accumulate power in one branch (Madison, 1788).

Hence, according to the theory of checks and balances, one branch should be able to supervise and monitor the two other branches without damaging their independence. Of course, this supervision should not become a means to pressure the judiciary and compromise its independence.

It is noteworthy to mention that when corruption is widespread in a society, then assigning full independence to the judiciary will create a breeding ground for corruption in the long run; Pimentel (2014) asserted that giving absolute independence to the judiciary in such societies only leads to an increase in corruption and a reduction in the rule of law. This scholar suggests that in the process of drafting a new constitution, authors will need to pay particular attention to the accountability of the courts.

Essential Qualities – Judicial Accountability. Judicial independence is a very important to establish the separation of powers. Now, the question is: how can judicial accountability and judicial independence be achieved simultaneously? Should the judicial branch be accountable like the executive and legislative branch? This is a topic of debate, and some might believe that making courts accountable will undermine their legitimacy. Others, such as the head of the Malaysian judiciary, believe that judges are, by default, accountable for their decisions because they make those decisions in a public forum (Le Seuer, 2012).

Some scholars believe that there would have to be a balance created between judicial accountability and judicial independence, in such a way that guarantees the independence of the judges and enables them to make a decision based on the facts of the case and the law without any fear, at the same time, without absolute independence which will give them immunity and allow them to ignore the law or even ignore the facts of the case (Geyh, 2008).

Judicial Independence and Accountability

Judicial independence and judicial accountability: which one is being compromised? Voigt (2008) argued that the judiciary can be designed in a way that is both accountable and independent. He asserted that judicial independence and judicial accountability should be complementary to each other, and both of them are the means to achieve judicial impartiality. He claims that judicial independence means that there should not be any pressure on judges (from parties, lawyers, or even political institutions outside the court), and judicial accountability means that judges are required to enforce the law precisely. These two important judicial attributes can complement each other in order to achieve the goal of being judicially impartial.

Monitoring the judicial system without compromising the independence of it: As Rios-Figueroa (2012) argues, in order to prevent corruption, the judicial branch should also be under continuous inspection to prevent creating "unchecked checkers" (p. 197). However, this continuous monitoring and inspection will not reduce corruption, unless there is judicial independence. Scholars, Voigt, and Gutmann (2015) conduct detailed research in which they assert that the supervision of the courts and their independence are complementary and serve to reduce judicial corruption. At the same time, monitoring the work of the courts can only lead to a reduction of corruption if judges have independence.

Rose-Ackerman argues that without judicial independence, politicians will try to misuse the courts and put pressure on judges to reduce political competition or to eliminate competitors, which will create prevalent judicial corruption. However, if the judicial branch receives absolute independency, then their very independence can create corruption because "no one has the authority to oversee them" (Rose-Ackerman, 2007, p. 24) and there is a possibility that this branch will become corrupted from within. She emphasises that it is not possible to achieve independence of the judiciary only by drawing up laws, but that the judges themselves should also act independently (Rose-Ackerman, 2007).

Contributory Factors for the Creation of Judicial Corruption

Having reviewed theories of Essential Qualities, this essay will next review contributory factors for the creation of judicial corruption.

Contributory Factors – Legal Culture. Research has shown that society's culture plays a significant role in the formation and spread of corruption. Public perception, such as how citizens see or consider paying or receiving bribes (bad or good), has an impact on reducing or spreading corruption. A study by Miller, Gradeland, and Koshechkina (2001) in Eastern Europe, in their research of citizen-official perception, suggested that there is a linkage between the reduction of corruption and public perceptions about corruption. It is obvious that the legal culture of society is important when it comes to examining corruption, especially because corruption can destroy the legal culture of society from within (Glenn, 2014).

Definition of legal culture has been a subject of debate in socio-legal research literature (Nelken, 2014). Friedman (1969), who was the first to use this term, defined legal culture as "the values and attitudes which bind the system together, and which determine the place of the legal system in the culture of the society as a whole" (p. 34); he categorised legal culture into: (i) Internal legal culture which deals with the behaviour of judges and lawyers; (ii) external legal culture which deals with the society's attitude to the system of justice and law in society (Friedman, 1994). Glenn (2014) asserted that legal traditions play a major role in the reduction of any crime.

Kurkchiyan focuses on judicial corruption in the context of legal culture from the perspective of the sociology of law, and she claimed that for a deep understanding of judicial corruption, it should be investigated in a local context, and one must pay attention to the following points: how well a judge defines themselves and how proud are they of themselves? How are they getting on in their social life? Plus, how far is corruption tolerated in that society? She asserts that these answers are all of significance. She further emphasises that in any society the judge behaves like other judges; she claims that in order to understand the behaviour of judges, one must focus on how judges see themselves and what corruption means for them, hence, it is necessary to take a careful look at the legal culture of the society (Kurkchiyan, 2007).

Contributory Factors – Impact of the Media on Judicial Corruption. Kaisaer (1995) reviewed the relationship between the media and the judiciary and asserted that transparency is one of the main pillars of democracy. He argues that considering the importance of the duties of the judiciary, it is necessary that society can fully trust the judicial branch. When the media is limited to reporting on the functioning of the judiciary, then citizens doubt and suspect that corruption and misuse of power are ongoing there.

Robertson (2007) claimed that all laws and regulations are worthless unless they are enforced by independent and impartial judges, and simultaneously that the free media monitor the judiciary and are enabled to expose any corruption (if they find any). McMillan and Zoido (2004) rightly stated:

> The news media are the chief watchdog. The checks and balances work as a system, so an independent judiciary and genuine political competition are important. But the media can provide oversight of the government even where the other checks and balances have broken down. Safeguards for the media; ensuring they are protected from political influence and are credible to the public, may be the crucial policies for shoring up democracy. (p. 91)

It is worth noting that there is a direct link between the existence of democracy and the freedom of media, with corruption. A study found that the more democracy and freedom of the press, the less chance of corruption (Bhattacharyya & Hodler, 2015).

Identifying judicial corruption to report it is not an easy task; as Robertson (2007) argues, the reporter must be knowledgeable about judicial systems, procedures, and law; hence, he emphasises the need for educating investigative journalists in this subject.

Lawyer's Roles in Forming Corruption. Scholars carried out research into the role of lawyers in the creation of judicial corruption, and they categorised these roles as the following:

1. Lawyers who play a direct role and make contact with the judges to pay bribes and ask for their demands.
2. Lawyers who understand from the behaviour of the courts that their client has paid a bribe but turn a blind eye.
3. Lawyers who have a reputation for being involved in judicial corruption but nobody takes any legal action against them.

The above-mentioned scholars also argue that corrupt lawyers will use the high load of cases and the slow pace of processing, to take bribes to expedite the processing of cases, and sometimes also find it beneficial to slow down the handling of cases to favour their interests (Tsunga & Deya, 2007).

Consequences of Judicial Corruption

Balogun (2003) rightly claimed that corruption, (depending on its size and shape), can lead to undermining the morality and ethics in society. It threatens the country's national security, disrupts order, and pushes the sustainability of society, plus it reduces economic growth, and is a barrier to sustainable development.

Undermining the Rule of Law. In order to understand the impact of judicial corruption, we need to consider the importance of the Rule of Law in society, and how judicial corruption will undermine the Rule of Law. Some scholars try to define the rule of law by "the goals" that the rule of law is intended to achieve including: existence of law and order, binding government by law, equality of everyone before the law, existence of predictable and efficient justice system, and lack of state violation of human rights (Belton, 2005).

However, some scholars claim that for better understanding of the rule of law, one must pay attention to the existence of institutions which uphold the rule of law in society, including (i) the existence of laws which are publicly known and relatively settled; (ii) the presence of an independent and uncorrupted judiciary; and finally (iii) the existence of law enforcement agencies that are capable of enforcing laws, executing judgements, and maintaining public peace (Belton, 2005).

In General, the existence of the rule of law can be measured by the following points:

1. Whether the law in that society is legitimate and approved by delegates elected during a free election, which coincides with the opinion of most

citizens being considered, while still ensuring the fundamental rights of minorities, are not violated.
2. Whether the law in that society is not against reasonable norms (e.g. internationally recognised human rights).
3. The citizens of the country also achieve political and cultural maturity, and the culture of society is also compatible with that law.
4. This law is applicable to everyone in a similar way.
5. There also exists an independent judiciary to ensure the smooth implementation of the law.

One of the EU affiliated organisations called the European Commission of Democracy through the law examines the concept of the rule of law, and in conclusion it lays down the following conditions:

- The existence of a transparent and democratic procedure for the formulation and adoption of laws.
- Legal certainty.
- Prohibition of the arbitrary enforcement of the law.
- Existence of fair and impartial and independent courts.
- Existence of the Courts for Judicial review which are authorised to review the performance of government officials and employees in compliance with regulations and laws.
- Respect for human rights.
- Non-discrimination and equality before the law for all (European Commission for Democracy Through Law, 2011).

On the above scale, we can see the importance of independent and impartial courts to establish the rule of law in society. Existence of Judicial corruption, even in a limited scope, will undermine rule of law (Knaul, 2012).

Undermining Good Governance. In Resolution no 288.66 of the United Nations (adopted by the General Assembly on 27th July 2012), it is stated that democracy, good governance, and the rule of law are essential for sustainable development. The question here is why, in this statement, there is equal attention given to both good governance and the rule of law? And what is its relevance to corruption in the judiciary? There is no doubt about the importance of good governance for prosperity and stability in a country. Research has shown that there is a direct link between good governance and economic growth and the welfare of citizens (Kaufmann Kraay, & Zoido-Lobatón, 1999).

Traditionally, governance was about how a government exercises its political power. For example, The UN Capital Development Fund described governance as applying power in the field of politics and economics for managing the country (as cited in Hugh, 2013). In the 1980s, scholars reintroduced governance and Doeveren (2011) described this new definition as: a process of decision-making in which sovereignty is dispersed among governmental and nongovernmental actors who together participate in a political decision-making process that cannot be controlled from the centre (p. 342).

Kaufmann, Aart, and Lobatón (1990) defined good governance as "the traditions and institutions by which authority in a country is exercised" (p.5); they emphasise the point that governance means the way power is exercised in a country, including how the government chooses to oversee those who wield it and how to replace the power holders – also, the concept of effective government, the ability of government to adopt and implement sound policies, and of respect for the government and citizens for institutions that manage economic activities or social interactions. They categorised six dimensions which contribute to good governance: voice and accountability, political stability and the absence of violence, government effectiveness, regulatory quality, rule of law, and control of corruption.

1. Voice and accountability: Assessing the extent to which citizens of a country participate in the process of government selection and to what extent freedom of expression is the freedom to form associations and freedom of the press:

1. Political stability and absence of violence: Assessing the stability of a government and the extent to which a government may be overthrown by coup or unconstitutional terrorist acts.
2. Government effectiveness: Assessing the quality of public services and the extent to which these services are safe from political pressures. And what is the extent of the quality of adopted policies, as well as the extent the governance adheres to these policies.
3. Regulatory quality: Assessing to what extent the government should adopt its own private sector development policies and the extension of it.
4. Rule of law: Evaluating that all citizens, including law enforcement actors, are subject to the law.
5. Also, the quality of the implementation of contracts for private properties, the performance of law enforcement and courts, and the rate of crime and violence will be examined.
6. Control of corruption: Assessing the extent to which people who are empowered by the government use this power for personal purposes.

Violation of Human Rights. Corruption can lead to the violation of human rights. The international Council on Human Rights Policy (2007) addressed this issue, and categorised the impact of corruption into Indirect and Direct violations of human rights. It is obvious that corruption in the judiciary will violate the rights of citizens to have a fair trial and can be considered as a violation of Article 10 of the Universal Declaration of Human Rights. However, corruption can have an indirect impact on human rights too. This is where corruption leads to a chain of events, each of which is a violation of human rights in a different way. For example, the environment can be damaged as a result of corruption, (corruption will manifest itself in environmental organisations), or the result of corruption can be seen in the department responsible for providing health services, limiting access to health services for the citizens.

Violation of Women's Rights. Women's rights are severely restricted in Iran, and the government systematically suppress women. Therefore, it is important to consider the impact of judicial corruption on women's rights. Scholars have examined the issue of the effects of corruption on genders, and first posed a fundamental question as to whether gender discrimination in courts can be considered a type of judicial corruption; then rightly argued that the definition of corruption is not comprehensive and should include the extortion and sexual harassment resulting from abuse of power. It is argued that women are more vulnerable to the impact of judicial corruption, because women have less access to financial resources, and when bribery affects the decisions of the court, their access to justice is reduced. To further exasperate this, in some societies women's literacy levels are lower than men (Nyamu-Musembi, 2007).

The Spread of Organised Crimes. Rose-Ackerman (1999) insists that the spread of judicial corruption will lead to the spread of corruption in other institutions; among these institutions are the country's security systems and law enforcement agencies. Findings from Zhilla's (2011) research show that there is a direct relation between judicial corruption and the prevalence of organised crime. Beare argued that corruption is a pre-requisite for the formation of organised crime, and emphasises that extortion or illegal accumulation of wealth is only one of the consequences of organised crime; indeed the most dangerous part is that government institutions will become an executive arm for criminal organisations (as cited in Rider 1997, p. 65–76).

Consequences of Judicial Corruption on Democracy. Rose-Ackreman (1997) claims that judicial corruption has a huge negative impact on democracy; that the judicial system contaminated with corruption is not credible and cannot protect the fundamental rights of the citizen in accordance with the constitution of that country; and the judiciary cannot "check" the legislature or the executive branches.

The Costs of Judicial Corruption

Corruption (in any shape or form) will lead to the unjustifiable and unjust allocation of resources in the country (Rider, 1997), and is a major obstacle to economic development (Kaufmann, Kraay & Mastruzzi, 1997). In order to understand judicial corruption, one must consider concepts such as transaction cost. Here the transaction cost is briefly introduced, and the effects of judicial corruption on the economy will be reviewed:

Judicial Corruption and Economic Growth. Juin-jim and Chia-ying (2007) tried to shed light on the link between social norm and judicial corruption, and they claimed if in any judicial system, a substantial number of judges are willing to accept bribes in exchange for their judgement, then firms will be encouraged to violate law and regulations. In this scenario, the norms are the cause of corruption, then the more corruption there is, the more it becomes easier for the society to accept further corruption, and this corruption spreads like an avalanche. Hence, if there is an epidemic of corruption in a society then any efforts to reduce it will be less effective. Hence, tolerance of corruption, even for a short period, would have serious consequences for the future of that society. Juin-jrm and Ying (2007) emphasise that when a high-Corruption Equilibrium is created, it will be very costly to counter it.

Judicial Corruption and Transaction Costs. Transaction costs are expenses and are incurred during a transaction when a firm (or a person) tries to collect information in the sale or purchase of goods, or for negotiating with the opposite party or for protecting its interests (Transaction Costs, 2014). If the judiciary system is corrupt, these costs will be greatly increased and, in principle, a firm cannot predict or calculate it. For example, firms, when entering into a contract, will have to ask themselves the following questions:

1. If the other party fails to comply with the contract and if I file a complaint, would the other party violate and interrupt the justice system by paying bribes?
2. If the other party fails to comply with the contract, and I had to go to court, how much of a bribe should I pay to the judges or court's staff,

so that I could maintain my own rights and defend my interests in the contract?
3. If the other party pays more bribes then how can it be trusted that the judge will not refuse to fulfil his promise?

The existence of judicial corruption means an increase in transaction costs. When there is judicial corruption in any society, attaining Pareto efficiency will no longer be easy, while the rent-seekers will take advantage of the justice system's weakness. It goes without saying that judicial corruption on a large-scale causes corruption in other parts of government too and such widespread corruption leads to a reduction in GDP. De Soto (1989) argued that one of the imperative reasons for poverty in developing countries is the problems that the governments create for small business (i.e. excessive bureaucracy or existence of corruption), and these obstacles have more negative impacts on small businesses.

Amartya Sen, world-renowned economist and philosopher, in his speech at the World Bank addressed the importance of a non-corrupt judiciary (and the creation of the rule of law as a consequence); he argued that without the existence of the rule of law, one cannot attain a free market, and insisted that due to a lack of the rule of law, citizens' fundamental rights, including the right to property, cannot be protected, and in turn, enforcing any contracts will be difficult (Sen. 2000).

Combating Judicial Corruption

When considering ways to counter corruption, what needs to be considered is that combating corruption has a huge difference compared to fighting to eliminate other crimes. In order to counter corruption, the government should willingly participate and engage. McCormick and Paterson (2006) argue that the most important tool for combating corruption is the commitment of the government to fight corruption.

Furthermore, it is important to focus on the structure of the judiciary system. Scholars suggest that the most important tool for preventing corruption is the proper design of the structure of an entity, as well as intelligent formulation of the decision process (Cooter & Garoupa, 2000).

The following recommendations for reducing corruption are suggested:

(1) Make sure that the salaries of judicial personnel remain at least constant in real terms, i.e. insure their certainty, (2) insure that court decisions are regularly

> published, (3) do away with the monopoly of the prosecutor to prosecute criminal acts, (4) reduce the number of independent procedural actions that need to be taken to produce an enforceable court decision and (5) increase the necessity for judges to justify their decisions in legal terms. (Voigt and Gutmann, 2015, p. 16)

Besley and McLaren (1993) suggested that paying adequate salaries can contribute to the reduction of corruption. However, judicial corruption is a particular kind of corruption, and paying adequate salaries has little impact on the creation or reduction of judicial corruption. Buscaglia (1999) explored the causes and consequences of judicial corruption by examining the performance of several courts and the judges in several countries. He suggested that the following conditions are the fundamental reasons for corruption to occur:

1. Lack of transparency in assigning responsibilities to court staff,
2. The high volume of cases and the complexity of the judicial process and the possibility of exercising discretion,
3. Absence of proper channels to share precedents,
4. The lack of other options for recourse such as the Dispute Resolution Council to replace and compete with the courts.

International Transparency (2003) conducted an international poll on the payment of bribes to judiciary in sixty different countries, and the findings of that study indicate that there is a direct relationship between the existence of the rule of law in a country and corruption in the courts. International Transparency has confirmed in an article that, in general, the following four actions could lead to a reduction in judicial corruption:

1. Appointment of judges based on ability and competence.
2. Providing adequate salaries for judges and court staff.
3. Accountability and punishment of corrupt judges and employees
4. Transparency in court performance and permission for the press to report any shortcomings in the courts.

In conclusion, the above scholar believes there is a direct relationship between the complexity of the judicial process and the extent of judicial corruption.

International Standards and Conventions for Countering Corruption

This section will attempt to review existing norms and international laws relevant to the subject of this research.

Universal Declaration of Human Rights. Article 10 of the Universal Declaration of Human Rights emphasises the rights of citizens to a fair trial, and states that every human being deserves to fully and openly have access to an impartial, independent, and fair judicial system, so that the court's duties will be to review any criminal charges against them. It is to be noted that a corrupt judicial system is a violation and defect of the UDHR.

International Covenant on Civil and Political Rights. Article 14 of the International Covenant on Civil and Political Rights deals extensively with the rights of citizens to benefit from a fair judicial system, and Article 14 (1) deals with the equality of all before the courts, and the fairness of the courts. In 2004, the United Nations Commission on Human Rights (UNHRC), underlined this in a Declaration on the Independence of the Judicial System of the States and its Importance.

The Bangalore Principles of judicial conduct. The Bangalore Principles is one of the most important international documents on ethical standards in the judiciary. The draft of this document was originally submitted in 2001 and was approved by the United Nations in its 2003, 59th summit. It should be noted that this bill does not have any enforcement guarantees. There is a clear indication of the conduct and standards governing the performance of judges in this document. Its outline is as follows:

- Judges should act independently and decide only on evidence and reality
- Judges should act in a totally impartial manner.
- Judges should avoid creating any inappropriate relationship with either party.
- In order to be publicly trustworthy, the judge must display appropriate behavioural standards.
- Judges, and their family members, should not accept any gifts from the parties to the dispute.
- The judge should not allow a member of his office to take a gift or request a loan to take advantage of financial benefits.

Recommendations from the United Nations Office on Drugs and Crime. The United Nations Office on Drugs and Crime (UNODC) offered a draft for an International Anti-Corruption Convention, which was approved in 2003. Its outline is as follows:

1. Article 7 calls for transparency in the selection and supervision of the work of those who are prone to corruption in their jobs. It also called on

the members of the UN to prevent the spread of corruption by providing education, and by adopting the necessary rules for the formation of the corruption.

2. Article 11 emphasises the importance of a non-corrupt judiciary and recalls that UN members should work towards strengthening standards and the conduct of judges and the judiciary's employees.
3. Article 13 referred to the need for the participation of citizens from non-governmental organisations and the private sector in the fight against corruption and called on the members of the UN to assist this partnership by formulating the proper laws.
4. Articles 15 and 16 call for the passing of laws to combat bribery.

It should be noted that despite the signing of this covenant and its approval by the Islamic Assembly in Iran, The Guardian Council opposed it. Following the submission of this Covenant to the Expediency Council in 2003, the Assembly appended it by adding the following:

> The Islamic Republic of Iran demands that the provisions of article 66, paragraph 2, of the Convention on the Referral of any dispute arising out of a fault or its implementation not resolved by negotiation shall not be considered by the International Court of Justice. (Larijani, 2009)

Reviewing Previous Research on Judicial Corruption in Iran

The author has been unable to find any academic research in Persian or in English about judicial corruption in Iran, but there are a few reports in the media about corruption in the judiciary.

A journalist interviewed several human rights lawyers in Iran about corruption by judges in the judiciary. Three lawyers have been independently interviewed, and they insisted that the most corrupt part of the judiciary is the disciplinary court for the judges (Tavasolian, 2016).

The only research that even indirectly deals with judicial corruption in Iran is an article in the *Quarterly Journal of Criminal Law* titled "Health Promotion in the Judiciary" (Salehi, 1993), which only addressed the relevant laws in Iran to combat judicial corruption.

Rule of Law in Iran

Scholars examined the rule of law and its relationship with the separation of power in Iran. Although the results of their research help the reader to understand the role of the judiciary in violating human rights in Iran, judicial corruption has not been addressed (Bahraeini, Nayyeri & Sheeran, 2014).

Independence of Judiciary:

Barlowe (2015) examined the Iranian judiciary, and claims *the Guardianship of the Islamic Jurist* (Velâyat-e Faqih) has fundamentally taken into question the credibility of the judiciary in Iran, and it has transformed the Iranian judiciary into tools for a religious regime to suppress any opposition. The problems of the Iranian judiciary are firstly a lack of independence and the inability to carry out its supervisory duties on other political institutions. This is due to the Supreme Leader having unlimited powers and able to change the head of the judiciary. Secondly, a special clergy court is also used as a tool, so it can punish clerical judges who fail to comply with the Supreme Leader. The result of these conditions is the lack of independence of the judiciary. The Supreme Leader and his executive authority are the most important barrier for due process in Iran.

Other research that elaborates on the lack of independence and corruption in the judicial system is the article written by an Iranian lawyer who lives in exile. In an article titled "Who Are the Judiciary in The Islamic Republic", she addressed the issue of the absence of independence in the judiciary. She explains that judges must have the following conditions to choose and to arrive at a position of authority: (1) Male gender, (2) Belief in the regime and its principles, (3) Iranian citizenship, (4) Not being born of parents not married to each other, (5) Having mental health and the ability to judge, (6) No criminal records, (7) Bachelor of Law, theology, or graduated from Islamic religious school (Seminary).

The above scholar referred to Articles 156 and 157 of the constitution and the structure of the judiciary, which concludes that the head of the judiciary has unlimited control over all judges. Since the head of the judiciary is only accountable to the Supreme Leader, the whole judicial system in Iran suffers from a lack of independence (Kar, 2012).

Reporters Without Borders ranked Iran 170 out of 180 countries in the World Press Freedom Index (Reporters Without Borders, 2017).

References

Ackerman, S. (n.d.). The pursuit of absolute integrity: How corruption control makes government ineffective – Anechiarico, F, Jacobs, J. B. *Journal of Policy Analysis and Management, 16*(4), 661–664.

Alsheban, A. (2017). *IOSR Journal of Humanities and Social Science* (IOSR-JHSS), *22*(5), Ver. II (May 2017), 37–44. e-ISSN: 2279-0837, p-ISSN: 2279-0845.

Anand, V., Ashforth, B., & Joshi, M. (2004). Business as usual: The acceptance and perpetuation of corruption in organizations. *Academy of Management Executive, 18*(2), 39–53.

Anand, V., Ashforth, B., & Joshi, M. (2005). Business as usual: The acceptance and perpetuation of corruption within organisations. *Academy of Management Executive, 19*(4), 9–23. http://84.89.132.1/-lemenestrel/IMG/pdf/anand_et_al._ame_2004.pdf

Bahraeini, R., Nayyeri, M., & Sheeran, S. (2014). *Electoral Process in Iran: Analysis of Political Participation and Iran's Compliance with International Human Rights Obligations.* University of Essex. https://www.essex.ac.uk/hri/documents/electoral-process-in-iran.pdf

Balogun, M. J. (2003). Causative and enabling factors in public integrity: A focus on leadership, institutions, and character formation. *Public Integrity, 5*(2), 127–147.

Barlowe, S. (2015). What's Islam got to do with It – Obstacles in securing fair trial rights under Iran's repressive regime. *Cardozo Journal of International and Comparative Law,* (3), 601.

Becker, G. S., & Stigler, G. J. (1974). Law enforcement, malfeasance, and compensation of enforcers. *Journal of Legal Studies, III,* 1–19.

Begovic, B. (2004). *Corruption in Judiciary, Centre for Liberal -Democratic studies,* Belgrade, Retrieved from: pdc.ceu.hu/archive/00002541/01/Corruption_in_judiciary.pdf (Accessed 31-03-2016).

Belton, R. K. (2005). *Competing Definitions of the Rule of Law: Implications for Practitioners.* (2005). Carnegie Endowment for International Peace. Carnegie Endowment for International Peace (2005) Stable. https://w2ww.jstor.org/stable/resrep12779

Besley, T., & McLaren, J. (1993). Taxes and bribery: The role of wage incentives. *Economic Journal, 103*(416), 119–141. https://doi.org/10.2307/2234340.

Bhattacharyya, S., & Hodler, R. (2015). Media freedom and democracy in the fight against corruption. *European Journal of Political Economy,* 3913–24. doi:10.1016/j.ejpoleco.2015.03.004.

Bracking, S. (2007). *Corruption and development: The anti-corruption campaigns.* Basingstoke: Palgrave Macmillan.

Brooke, R. (2002). *Judicial Independence* — Its History in England and Wales, The Right Honourable Lord Justice Brooke, can be retrieved at: www.judcom.nsw.gov.au/publications/education-monographs-1/monograph1/fbbrook.htm (accessed 31-03-2016).

Brooke, R. (2009, March 5). *Judicial Independence — Its History in England and Wales.* Retrieved from https://web.archive.org/web/20090612153459/http://www.judcom.nsw.gov.au/publications/education-monographs-1/monograph1/fbbrook.htm

Brooks, G., Walsh, D., Lewis, C., & Kim, H. (2013). *Preventing corruption: Investigation, enforcement and governance.* Basingstoke: Palgrave Macmillan.

Brytting, T., Minogue, R., & Morino, V. (2011). *The anatomy of fraud and corruption.* [electronic resource]: Organizational causes and remedies. Farnham, Surrey, England; Burlington, VT: Gower.

Buscaglia, E., & Dakolias, M. (1999). *An analysis of the causes of corruption in the judiciary. Law and Policy in International Business, 30*, 95–116.

Caiden, G., & Dwivedi, O. (2001). Official ethics and corruption. In G. Caiden, G. Dwivedi, & J. Jabbra (Eds.), *Where corruption lives*, Bloomfield: Kumarian Press.

Caiden, G. E., Dwivedi, O. P., & Jabbra, J. G. (2001). *Where corruption lives.* [electronic resource]. Bloomfield, CT: Kumarian Press.

Chemerinsky, E. (1989). Ideology, judicial selection and judicial ethics. 2 *Georgetown Journal of Legal Ethics,* 643–664. Available at: http://scholarship.law.duke.edu/cgi/viewcontent.cgi?article=2145&context=faculty_scholarship (accessed 31-03-2016).

Clarke, R. (1980). Situational crime prevention: Theory and practice. *British Journal of Criminology, 20*, 136–145.

Clarke, R. V., & Mayhew, P. (1989) Crime as opportunity. A note on domestic gas suicide in Britain and the Netherlands. *British Journal of Criminology, 29*(1), 35–46.

Cohen, L., & Felson, M. (1979). Social change and crime rate trends: A routine activity approach. *American Sociological Review, 44.* doi:10.2307/2094589.

Cooter, R., & Garoupa, N. (2000). The vicious circle of distrust: A mechanism to deter bribes and Other Cooperative Crimes. https://doi.org/http://www.escholarship.org/uc/item/83c0k3wc.pdf.

Cressey, D. (1953). *Other people's money: A study in the social psychology of embezzlement.* Glencoe: Free Press.

Dahlstrom, R., & Nygaard, A. (1999). An Empirical Investigation of Ex Post Transaction Costs in Franchised Distribution Channels. *Journal of Marketing Research*, 36(2), 160–170. doi:10.2307/3152090.

De Graaf, G. (2007). Causes of corruption: Towards a contextual theory of corruption. *Public Administration Quarterly,* (1/2), 39.

De Soto, H. (1989). *The other path.* New York: Harper and Row.

Doeveren, V. (2011). Rethinking good governance. *Public Integrity, 13*, 4. doi:10.2753/PIN1099-9922130401.

European Commission For Democracy Through Law. (2009). *Report On The Rule Of Law,* Study No. 512/ 2009, Strasbourg, 4 April 2011, Retrieved from: www.venice.coe.int/webforms/documents/default.aspx?pdffile=CDL-AD(2011)003rev-e (accessed 31-03-2016).

Fehr, E., & Fischbacher, U. (2005). The economics of strong reciprocity. In H. Gintis, S. Bowles, R. Boyd, & E. Fehr (Eds.), *Moral sentiments and material interests. The foundations for cooperation in economic life* (pp. 151–193). Cambridge: MIT Press.

Friedman, L. (1994). Is there a modern legal culture?. *Ratio Juris*, 7(2), 117–131, July 1994, can be retired (partially): http://goo.gl/BkubCv (accessed 04/01/2016).

Friedman, L. M. (1969). Legal culture and social development. *Law & Society Review, 4*(1), 29–44.

Geyh, C. (2008). Methods of judicial selection & their impact on judicial independence. *Daedalus, 137*(4), 86–101.

Geyh, C. (2014a). The dimensions of judicial impartiality, 65 fla. *L. Rev. 493* (2014). Available at: http://scholarship.law.ufl.edu/flr/vol65/iss2/4

Geyh, C. (2014b). *The Dimensions of Judicial Impartiality*. Can be retrieved at: scholarship.law.ufl.edu/cgi/viewcontent.cgi?article=1138&context=flr

Glenn, P. (2014). *Legal traditions of the world: Sustainable diversity in law.* Oxford University Press. Retrieved from (partially): https://goo.gl/X9TtwC (accessed 3-11-2015).

Hobbes, T. (1998). *Hobbes: On the citizen*. Cambridge: Cambridge University Press, 20 Aug 1998.

Hobbes, T. (2001). *Leviathan. [electronic esource] : 1651.* Infomotions, Inc.

Hoffmann, J. P. (2002). A contextual analysis of differential association, social control, and strain theories of delinquency. *Social Forces, 81*(3), 753–785.

Hough, D. (2013). *Corruption, anti-corruption and governance.* Basingstoke: Palgrave Macmillan.

Hughes, P. (2000). Judicial independence: Contemporary pressures and appropriate responses. *Can. B. Rev., 80,* 181 (2001) https://heinonline.org/HOL/LandingPage?handle=hein.journals/canbarev80&div=12&id=&page=

Huntington, S. (1989). *Modernization and corruption. In political corruption. A handbook.* Heidenheimer, New Brunswick: Transaction Publishers, can be retrieved at: http://www.brandonkendhammer.com/pols340_winter2012/wp-content/uploads/2011/12/Political-Corruption-pp.-253-264.pdf (accessed 31-03-2016).

International Transparency (2003)

Judgement of first January 1982, PIERSACK v. BELGIUM. 8692/79, CLI:CE:ECHR:1982:1001JUD000869279

Juin-jen, C., & Chia-ying, L. (2007). The negligence rule in the presence of judicial corruption and social norms. *Atlantic Economic Journal, 35*(2), 203–215. doi:10.1007/s11293-007-9068-8.

Kaisaer, H. (1995). *"The Media And The Judiciary In The Democratic Process"*. Dalhousie University. Can be retrieved from: cjei.org/publications/kaiser.html (accessed 04/01/2016).

Kar, M. (2012). *Who are the judges in the Islamic Republic of Iran*. London: Legatum Institute.

Kasravi, A. (1945). *Tarikhe-h- mashroteh- Iran*. [History of Persian constitutional revolution]. Tehran: Amirkabir publication.

Kaufmann, D., Aart, K., & Lobatón, P. (1999). *Governance matters.* World Bank. Retrieved from: https://goo.gl/h3Fs7V; (accessed 31-03-2016).

Kaufmann, D., & Kraay, A. (2008). *Governance indicators: Where are we, where should we be going?* Oxford University Press. doi:10.1093/wbro/lkm012.

Kaufmann, D., Kraay, A., & Mastruzzi, M. (2006). *Measuring corruption: Myths and realities.* Washington, DC: The World Bank.

Kaufmann, D., Kraay, A., & Mastruzzi, M. (2009). *Governance Matters VIII.* The World Bank Development Research Group Macroeconomics and Growth Team.

Kaufmann, D., Kraay, A., & Mastruzzi, M. (2010). *The worldwide governance indicators: Methodology and analytical issues.* World Bank Policy Research Working Paper No. 5430.

Kaufmann, D., Kraay, A., & Zoido-Lobato´n, P. (1999). *"Aggregating Governance Indicators."* Policy Research Working Paper 2195. Washington, D.C: World Bank.

Khandan, R. (2015, May 20).Soltani ra azad konid [Fee soltani]. Facebook. Retrieved from https://goo.gl/YVP0da

Khosravi, M. (2011). Hakemiat ghanon chist [Rule of Law, law as a norm]. Can be retrieved at: http://yasharparsa.com/?p=1670

King, R. D., & Wincup, E. (2008). *Doing research on crime and justice.* Oxford: Oxford University Press.

Klerman, D., & Mahoney, P. (2005). The value of judicial independence: Evidence from eighteenth century England. *American Law and Economics Review, 7*(1), 1–27.

Klitgaard, R. (1988). *Controlling corruption.* Berkeley, CA: University of California Press.

Klitgaard, R. (1998). Combating corruption. *UN Chronicle, 35*(1), 90.

Klitgaard, R. (2006). Introduction: Subverting corruption. *Global Crime, 7*(3/4), 299–307. doi:10.1080/17440570601063724.

Klitgarrd, R. (2008). *A holistic approach to the fight against corruption.* the Second Session of the Conference of State Parties to the United Nations Convention against Anti-Corruption, can be retrieved at: www.cgu.edu/PDFFiles/Presidents%20Office/Holistic_Approach_1-08.pdf

Knaul, G. (2012). Report from *The United Nations Special Rapporteur on the independence of judges and lawyers.* Retrieved from: available at: http://www.ohchr.org/EN/NewsEvents/Pages/DisplayNews.aspx?NewsID=12692&LangID=E#sthash.198TkyID.dpuf (accessed 31-03-2016). Koppen, De Poot, & Blokland, 2010).

Kurkchiyan, M. (2007). *Judicial corruption in the context of legal culture.* Cambridge: Cambridge University Press.

La Porta, R., De Silanes, L., Eleches, C., & Sheleifer, A. (2004). Judicial checks and balances. *Journal of Political Economy, 112*(2), 445–470. https://doi.org/10.1086/381480.

La Porta, R., Florencio Lopez-de-Silanes, Shleifer, A., & Vishny, R. (1997). Trust in large organizations. *The American Economic Review, 87*(2), 333–338. Retrieved from http://www.jstor.org/stable/2950941

La Porta, R., Florencio, L., Shleifer, A., & Vishny, R. (1999). The quality of government. *Journal of Law, Economics, & Organization,* (1), 222.

Lahidji, K. (2012). *The history of the judiciary in Iran.* London: Legatum Institute.

Lambsdorff, J. (2002). Making corrupt deals- contracting in the shadow of the law. *Journal of Economic Behavior & Organization, 48,* 222–241.

Lambsdorff, J. (2005). Consequences and causes of corruption: What do we know from a cross-section of countries? Passauer Diskussionspapiere - Volkswirtschaftliche Reihe, No. V-34-05 available at: http://hdl.handle.net/10419/55031

Lambsdorff, J. G. (2007). *The institutional economics of corruption and reform: Theory, evidence and policy.* Cambridge: Cambridge University Press.

Lambsdorff, J., & Nell, M. (2007). *Fighting corruption with asymmetric penalties and leniency,* cege Discussion Papers, No. 59. Göttingen: Universität Göttingen Center for European, Governance and Economic Development Research (cege).

Le Seuer, A. (2012). *The Chief Justice of Malaysia addressing Commonwealth Lawyers Association* 'Judicial Accountability Workshop' in April 2002, cited by Andrew Le Seuer (n 75) 52.

Lessig, L. (2013). Foreword: "*Institutional corruption*" defined. *Journal of Law, Medicine and Ethics, 41*(3), 553–555. doi:10.1111/jlme.12063.

Levenstein, R. H., & Sisco, M. (2016). Crisis of knowledge: The importance of educating the public about the role of fair and impartial courts in our system of government. *Florida Bar Journal, 90*(5), 34–37.

Levi, M. (2003). The Roskill Fraud Commission revisited: An assessment. *Journal of Financial Crime, 1,* 38.

Li, L. (2012). The 'Production' of corruption in China's courts: Judicial politics and decision making in a one-party State. *Law & Social Inquiry, 37*(4), 848–877. doi:10.1111/j.1747-4469.2012.01285.x.

Lindstedt, C., & Naurin, D. (2010). Transparency is not enough: Making transparency effective in reducing corruption (La transparence ne suffit pas: rendre la transparence efficace dans la lutte contre la corruption) (La transparencia no basta: Cómo crear una transparencia efectiva para reducir la corrupción). *International Political Science Review/ Revue internationale de science politique,* (3), 301.

Locke, J. (1632). *Two treatises of government.* London: Thomas Tegg.

Locke, J., & Laslett, P. (2003). *Two treatises of government* (Student ed., Cambridge texts in the history of political thought). Cambridge: Cambridge University Press.

Lynch, T. D., & Lynch, C. E. (2003). Corruption, reform, and virtue ethics. *Public Administration Review, 63*(3), 370–371.

Macaulay, b. (1889). *The history of England from the accession of James the second.* Popular Edition in Two Volumes I. London: Longmans.

Macaulay, M. (2012). *Corruption in the UK.* London, UK: Teesside University and TI-UK.

Mayne, G. (2007) *"Judicial integrity: The accountability gap and the Bangalore Principles",* Cambridge University Press.

McCormick, J., & Paterson, N. (2006). The threat posed by transnational political corruption to global commercial and development banking. *Journal of Financial Crime, 13*(2), 183–194.

Mcilwain, H. (1913). The tenure of English judges. *PoL. Sci. REV., 217,* 218 (1913). Retrieved from: https://archive.org/details/jstor-1944895 (accessed 31-03-2016).

Medema, G., & Zerba, R. (1999). *The Coase theorem.* Retrieved from: encyclo.findlaw.com/0730book.pdf (accessed 28/03/2016).

Melton, J., & Ginsburg, T. (2014). Does De Jure Judicial Independence Really Matter? A Revaluation of Explanations for Judicial Independence (Coase-Sandor Institute for Law & Economics Working Paper No. 612, 2014). Chicago: The University of Chicago.

Miller, W., Gradeland, T., & Koshechkina, Y. (2001). *A culture of corruption: Coping with government in post-communist Europe.* Budapest: Central European University Press. (accessed 28/06/2016). Can be retrieved partially at: https://goo.gl/XDdRWE

Modona, G. (2012). *External and internal aspects of the independence of the judiciary.* OECD: Proceedings of the Regional Seminar.

Montesquieu, C. (1949). *The spirit of the laws* (Hafner library of classics; 9). New York: Hafner.

Montinola, G., & Jackman, R.W. (2002). 'Sources of corruption: A cross country study.' *British Journal of Political Science, 32,* 147–70.

Moschtaghi, R. (2010). *Rule of law in Iran, Freie university* (Berlin), retrieved from: www.wikis.fu-berlin.de/display/SBprojectrol/Iran (accessed 31-03-2016).

Musembi, C. (2007). *Gender and corruption in the administration of justice.* London: Cambridge University Press.

Nassiri, M. (1995). *Iran's judicial system after the revolution.* London: Legatum Institute.

Nelken, D. (2010). *Comparative criminal justice: Making sense of difference.* London: SAGE Publications Ltd.

Nelken, D. (2014). Thinking about legal culture. *Asian Journal of Law and Society, 1*(2), 255–274.

Newburn, T. (2002). Atlantic crossings: 'Policy transfer' and crime control in the USA and Britain. *Punishment & Society, 4*(2), 165–194. doi:10.1177/14624740222228536.

Newburn, T. (2013). *Criminology.* London: Routledge.

Nohlen, D. (2001). *"Iran": A data handbook.* I. Oxford: Oxford University Press.

Pasquino, P. (2003). *Prolegomena to a theory of judicial power: The concept of judicial independence in theory and history* (accessed 07-11-2016). Can be retrieved at: http://www.heinonline.org/HOL/Page?handle=hein.journals/lpict2&div=8

Pimentel, D. (2014). Culture and the rule of law: Cautions for constitution-making. *Fordham Int. Law Journal, 37,* 101. Retrieved from: www.fordhamilj.org/files/2014/04/Pimentel_FILJOnline.pdf (accessed 04/01/2016).

Punch, M. (2000). Police corruption and its prevention. *European Journal on Criminal Policy and Research, 8,* 301–324.

Rider, B. K. (1997). *Corruption: The enemy within.* London: Kluwer Law International.

Robertson, G. (2007). The media and judicial corruption. In D. Rodriguez & L. Ehrich (Eds.), *Global corruption report 2007.* Cambridge: Cambridge University Press.

Robertson, G. (2014). *Judicial independence: Some recent problems.* International Bar Association's Human Rights Institute (Ibahri); Thematic Papers No 4.

Rose-Ackerman, S. (1999). *Corruption and government: Causes, consequences and reform.* Cambridge, United Kingdom: Cambridge University Press.

Rose-Ackerman, S. (2001). *Political corruption and democratic structures.* In A. K. Jain (Ed.), *The political economy of corruption* (pp. 111–141). New York: Routledge.

Rose-Ackerman, S. (2004). *The challenge of poor governance and corruption.* Cambridge University Press

Rose-Ackerman, A. (2007). Judicial independence and corruption. In D. Rodriguez & L. Ehrich (Eds.), *Global corruption report 2007.* Cambridge: Cambridge University Press.

Ross, I. (2016). *Exposing fraud: Skills, process and practicalities.* Chichester: Wiley.

Salehi, Z. (1993). Ertegha dar dastgah-e- ghaza [Promotion in the judiciary]. *Criminal Law Journal,* no 1, 1993.

Scott, R. (1995). *Institutions and organizations.* Thousand Oaks: SAGE.

Sen, A. (2000). *'What Is the Role of Legal And Judicial Reform In The Development Process?'* Speech delivered at the World Bank Conference on Legal and Judicial Reform. http://www1.worldbank.org/publicsector/legal/legalandjudicail.pdf (accessed 04/01/2016).

Shihatam, I. (1997). Corruption-a general review with an emphasis on the role of the World Bank. *Penn State International Law Review, 15*(3), Article 2. Available at: http://elibrary.law.psu.edu/psilr/vol15/iss3/2

Siegel, L. J., & McCormick, C. (2006). *Criminology in Canada: Theories, patterns, and typologies* (3rd ed.). Toronto: Thompson.

Situngkir, H. (2011). *The structural dynamics of corruption-artificial society approach*. Bandung Fe Institute. retrieved from: https://arxiv.org/ftp/nlin/papers/0403/0403042.pdf

Sullivan, J. D., & Shkolnikov, A. (2004). *Combating corruption: Private sector perspectives and solutions*. Washington, DC: CIPE. Retrieved 26/11/2016, from: https://goo.gl/kvASCm

Sutherland, E. (1939). *Principles of criminology*. Philadelphia: Lippincott

Sutherland, E. (1940). White-collar criminality'. *American Sociological Review, 5*, 1–12.

Swamy, A., Knack, S., Lee, Y., & Azfar, O. (2001). Gender and corruption. *Journal Of Development Economics*, 6425–55. doi:10.1016/S0304-3878(00)00123-1.

Tavassolian, N. (2012). *Reform within the judiciary of Iran*. London: Legatum Institute.

Tavasolian, N. (2016). *Fasedtarin bakhsheh ghoveh ghazei* [Most corrupt part of the Iranian judiciary]. IranWire, available at: https://iranwire.com/fa/features/4020

Teorell, J. (2007). *Corruption as an institution: Rethinking the nature and origins of the grabbing hand*. Göteborg University. Retrieved from: www.qog.pol.gu.se/digitalAssets/1350/1350653_2007_5_teorell.pdf (accessed 04/01/2016).

The World Bank. (1997). *Helping countries combat corruption the role of the World Bank*. Retrieved from: www1.worldbank.org/publicsector/anticorrupt/corruptn/corrptn.pdf (accessed 31-03-2016).

Thompson, S. (2013). *Two concepts of corruption* (August 1, 2013). Edmond J. Safra Working Papers, No. 16. Available at SSRN: https://ssrn.com/abstract=2304419 or http://dx.doi.org/10.2139/ssrn.2304419

Thoumi, F. E. (1987). Some implications of the growth of the underground economy in Colombia. *Journal of Interamerican Studies and World Affairs*, (2), 35.

TI's Global Corruption Barometer, conducted annually since 2003, is part of Gallup's Voice of the People Survey.

Transparency International. (2007a). Executive summary: Key judicial corruption problems. In D. Rodriguez & L. Ehrich (Eds.), *Global corruption report 2007*. Cambridge: Cambridge University Press

Transparency International. (2007b). *Global corruption report 2007*. Cambridge: Cambridge University Press.

Transparency International. (2014). *Corruption perceptions index 2014*. Retrieved March 1, 2017, from https://www.transparency.org/cpi2014/results

Transparency International. Toolkit. (2007). *Combating corruption in judicial systems advocacy toolkit*, transparency international. Berlin: Cambridge University Press.

Treisman, D. (2000). The causes of corruption: A cross-national study. *Journal of Public Economics*, 76399–457. doi:10.1016/S0047-2727(99)00092-4.

Trochev, A. (2010). *Meddling with justice. Demokratizatsiya*, *18*(2), 122–147.

Tsunga, A., & Deya, D. (2007). *Lawyers and corruption: A view from East and Southern Africa*. In D. Rodriguez & L. Ehrich (Eds.), *Global corruption report 2007*. Cambridge: Cambridge University Press.

van Koppen, M. V., de Poot, C. J., & Blokland, A. A. J. (2010). Comparing criminal careers of organized crime offenders and general offenders. *European Journal of Criminology*, *7*(5), 356–374. doi:10.1177/1477370810373730.

Voigt, S. (2008). The economic effects of judicial accountability: Cross-country evidence. *European Journal of Law & Economics, 25*(2), 95. doi:10.1007/s10657-007-9035-5.

Voigt, S., & Gutmann, J. (2015). On the wrong side of the law – Causes and consequences of a corrupt judiciary. *International Review of Law & Economics*, 43156–166. doi:10.1016/j.irle.2014.04.005.

Wilson, J. (1968). *Corruption is not always scandalous.* New York Times Magazine, April 28,

Wilson, J. Q., & Kelling, G. L. (1982). Broken windows: The police and neighborhood safety. *Atlantic Monthly, 211*, 29–38.

Yar, M. (2005) The novelty of 'Cybercrime': An assessment in light of routine activity theory. *European Journal of Criminology, 2*(4), 407–427.

Zhilla, F. (2011). Organised crime and judicial corruption in the Western Balkans: Are customary norms playing any role?. *Journal of Financial Crime, 18*(4), 387–404. doi:10.1108/13590791111173713.

Zyglidopoulos, S. C., Fleming, P. J., & Rothenberg. (2009). Rationalization, overcompensation and the escalation of corruption in organizations. *Journal of Business Ethics January 2009, 84*(Supplement 1), 65–73. doi:10.1007/s10551-008-9685-4.

3

The Complex Structure of the Iranian Judiciary

History of the Criminal Justice System in Iran

In this section, we will briefly examine the history of the judicial system of Iran. In order to understand corruption in the judiciary, it is necessary to know when and at what stage the system was formed.

Safavid Empire Era (1501–1736)

The concept of justice in Islam is not similar to modern liberal notions; it is more like Aristotle's definition of justice (Enayat, 2013, p. 10). In Islam, the ulama are the guardians, transmitters, and interpreters of religious knowledge in Islam. The ulama regard themselves as "heirs of the prophets" (Fierro, 2010, p.679).

For many years, rulers invited ulama into their circles to enhance the ruler's religious legitimacy (Fierro, 2010). The traditional interpretation of Islam gives the ruler absolute power; therefore, the ulama never see themselves needing to restrict the ruling power by creating any institute to reduce and then separate powers. The root for using shar'ia law (Islamic law) as a source in courts in Persia can be seen in the Safavid Empire era. Scholars have claimed that during the Safavid period, the government was obliged to establish order, implement Shari'a

Law, and so in return the ulama would confirm the legitimacy of the government (Enayat, 2013).

The Qajar Dynasty (1789–1925)

In the Qajar era (the ruling dynasty of Iran from 1794 to 1925) there was the dual legal system of *"shar" and "orf" courts* in Iran *(Enayat, 2013).* Shari'a court law was based on Jaʿfari jurisprudence which is the school of jurisprudence in Twelver Shi'a Islam (Zamiran and Ebadi, 1996). This kind of Court deals with disputes about property and commercial contracts. However, most criminal offences (especially serious ones) were dealt with by the Orf Courts (Enayat, 2013).

During the Qajar era, the Shah had absolute power, and the Courts were in full possession of him, and although there were "Shaykh al-Islām",[1] this type of authority had no power against the Shah (Enayat, 2013). The initiation of institutional changes in the judiciary in Iran dates back to Naser al-Din Shah's time, and some scholars believe that he attempted to reduce the influence of the Grand Ayatollahs (mujtahids) on the Courts (Amin, 1992). From what has been mentioned above, seemingly the first fundamental change in Iran's judiciary system was during the time of Nasir-Din Shah, which was also the era of the creation of the Minister of Justice. Naser-Din Shah, in 1859, established a board of ministers called State Government, with six ministers delegated, one of which was a Justice Minister. Naser-Din Shah's next step was the establishment of "the secretary office for Court of Justice", which was exclusively controlled by the Minister of Justice and was the centre where people could file a complaint; and officers could decide if the case should be dealt in Orf Court (in which he would himself issue a ruling); otherwise, he would refer the case to a Faqīh (Islamic jurisprudence) for ruling (Madani, 1980).

In 1862, Naser-Din Shah established "Divaan Mazalem" or the Disciplinary Tribunal. This tribunal was in fact a court where the king or his agent dealt with the cases. Madani (1980) stated that the major part of the claims that the Shah considered were related to princes and Khans (noblemen). Other disputes, often related to the rights of ordinary individuals, were referred to Ayatollahs. Usually when filing a lawsuit, the mujtahid invited both parties to investigate, and by both parties being present he would assess their claims based on the rules and reasons known in the Shari'a of Islam and the examination of evidence. Haghdar (2011) describes courts in Naser-Din Shah's era and claimed that Courts were established to deal with public claims and complaints, and even a booklet with title "The Rules of The Supreme Administrative Court's Booklet" was published, but in fact neither the organisation nor the effectiveness of the law was enforced.

The next major step in the process of change in the judiciary occurred when Mirza Hosein Sepahsalar was appointed the Minister of Justice by Naser-Din Shah in 1870. In the first act, that was unprecedented in the history of Iran's judicial system, Sepahsalar urged Naser-Din Shah to order his governors to not issue any judgement, and to give monopoly of issuing judgements to the Courts. This was the first attempt towards independence of the courts. Another major step endeavoured by him was to reduce corruption in the judicial system (Introduction to ancient Iran's judicial system, 2001).

For the first time, Sepahsalar introduced a new law on the 20th June 1871, with the title of "The Act for The Ministry of Justice and The Courts"[2]. According to this law, other parts of the government were not allowed to interfere in judicial process or influence the court in the issuance of judicial orders (Haghdar, 2016). Sepahsalar made much effort to reduce the influence of the Ayatollahs on the Courts, and ordered that physical punishment and amputation of body parts stop. Although Sepahsalar was celebrated for his attempts to promote justice, it was still not available to all ordinary citizens. Kasravi (1943) even claims that there was no real court in that era in Iran.

The lack of access to justice for ordinary people is one of the most important factors in the formation of the Persian Constitutional Revolution,[3] to the point where it was initially called the "Movement for the House of Justice".[4]

Criminal Justice System after the Constitutional Revolution

The importance of the independent judiciary in the contemporary political history of Iran is so great that the establishment of "the House of Justice" is one of the main demands of the constitutional revolution. Of course, some people argue that the establishment of the house of justice was merely a slogan and the main goal of the movement was the creation of the National Assembly (Fallah, 1998); however, most scholars believe the non-existence of a proper judiciary played a major role in the engagement of ordinary citizens, and their protests led to the formation of the Constitutional Revolution. In addition, they refer to the contradictory judgements of Shari'a courts as another reason (Arjomand & Brown, 2013).

By looking at the demands of the protestors in the early stages, one can see that they asked for the creation of a proper court in every city of Iran. In Clause 4 of the letter from protestors (their official demands), they stated: "Establishing a justice system in Iran, to deal with claims, complaints, and the suppression of the minority in an equitable manner" (Kasravi, 1943, p. 34). This is how the constitutional revolution forced Mozaffar ad-Din Shah[5] to issue a decree on the 4th of August of 1906. In his decree, he ordered his chancellor to establish an independent judiciary in Iran.

The next important development happened on the 6th of October 1907, when the next Shah was forced to sign an amendment of Constitution. That amendment (Articles 73 and 74) stated that nobody was allowed to create any court outside the law. Although the authors of the constitution were inspired by the constitutions of European countries, and had introduced tribunals as the only source for dealing with crimes, they still allowed Ayatollahs to judge religious affairs.

Other principles of the amendment of the Constitution tried to ensure citizens' access to the court, as well as the process of appointing judges, to be transparent. It also confirmed the openness of the courts and the transparency of the verdicts:

> Art. 76. All proceedings of tribunals shall be public, save in cases where such publicity would be injurious to public order or contrary to public morality. In such cases, the tribunal must declare the necessity of sitting clausis foribus (court in closed session).
>
> Art. 77. In case of political or press offenses, where it is desirable that the proceedings should be in private, this must be agreed to by all the members of the tribunal.
>
> Art. 78. The decisions and sentences emanating from the tribunals must be reasoned and supported by proof, and must contain the articles of the Law in accordance with which judgement has been given, and they must be ready publicly.
>
> Art. 79. In cases of political and press offences, a jury must be present in the tribunals.
>
> Art. 80. The presidents and members of judicial tribunals shall be chosen in such manner as the laws of justice determine, and shall be appointed by Royal Decree.
>
> Art. 81. No judge of a judicial tribunal can be temporarily or permanently transferred from his office unless he be brought to judgment and his offence be proved, save in the case of his voluntary resignation.
>
> Art. 82. The functions of a judge of a judicial tribunal cannot be changed save by his own consent.
>
> Art. 83. The appointment of the Public Prosecutor is within the competence of the King, supported by the approval of the ecclesiastical judge.

Art. 84. The appointment of the members of the judicial tribunals shall be determined in accordance with the law.

Art. 85. The presidents of judicial tribunals cannot accept salaried posts under government, unless they undertake such service without recompense, always provided that [in this case also] there be no contravention of the Law.

Art. 86. In every provincial capital there shall be established a Court of Appeal for dealing with the judicial matters in such ways as is explicitly set forth in the laws concerning the administration of justice.

Art. 87. Military tribunals shall be established throughout the whole Kingdom according the special laws. (Persian Constitution of 1906, cited by Shuster, 2013))

Enayat (2013) believes that the law and justice has been at the heart of the ideology of constitutional revolution (2013, P). The author of the Constitution had some inspiration from Europe. Their Constitution believed that any citizen is equal before the law and must have access to justice. However they also had to follow the traditions of the society in Iran (as a Muslim-majority country). Therefore, in Article 2 of the amendment, it stated:

> Art. 2. At no time must any legal enactment of the Sacred National Consultative Assembly, established by the favour and assistance of His Holiness the Imam of the Age (may God hasten his glad advent!), the favour of His Majesty the Shahinshah, of Islam (may God multiply the like them!), and the whole people of the Persian Nation, be at variance with the sacred rules of Islam, or the laws established by His Holiness the Best of Mankind (on whom and on whose household be the blessings of God and His peace). (Persian Constitution of 1906)

Judicial System during the Post-constitutional Period

In the aftermath of the victory of the Constitutional Revolution, due to the lack of specific laws and disciplinary procedures, the judicial system of the country faced a crisis. According to the second principle of the amendment to the constitution which ordered the issuance of a sentence subject to its compliance with Islamic law, there was a great deal of restriction on the court. Even creating new laws was opposed by the Ayatollahs. Amin (2012) insisted that even a few years after signing the constitution, judges (assigned by the Ministry of Justice) did not dare refer to their decisions as judgements.

Eventually on the 17th July 1911, a new law of the Principles of the Judiciary[6] was passed by the National Assembly. According to this law, the courts of Iran took on a new form and structure. On the 9th November 1911, another law called the Provisional Laws of the Principles of Legal Trials[7] was approved by the National Assembly. This law emphasised that religious matters (marriage, divorce, etc.) should be taken into Sariah courts and cases relating to matters, such as taxes and state privileges, should be taken to the Orf court. After 1921, Reza Khan (Later Reza Shah) rose to power, dissolved the previous government, and changed the Prime Minister. For a few years, he was the Commander-in-Chief of the Army, and later became the new Shah.

Reza Shah appointed Ali Akbar Davar as the new Minister of Justice on the 9th of February 1927. Davar had dissolved the judiciary only 48 hours after his appointment of the Justice Minister with the permission of the National Assembly, and then presented the modern Judiciary. During this process, efforts were made to regulate the judges' performance, and they were replaced with new judges who had legal knowledge. Therefore, over a short period of time, the majority of clerics lost their jobs as judges.

Ali Akbar spoke in the House of Representatives when he defended his plan to redesign the judiciary, and stated: "This court system, which came from the first constitution and is based on citizens demands, . . . I thought of it and did not see any way to reform it, unless to change it from the foundation . . .." (as cited in Haghdar, 2016). In 1933, Sariah Courts jurisdiction was limited to divorce tribunals.

Although many believe that the new judicial structure in Iran is due to the Davar's action and the efforts of Reza Shah, Enayat (2013) insisted that Davar did not carry out the reform alone, and the creation of a new legal structure was at the heart of the constitutional movement. Subsequently, on the 16th of September 1946, the National Assembly passed the Civil Procedure Law. Of course, the law was amended in 1952. After the 1953 Iranian coup d'état and considering that Mohammad Reza Shah Pahlavi had a much wider power, independence of the judiciary was undermined. Mohammad Reza Shah extended the authority of the military and security courts, and with the creation of specialised commissions in the municipalities, the task of reviewing and resolving disputes in some matters was turned over to these commissions.

In 1963, Mohammad Reza Shah presented his far-reaching series of reforms in Iran known as The White Revolution. He created "fair houses"[8]as mediate council in the villages.

Arjomand focused on the appointment of the highest judicial authority, the minister of justice, and recalls that many judges initially joined the cabinet. But at the same time, only 6% of those who were previously in the judicial system were appointed to the position of Justice Minister between the years of 1906 and 1979. But more than 41% of them were previously in the post of Minister of the Interior, and 16% were Minister of Economy. Arjomand argues that such behaviour undermined judges and their importance in Iran (Arjomand, 2013).

It is clear that Pahlavi I and II made a very extensive effort to modernise the country; they also endeavoured to move the judicial system away from its Islamic Origins (Entesar, 1988 as cited by Barlow, 2015).

The Main Achievement in the Judiciary after the Constitutional Revolution

These achievements can be listed in the following categories:

- Establishing the official procedure so citizens could easily find out what their rights were in the courts,
- Attempts to appoint people with legal knowledge and experts as judges,
- Preventing the issuance of contradictory judgement in different parts of the country and trying to create precedents,
- An attempt to create a new order in the country using courts and the Prosecution office,
- Establishing a place in society for lawyers and creating an association for them as a civil institution.

Major Changes in the Judicial System of Iran after the 1979 Islamic Revolution

Arjomand(1989) accepted that after the revolution, the government made attempts to modernise Shari'a, but emphasised that after the 1979 Revolution, Iran's transformation was a traditionalising of a nation which had been modernised before.

It can be claimed that the result of the 1979 revolution in Iran's judicial system has been a great effort to traditionalise the system. In the following points, the most significant changes in Iran's judiciary after the 1979 Revolution will be reviewed (in a separate section, there will be detailed discussions on how the special Clerical Court was formed).

After Khomeini took control of the country in 1979, he assigned Sadeq Givi Khalkhali as the Shari'a ruler or head of the newly established Revolutionary Courts on the 24th of February 1979. He is known in Iran as the "hanging judge". However, on the 15th February 1979, ten days before Khomeini assigned him any judicial authority, Khalkhali executed four citizens without any judicial authority.

On the 7th of March 1979, a bill on the reform of the Judiciary was approved by the revolutionary council, which had extensive powers, including the right to dissolve courts and judicial authorities. Those departments that were redundant were identified and re-established after settlement.

On the 16th of March 1979, the Supreme Court and its prosecutor's office, and the judicial review courts were dissolved.

On the 4th of April 1980, the Supreme Court[9] was created with a new structure.

In June 1980, the Revolutionary council approved the regulation that led to the establishment of the Revolutionary Courts formally. The Shari'a courts were replaced by the Revolutionary Courts. Based on that regulation, the formation and dissolution of this court were set out in the rules:

> Article 1: the reason for the formation of this court was to investigate the crimes committed before the victory of the revolution in order to consolidate the Pahlavi regime and to establish and prevent maintain the influence of foreigners, or after the victory of the revolution against the Islamic revolution of the Iranian nation. These courts were formed at the command of the leader of the Islamic Revolution in the centre of each province, an Islamic public revolutionary Prosecutor's Office. (Resolution about the Revolutionary Courts, approved by the Revolutionary Council, 1980, June 2, 2nd paragraph)

The use of Ayatollah Khomeini's book has been recognised as one of the main sources for the formulation of laws, and courts have also cited that book as law in their judgements. For example, the Guardian Council has officially announced that it will refer to this book in order to check whatever law passed by Parliament is against Islam or not.

In June 1980, the Bar Association founded by Davar in 1936, which was an independent institution, was suspended.

On the 27th of September 1981 after amending the Criminal Procedure Code, a new Criminal Court division was created (Islamic Penal Code, 1981).

On the 1st of May 1983, a new law was passed by the Islamic Consultative Assembly, which permitted the continued life of the Revolutionary Court (Act for Revolutionary Courts 1983).

Following changes to the constitution, according to Khomeini's recommendation, the institution of the Supreme Judicial Council was dissolved and was replaced by the head of the judiciary (Arjomand, 2013).

After Ayatollah Ruhollah Khomeini's death, Ayatollah Ali Khamenei rose to power. A constitutional referendum was held in Iran on the 28th of July 1989 and was approved by voters. In the amendment, they created a new post of Head of the Judiciary, who took over the role of the Supreme Judicial Council, and has a wide range of power, including the appointment and dismissal of judges, and the drafting of bills of law to be considered by the Islamic Consultative Assembly (Nohlen, 2001).

In 1999, the former head of the judiciary in Iran (Ayatollah Yazdei) insisted on making a change in the judiciary. Based on his request, the prosecutor's office was removed from the judicial system, and the task was given to the judge himself (Ahmadi, 2015).

Scholars believed in 1920 that Iranian law was adopted from Napoleonic law, which created the system of courts and tribunals. The prosecution and court system in Iran continued until 1994, after which the authorities claimed that they intended to implement Islamic law in the judicial system. This mode of action was done in such a way that the police were enabled to arrest offenders and take the perpetrators directly to court. In this system, the prosecution and the prosecutor's office were removed, and the police took their place instead (Ashori, 2014).

In 1999, a new law concerning the head of the judiciary was passed and in accordance with this law, the powers of the head of the judiciary were extended. Most importantly, he gave them judicial powers. Article 2 stipulates the following:

> The head of the judiciary has judicial positions. While carrying out inspections, if he finds court's verdicts or judgements violating the judicial ruling, it will be referred to a more competent authority. (Judiciary Act, 1999)

Under this law, the head of the judiciary oversees all courts and sentences issued in the country. As the chief judge, all courts are considered his jurisdiction.

In 2002, a new law was passed and a new prosecutor's office with general jurisdiction in the investigation of public and revolutionary crimes was established (Prosecutor Law, 2002). The Iranian newspaper (Mardomsalary) reported that the head of the judiciary announced in 2010 that efforts were being made by the judiciary to create a special task force as the "Intelligence Services of Judiciary" (Mohdeni, 2 August 2010).

Formation of the Special Clerical Court

The special Clerical Court is a Court that cannot easily be called a subsection of the judiciary. In fact, it acts as a parallel body. The existence of such a system has not been approved in the constitution, and even the Iranian Parliament has not endorsed the creation of such a body.

It should be noted that one of the demands made during the constitutional revolution was for courts to be legally created, in accordance with the amendment of the Persian Constitution of 1906, which was ratified more than 100 years ago.

Although the Persian Constitution of 1906 is no longer in force, even the current constitution expressly states in Article 159 that the formation of a court should be in accordance with the law, and states: "Article 159: The Ministry of Justice is the official source for submitting grievances and complaints. The composition of the courts and their competence are subject to the law." (The Constitution of the Islamic Republic of Iran)

Many scholars consider the revolutionary court as an unlawful organisation, but at least the revolutionary court is a subordinate of the judiciary and the parliament has ratified it. Meanwhile, the clerical court has no such legally recognised character.

Since many influential judges are clerical, this organ can itself act as leverage against independent judges. One scholar claimed that the Special Clerical Court has become a tool to put pressure on judges who are clergy, and if necessary, they will be punished (Entesar, as cited in Barlow, 2015). In order to understand how Ayatollahs justify the existence of this court, it should be noted that in their ideology, the Supreme Leader has absolute jurisdiction and authority over the judiciary, and as a result he can reformulate the shape of the court or create a new one. Ayatollah Hashemi Shahroodi (former head of judiciary) stated: "The Supreme Leader (Velâye-e Faqih) has absolute jurisdiction over judiciary." (Shahroodi, no date, p. 111).

On the 24th of May 1979, Ayatollah Khomeini ordered the establishment of the Special Clerical Court. Therefore, the Special Clerical Court was formed from the very beginning of the revolution on the orders of Khomeini. Its activities were reduced on request of Ayatollah Montazeri; however in 1987, the Special Clerical Court was restored (Arjomand, 2013).

Based on existing documents and evidence, the Special Clerical Court and its activities can be divvied into three stages:

- 1st stage: The first stage of the formation of the Special Clerical Court was proposed by Montazeri and confirmed by Khomeini in 1979.
- 2nd stage: In 1987, according to Khomeini's command, it was formed to repress the affiliates with Ayatollah Montazeri (Mohamadi, 2008).

- 3rd stage: In 1989 and following the appointment of Khomeini as the Supreme Leader, the Special Clerical Court was expanded (Arjomand, 2013).

Due to a lack of information and a lack of access to witnesses and preliminary information, little research has been done on the Special Clerical Court. Kankalar addressed this issue, and she described this court as the following:

- The main duty of the Special Clerical Court is investigating crimes committed by members of the clergy, but in practice it has become a means of suppressing opposition clerics.
- After reaching the Supreme Leader position, Khamenei expanded and established branches for this Court in 10 Iranian cities. He also prepared a regulation for this court and published it in October 1990. Although the regulation was published in the official newspaper of the country, the parliament did not approve it. Its publication in the official newspaper was an attempt to legalise it in accordance with the rules of judges and the prosecutors.
- Although the verdicts issued by this court are not subject to appeal, it seems that an appeal can be rendered in the first branch of the Special Court for the Clerical court.
- The verdicts of this court are not published anywhere, and proceedings take place behind closed doors. The defendants do not have the right to freely choose a lawyer either. They must choose their lawyer from the list of attorneys the court provides them with. The judges and the chairman of the court should be "Hojatoleslam", but they are not required to have legal education.
- The special clerical court also sentenced non-clergy citizens too, for example, the editor of a journal who was not at all clerical was sentenced to four months imprisonment. In some cases, this court has given immunity to clerics and refused to hear cases.
- It can clearly be seen that there is no accountability or independence with the Special Clerical Court, and all is monitored by Khamenei, to suppress his opponents (Arjomand & Brown, 2013).

At the time Khomeini ordered the creation of this court, in his own words, he said all courts and the Supreme Court of Justice must cooperate with the Special Clerical Court. In other words, the Special Clerical Court is superior to all other ordinary courts.

One of the most important cases investigated by this court is the execution of Mehdi Hashemi. He was one of the founders of the revolutionary guard and was sentenced to death in 1987 due to the disclosure of the Iran–Contra affair (Wilfrie, 2000).

The Current Structure of the Judiciary in the Islamic Republic of Iran

In this section, the structure of the judiciary and the existing courts are introduced. Obviously, instead of the administrative structure, focus will be on the hierarchy of the court.

Administration and Policymaking

The Supreme Leader. According to Article 157 of the Iranian constitution, the Supreme Leader appoints the head of the judiciary:

> In order to fulfil the responsibilities of the judiciary power in all of the judicial, administrative, and executive matters, the leadership designates for a period of five years a just scholar of jurisprudence (mujtahid), who is knowledgeable of judicial matters and is a competent administrator as the head of the judiciary power: the supreme position in the judiciary power. (The Constitution of the Islamic Republic of Iran)

Article 57 of the constitution, while declaring independence of the judiciary, affirms that all three powers must be under the supervision of the leader.

> The governing powers in the Islamic Republic of Iran consist of the legislative, the executive, and the judiciary powers. They operate under the supervision of the absolute authority of the command (velayat-i amr) and religious leadership (imamat) of the community of believers and according to the forthcoming articles of this law. These powers are independent of one another. (The Constitution of the Islamic Republic of Iran)

The head of the judiciary. According to Article 157 of the constitution, the Supreme Leader appoints the head of the judiciary for a term of five years, and according to Article 158 of the constitution, he will have vast powers such as the dismissal and appointment of judges, and the power to approve regulations and appeals.

It should be noted that according to Article 91 of the constitution, half the members of the Guardian Council are nominated by the head judiciary, and once approved by the parliament they will be appointed. The findings of Bahraini and her colleagues (2014) showed that the Guardian Council has a significant influence in holding elections and could exclude candidates. In reality, the Guardian Council manipulates elections in Iran.

The Supreme Court of Iran. The Supreme Court is the highest judicial body in the country, and its judgements and orders overrule all civil and criminal courts. According to Article 110 of the constitution, the Supreme Court can investigate any complaints against the president.

Ministry of Justice. The Minister of Justice is the only link between the judiciary and the executive branch and has no judicial authority.

The Prosecutor-General of Iran. According to Article 162 of the constitution the head of the Supreme Court and the Prosecutor-General of Iran are also an Ayatollah and will be appointed by the head of the judiciary.

General Courts

In Iran, the court system comprises of general and specialised courts. General courts enjoy the jurisdiction to deal with all cases, and only exclude cases that specifically fall under the rule of specialised courts.

Preliminary Courts (Dadgahe-y- badvi). This category comprises of the following courts:

- *Family Court.* Family disputes on divorce, marriage, alimony, custody, and such matters are the responsibility of this court.
- *Criminal Courts.* This court will hear cases about criminal offences. Of course, the prosecutor also cooperates parallel to this court. It should be noted that this court cannot deal with such crimes that fall under the jurisdiction of certain courts such as the Revolutionary Courts or the Clergy Courts.
- *Provincial Criminal Courts.* The investigation of crimes punishable by severe penalties, such as execution, life imprisonment, and stoning, as well as the investigation of press and political crimes are within the jurisdiction of this court. Also, according to the law, citizens' complaints about members of parliament or cabinet members, members of the Guardian Council and the Assembly of Experts, senior officials of the Armed Forces or the managers of

the Ministry of Intelligence will also be heard by this court. In most cases, the court will consist of three judges, but in cases where the death penalty or life imprisonment is a possibility, the court will have five judges.
- *Civil Courts.* It is responsible for dealing with civil disputes.
- *The Centres for Dispute Resolution (Shoraye-e- hal ekhtelaf).* In order to reduce court cases, claims, and complaints, some cases will be heard by the Dispute Resolution Council. The jurisdiction of this council includes the following: (a) Civil and legal affairs, and (b) The private aspects of unforgiveable crimes.

Appellate Courts (Dadgah-a-hay-e tajdeed-e-nazar). This category comprises of the following courts:

- Appellate court of province (dadgaheh tajdid-e nazar-e ostan) who deals with appeals from the decisions of preliminary courts.
- The Supreme Court of Iran (Divane- aley-e keshvar) is the highest juridical authority and deals with civil and criminal appeals. Article 161 of the Iranian constitution: "The Supreme Court is to be formed for the purpose of supervising the correct implementation of the laws by the courts, ensuring uniformity of judicial procedure, and fulfilling any other responsibilities assigned to it by law, on the basis of regulations to be established by the head of the judicial branch."

Specialised Courts

This category comprises of the following courts:

- *Revolutionary Courts (Dadgahe-e- enghelab) deals with* crimes against national security, moharebeh (waging war against God), and Mofsed-e-filarz (spreading corruption on Earth), assassination of political officials, insulting Khomeini or Khamenei, conspiracy against the government of the Islamic Republic, military coup, espionage, gambling, abuse of public property, and all other crimes relating to drugs and smuggling are the responsibility of this court.
- Court of Protection deals with children and mentally unfit persons. It is within the jurisdiction of this court to deal with children's affairs and those who do not have mental health capacity.
- Young Offender's Court has the duty to investigate crimes committed by children under the age of 18.

- Review Courts *(Divane-e- edalate – edari).* The duty of this court is to deal with members of the public's complaints against civil servants, government agencies, or the violation of government regulations.
- The Special Court for the Clergy and its Special Prosecutor's Office (dadgah vijeh rohanit). This court has the jurisdiction to deal with all the crimes committed by clergymen.
- The disciplinary Court for the Judges investigates claims against judges.
- The Special Court for the investigation of State Employees Crimes investigates crimes such as bribery and embezzlement by civil servants.
- Judiciary Organisation of the Armed Forces. It is this court's responsibility to handle the crimes of the Armed Forces as well as the Ministry of Intelligence.

Charts

Structure of the Iranian Judiciary

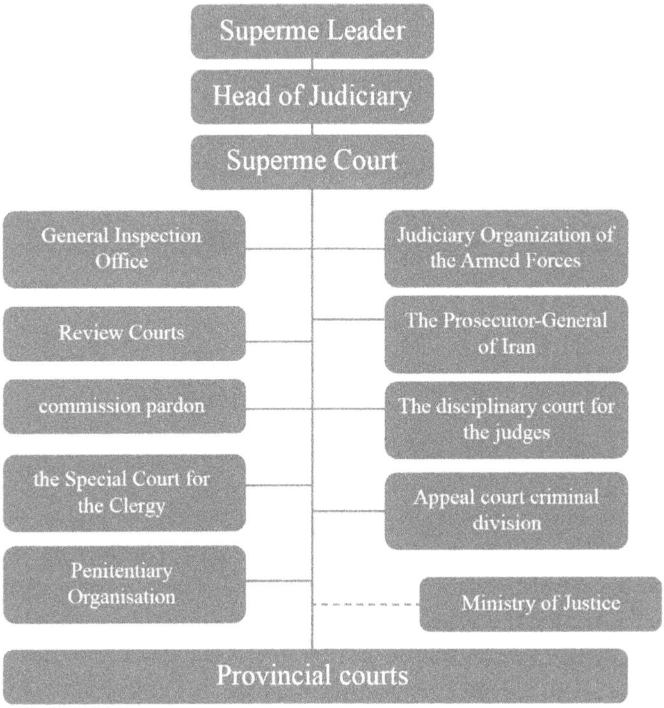

Figure 3.1: Structure of the Iranian judiciary. Source: Author.

Structure of the Judiciary (Provincial Courts)

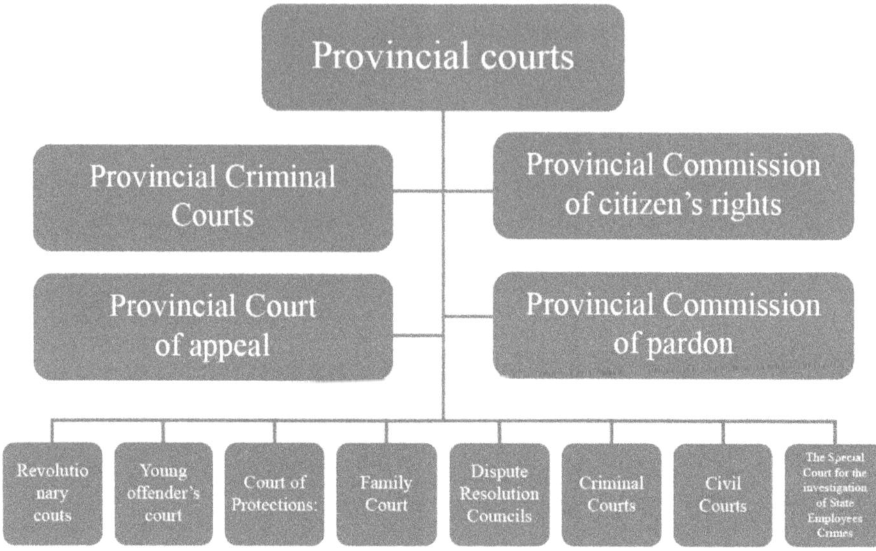

Figure 3.2: Structure of the judiciary in The Islamic Republic of Iran (Provincial courts). Source: Author.

Definition of the Judge and the Judiciary

To understand the causes of corruption in the judiciary, it is necessary to know how law and Shari'a law define a judge; then we need to understand what the extent of the authority of the judge in Iran is.

The Legislator's and Shari'a Perspectives of a Judge

The following is said in the preamble to the constitution:

> The judiciary in its preservation of the rights of the people, and in accordance with the line followed by the Islamic revolution, and in its prevention of deviations within the Muslim nation, plays a crucial role. Therefore, provisions must be made to create a judicial system that is based on Islamic justice and is composed of just judges who are aware of the precise criteria laid down in Islam. Given the sensitive nature of the judiciary and the need for its ideological correction, the judiciary must shun any unhealthy relations and connections. This is in accordance with the Qur'anic verse, 'When you pass judgment among men, judge with fairness' (The Constitution of the Islamic Republic of Iran).

In the school of jurisprudence (fiqh) in Twelver Shi'a Islam, the bench of a judge belongs to the Prophet and his successors. In fact, the judge is regarded as the successor of the Prophet on the bench (The book Al-Kāfī, vol. No 7, Page 407). In the eyes of the Shi'a jurists, in the absence of the twelfth Imam, this duty is left to the jurists who have adequate knowledge of Ahl al-Bayt[10] (Wasā'il al-Shīʿa, Vol no 8, page 98). Hence, some jurists have argued that a judge should by necessity be an individual who is qualified to exercise ijtihad in the evaluation of Islamic law (mujtahid). Under the current laws and procedures for the appointment of judges, there is no need for the judge to be a mujtahid, but they should be completely familiar with Islamic law.

Authority of Judges

One of the most important reasons for the corruption in the judiciary is the wide discretion given to judges, and in some conditions, the judges can even act beyond the law. According to procedural law, the judge is allowed to act as Mujtahid; therefore, the judge is allowed to ignore any law which he thinks is against Shari'a law. For example, Article 3 of the Civil Procedure refers to some of the judge's duties, and states that Court judges are obliged to comply with applicable laws and regulations in a manner that is appropriate to issue their judgements. If the laws of the subject are not clear or are contradictory, or if there is no law in that subject, then judges are allowed to issue their judgement based on authentic Islamic sources, fatwas.

In fact, the judges can invoke authoritative Islamic sources instead of the law, despite the fact that there is no distinct definition of these sources and these sources may be considered valid from one person's perspective and not valid from another. This situation contradicts legal certainty, and undermines the rule of law.

On the other hand, the sources of jurisprudence are not easy for the citizens to understand; in fact, citizen's access to the rules are reduced. Citizens cannot figure out what the law stipulates regarding different issues. It should be noted that certainty of the law and understanding of the law are the most important foundations of the rule of law.

The Principle of the Discretion of the Judge (Elme-Qazi)

Because of the importance of the judge's knowledge in the creation of corruption, next this essay will review the judge's knowledge and notion behind it.

First, it is necessary to provide explanations about the duty of each Muslim. There are three types of duty in Islam:

- The duty of each person to god, for example, praying (Hagho-al- Allah).
- The duty of each person to other members of the society, for example, paying back loans (Hagho-al-naass).
- The duty of each person to themselves, for example, not harming themselves (Hagho-al-nafs).

Khomeini published a book called Tahrir al-Wasilah (1964), which is his commentary on a traditional theological text. After the revolution, this book became the main reference for the formulation of laws and many judges cite from it when they cast their judgement. Khomeini referred to a judge's knowledge and said: "Issue no 8: the judge can issue a judgement in any matter related to the duty of person toward his god or other member of society only based on his personal knowledge without requiring witnesses or any evidence." (Khomeini, 1964, p. 367)

In fact, according to this decree, judges are empowered to take actions regardless of the existence or non-existence of evidence.

Scholars have criticised this usage of judge's knowledge for issuing judgements; for instance, Abd al-Razzāq al-Sanhūrī) who drafted the Egyptian Civil Code of 1948) argued that a judge's knowledge should not be a reason for judgement, because parties cannot evaluate it. Secondly, the right to dispute will be quashed. Even if the judge gives one party to dispute his personal knowledge, the judge will be demoted to one of the parties to the dispute (Arabian, no date).

Knowledge in jurisprudence terms means certainty and is also called ordinary knowledge (Jafari-Langaroodi, 1987). Hosseinpoor (2007) in the *Jurisprudence Journal* defined the judge's knowledge as follows: "The judge's knowledge comes from his senses and has a wide range that includes method of discovery of crime" (p.55).

According to the theory of The Guardianship of the Islamic Jurist, the judge represents the Supreme Leader, and the Supreme Leader is considered representative of God. Ayatollah Shahroodi, the former head of the judiciary, has written a long article about judges' knowledge and has tried to justify using judges' knowledge in issuing judgements. He argued that the Supreme Leader sits as a replacement of the Prophet, and will have absolute right to use his knowledge in the process of issuing judgement (as a representative of god). Furthermore, the Supreme Leader's right is transferable, and he can appoint any judge and assign his authority to him (Shahroodi, no date, page 110–111). By relying on the above justifications, Iranian parliament passed the penal code, and Article 211 of the Islamic Penal Code allows judges to use their knowledge and issue any judgement based on it.

Impact of judge's knowledge as a result of criminal cases. One of the most important challenges facing the Iranian judiciary is that a judge can use his power to issue any judgement based on his personal knowledge. In other words, the judge can issue a verdict based on his opinion or knowledge without regard to the contents of the case. Although in civil cases, the judge has less chance to rely on his knowledge as in such cases the judge is obliged to follow certain grounds for issuing a judgement based on documents, statements, witnesses, swearing on oath, local investigations, and expert reports. Of course, Article 1335 of the Civil Code allows the judge limitations to use his knowledge; if one of the parties has sworn on oath, he can use his knowledge.

It should be noted that the Human Rights Watch fiercely criticises using judge's knowledge as a means for issuing judgement and calls for its removal (Human Rights Watch, 2012).

Jury in the Judiciary System of Iran

Currently, only for political crimes and crimes committed by the media, courts are allowed to use a jury (Mashadi, 2010). In fact, in the school of jurisprudence (fiqh) in Twelver Shi'a Islam, judges are not allowed to use other people's opinions to issue a judgement; therefore, the presence of a jury is not allowed (Zeydan, 1984).

Examining Anti-Corruption Laws in Iran

Judicial Immunity for Judges

According to Article 42 of the ACT for establishing the judiciary, judges are immune from any legal proceeding against them. However, according to advisory judgement from the Supreme Court of Iran, if the judge is suspended, his immunity will become invalid (Advisory no 7/3770 of the Supreme Court).

According to Article 8 of the ACT for establishing General Courts, the Criminal Court in Tehran has jurisdiction to hear any criminal case against judges; however, according to another law (Supervision of judges law), that court must seek permission from the attorney general to suspend any judge (and suspend his immunity), then they can hear the case against him.

The Iranian Parliament passed the above law (Supervision of Judges Act) on 09/10/2011. This act creates a special court to hear cases against any misconduct by any judge. According to that law, there is widespread authority dedicated to such courts. Article 11 outlines the duties and powers of the courts as the following:

- Inspection and detection of any violation of the law enforcement of judges and prosecution of the judges in any position or rank.
- Continuous monitoring of the performance of the judges, assessment, and investigation of inappropriate behaviour with respect to dignity and their privacy.
- Proposed suspension of a judge from judicial service to Supreme Court.
- Proposals encouraging outstanding services by the judges to the head of the judiciary.
- Proposal for the transfer of judges to the head of the judiciary in the implementation of Article 164 of the constitution.
- Inspection and preparation of reports on the performance of judges according to the request of the head of judiciary.
- According to Article 13 of the above law, the Supreme Disciplinary Court of Judges can impose a wide range of penalties on judges, including reduction of salary, demotion, and termination of contract. The above law forbids judges from receiving any gifts, and describes it as misconduct.

Bribery as a Crime in the Penal Code

In 1987, the Expediency Council passed a law about bribery. In Article 3, it stated that anyone who works for any part of government (including the judiciary) accepting or receiving any money or gifts (directly or indirectly) will be in breach of the law, and will be prosecuted for bribery. According to the above law, receiving a bribe can carry a punishment of five-year imprisonment. Furthermore, Article 592 of the Islamic Penal Code stated that anybody paying a bribe will face imprisonment of between 6 months and 3 years or 74 lashes.

Anti-corruption Methods

To prevent bribery, the human resources division of the judiciary uses the following rules:

1. Regulations on the prevention and combating of bribery in presidential institutions – department of justice – management, and planning organisation
2. Regulations on administrative offences

The above-mentioned regulations attempt to first train staff and then create a system of recording offenders' information to combat repeating this violation.

The Role of the Judiciary in the Massacre of Political Prisoners in the 1980s

In the summer of 1987, Ayatollah Khamenei (funder and previous Supreme Leader of the Islamic Republic of Iran) ordered that several thousands of political prisoners had to be executed. Several survivors, as well as Abrahamian (1999), claimed that a commission consisting of three judges (Nayeri, Ashraghi and Mobasheri) were responsible for all cases brought before the court, and it was not the case that there was no court for individuals. In fact, in unjust trials, commission members with a few simple questions decided whether the defendant was a Mohareb (Enemy of god) or not. These special judicial commissions asked the following questions from prisoners:

- Do you still believe in your previous political ideologies?
- Do you accept the legitimacy of the Islamic Republic of Iran?
- Do you pray on a daily basis?
- Are you willing to publicly condemn your political party? (Shahrooz, 2007)

When any prisoner failed to condemn their own political party, or stated they did not pray, then the court sentenced them to death. That special court sentenced thousands of political prisoners to death (Robertson, 2006).

Iranian judiciary officials (past and current) never condemn this massacre. For example, Sadiq Larijani, the head of the Iranian Judiciary, claimed those executions were lawful (Larijani, 2017).

In December 2005, the Human Rights Watch released a report, which officially accused Poor-Mohamadi (who was involved in those executions) of crimes against humanity (HRW. 2005). This person was then appointed as minister in 2015.

The Evil Judges

In the last four decades, three judges in Iran attracted more attention (compared to others), and most Iranian citizens know them.

- Sadiq Khalkhali: After the Iranian revolution in 1979, Khomeini appointed Sadigh Khalkhali as Special Judge. In an interview, he acknowledged that he ordered more than 400 executions. Even though he was a judge, he set a prize of 100,000 Dollars for the assassination of Mohammad Reza Shah Pahlavi. There is no exact number of people executed on his order. Some people estimate it to be up to 8,000 (Masumi, 2015).
- Saeed Mortazavi was born in 1968. In Iran, journalists refer to him as the "Butcher of the Press" (Ghaemi, 2014). Human Rights activists hold him responsible for his role in the murder of Canadian Photographer Zahra Kazemi (Human Rights Documentation Centre, 2006). He also served as the prosecutor general for the revolutionary court in Tehran (VOA, 2011). The following are noteworthy: After the Green Movement in Iran, and the murder and rape of a number of detainees in 2009, the Iranian parliament established the Committee of Investigations, and considered Mortazavi responsible for the incident. One MP reported: "We believe that one of the important parts of this case is related to someone who sent them unduly to Kahrizak" (DW, 2012). In 2011, the European Union, sanctioned Mortazavi for violating human rights (European Law, Council Regulation, 12 April 2011, No. 359/2011).
- Gholam-Hossein Mohseni-Eje'i is a jurist and prosecutor who currently serves as the second-highest official in the Judicial system of Iran. One of the witnesses of this research, Hooshang Bouzari, opened a file against Mr Mohseni at the Canadian High Court in Ottawa for kidnapping and extortion because Mr Bouzari, was forced to give more than $3 million in bribes to Mohseni-Eje'i, to release him. Mr Bouzari also provided the author with proof of payment of ransom to Mohseni-Eje'i, which is published in this book for the first time (See chapter 10, section 4-2). It should

be noted that these sums have been credited to the court's account, which, at that time, was a semi-personal account of officials such as Mr Mohseni.

The Committee of Inquiry of the Islamic Consultative Assembly

On the 16th of January 2009, by relying on Article 76 of the constitution, which authorised the investigation of all matters of the country to the parliament, parliamentarians declared that they were going to investigate the judiciary.

The head of the judiciary refused to cooperate with the parliament and two years later, sent a letter to the parliament claiming that because the judiciary is part of the Supreme Leader's administration, parliament is not allowed to investigate the judiciary (the letter is available in chapter 10, section 4-1, page 279). Following this, Khamenei, the Supreme Leader, opposed investigating judicial cases.

The process of the investigation of the parliament, even though it has been restricted to a small section of the judiciary, did not reach an answer. It is cited in the MPs report:

Not only none of the correspondence with more than 300 questions posed by the board as representative of the people, but also as guardians and law enforcers, despite the explicit prohibition of half the provisions of the internal rules of the parliament and Article 76 of the Constitution chose a time-wasting option in the accountability process (Iranian Parliament, (2012).

Notes

1 A title conferred by the Shah to a mujtahid to act in official capacity including advising the sultan on religious matters, legitimising government policies, and appointing judges
2 Ghanon-e- adlieh-e- azam va edalatkhaneh-hay Iran
3 Enghelāb-e Mashrūteh
4 Nehazateh-e Edalat-khaneh
5 Mozaffar ad-Din Shah Qajar (23 March 1853–3 January 1907), was the fifth Qajar king of Persia (Iran).
6 Ghanon-e- osol-e- Adlieh va Mahazer Shaireieh va ahkame solhieh
7 GHanone-e movaghateh osol mohakemat hoghoghi
8 Khaneh-e- Ensaf

9 Divan-e Aliey-e keshvar
10 The family of the Islamic Prophet Muhammad

References

Ahmadi, N. (2015, 3 June). *Ghoveh Ghazaei dar gozar tarikh* [History of Iranian judiciary]. Isna. https://bit.ly/35elobh

Amin. H. (1992). *Dadresi va nezame ghazeie iran.* [Judicial system in Iran]. Tehran: Daftareh Zamiran Pazhohesh Publication.

Amin, S. (2012). *Moshirodoleh va khanedanesh.* [Moshiro-al-doleh- and his family]. Available at: http://goo.gl/4u2mng

Arjomand, S. A. (1989). History, structure, and revolution in the Shi'ite tradition in contemporary Iran. *International Political Science Review, 10*(2), 111.

Arjomand, S. A., & Brown, N. J. (2013). *The rule of law, Islam, and constitutional politics in Egypt and Iran.* [electronic resource]. Albany, NY: State University of New York Press.

Arvidsson, A. (2010). *Corruption in the judiciary-balancing accountability and judicial independence.* Oslo: Orebro University.

Ashori, M. (2014). *Keshvar hanoz asar hazfe dadsar ra tahmol mikonad.* [adverse impact of elimination of Prosecutor Office. Isna. http://www.irna.ir/fa/News/81881794/

Barlowe, S. (2015). What's Islam got to do with it – obstacles in securing fair trial rights under Iran's repressive regime. *Cardozo Journal of International and Comparative Law*, (3), 601–630.

Enayat, H. (2013). *Law, state, and society in modern Iran.* London: Palgrave Macmillan US.

Entessar, N. (1988). Criminal law and the legal system in revolutionary Iran. *Boston College Third World Law Journal*, 91–101.

Fallah, H. (1998). Edalatkhaneh Dolati, Vezarat adlieh ya majles? [Judiciary, ministry of Justice, or Parliament?]. *Journal of Alzahrah University.* No 1. Serial 75. 1998.

Ferrer, A. (2014). *Blind justice: A case for judiciary impartiality in the Philippine Supreme Court.* Can be retrieved at: https://goo.gl/Vq4hNQ (accessed 04/01/2016).

Fierro, M. (2010). *The 'ulamā'. In the new Cambridge history of Islam* (Vol. 2, pp. 679–704). Cambridge: Cambridge University Press.

Haghdar, A. (2011). *Tajadod hoghoghi dar iran* [Modernity and law in Iran]. Available at: http://cheragheazadi.org/index.php/archives/1782

Haghdar, A. (2016). *Tahvolat siasi in Iran.* [Political change in Iran] Adbiat Publication. Istanbul.

Jafaari langarodi, M. (1987). Daireh-al-moraefe eslami [Islamic encyclopedia]. Tehran: Jamaran Publication.

Khosravi, M. (2011). Hakemiat ghanon chist [Rule of Law, law as a norm]. Can be retrieved at: http://yasharparsa.com/?p=1670

Madani, J. (1980). *Zamaneh Journal.* Number 7 and 8.

Mohseni, M. (2010, 2 August). *Ijade herasat.* [creating intelligence service] Mardomsalari newspaper. Can be retrieved at: http://goo.gl/omMyYb

Nohlen, D. (2001). *"Iran": A data handbook.* I. Tehran: Oxford University Press.

Shahroodi, M. (no date). *Elme- ghazi* [Judge's knowledge]. Tehran: Adlieh Publication. Available at: https://goo.gl/WN9D6M

Shuster, W. (2013). *The strangling of Persia*. Iran: Read Books Ltd.

Wilfrie, B. (2000). *Who rules Iran?: The structure of power in the Islamic Republic.* Washington, DC: The Washington Inst. for Near East Policy ISBN 0-944029-39-6.

Zamiran, M., & Ebadi, Sh. (1996). *Sonnat and tajadod dar hoghogh-e-iran.* [traditions and modernity in Iranian law]. Tehran: Ganj Publication.

4 Research Methodology

Research Approach

Introduction of Applicable Research Methods

Firstly, the two qualitative and quantitative approaches will be introduced.

1. Quantitative methods: A quantitative approach is a research method that attempts to explain a social phenomenon or prove a theory with the help of statistics and measurements of variables.
2. Qualitative methods: As described by Strauss and Corbin (1990) a research method that offers results other than quantitative statistics and methods is called a qualitative approach.

The Research Approach of This Treatise

Under normal circumstances it is possible to investigate corruption using the quantitative method by collecting statistics. But this approach is not feasible in Iran. Therefore, a qualitative approach has been chosen as the research method.

It is not possible to select a quantitative approach as criticism of the judiciary in Iran can have serious consequences. Hence, access to first-hand information such as the submission of questionnaires to ordinary judiciary clients is not available. There is no statistical information available with regard to judicial corruption in Iran.

Scholars believe that, if a field of research is known to a great enough extent, a preliminary modelling of the hypothesis can be made, and a theory presented about it, then the positivist and quantitative approach can be used. But if the information available about a particular phenomenon is so small that even recognising the unknown issues is problematic, then they should use the qualitative methods (Paul, as cited by Hariri, 2000).

Patton believed the qualitative approach is similar to how medical students try to understand the anatomy of the human body, and claims social scientists try to study a group of individuals or institutions to understand how those individuals or institutions operate (Patton, 2015).

Since the purpose of this study is to achieve a proper understanding of the phenomenon of corruption in the judiciary, efforts have been made to select individuals who have personally experienced this phenomenon. "Purposive sampling" facilitates researchers to find witnesses with the utmost exposure to the nature of their researches (Silverman, 2014, p. 61; Patton, 2015, p. 46).

Credibility of Qualitative Methods

Silverman (2006) claims a body of research will be credible only if other researchers perform the same research in a different location and time, and they find similar outcomes. In order to obtain the necessary accreditation for this research, the method advocated by Silverman (2006) will be used. He recommended that in order to gain credibility in a qualitative research, it is necessary for the researcher to provide a completely transparent method of this research so that every step taken is understandable by other researchers. Other scholars can then adopt similar methods. One of the most important concerns of the researcher during the conduct of qualitative research is to ensure the accuracy of the research materials. To ensure the accuracy of the results obtained, it is necessary to try and get the results compared with the initial theory.

Hence, during this research, based on the above advice, attempts will be made to keep the research method as transparent as possible, including questions and answers which will be in Appendix no 9. Also, during data analysis, attempts have been made to include quotations directly.

Data Collection

In qualitative research, one of the most effective research methods is the interview. The interviewer can focus on the experiences and views of the interviewee for gathering data as accurately and in as much detail as possible (Bryman, 2008). Mayring (2007) believed a qualitative approach will allow the researcher to collect background information as well as obtain information to be considered; at the same time, the researcher can consider other research theories.

In this research, a semi-structured interview method is chosen to collect information from ordinary interviewees. Based on the definition given in this structure, an interview is conducted on the basis of a predefined framework, and the purpose of the interview is still pursued. At the same time it gives the interviewer the opportunity to ask relevant questions with the most detailed answers from the interviewee (Powell, 2006).

Since the researcher can ask new questions, they are given the opportunity to hear the personal views as well as experiences of the interviewee. It should be noted that one or more structured interviews with specific questions cannot lead to the discovery of the truth. In light of this limitation, the researcher is required to be prompt in assessing the situation, and based on the information obtained, to raise questions in line with new information or explanations.

Other information has also been used in this study. This is secondary information that has not been directly collected by the author (e.g. the report of the Islamic Consultative Assembly investigation committee from the judiciary).

Drafting the Interview Guide

Before the questions and the framework of the interview for this research were developed, an investigation into existing research was carried out and attempts were made to become acquainted with the corruption.

Afterwards, attempts were made to identify and document organisations' charts and governing structure.

After gaining a clear understanding of judicial corruption and the structure of the judiciary, the interview guide was prepared. It should be noted that a "semi-structured interview method" has been selected so that the interviewee can be allowed to answer questions with the expression of language comfortable for them.

How the Author Conducted the Interviews

The framework of the interview is presented in an exhaustive table in the next section. Initially, the following points will be highlighted during and before the interview:

- The interviewee is reminded that they are not obliged to answer. There will be no intention to judge them; the sole purpose is scientific inquiry.
- It will be assured to the interviewee that there will be no intention to condemn them and I will not comment on their behaviour.
- It will be explained to the interviewee that their honesty and the presentation of an accurate and fair picture of the events that have taken place will be very important for the quality of this research.
- The interviewee will be clearly told what the purpose of the interview is and what topics should be focused on. The meaning of corruption in the judiciary will be explained to the interviewee.
- The interviewee will be informed that they are to be questioned about corruption in the judiciary; they will be asked to choose an alias if they are in Iran, and they will be asked to give rough ages of themselves with a difference of five years more or less for their own safety.
- The interviewee is requested to confirm that they will allow the use of their experiences and events that have occurred to them, and with their permission to refer to their quotes in this research.
- During the interview, notes will be taken, and the person's remarks will be written down.

Interview Guide (Ordinary Citizens)

For collecting data from ordinary citizens, participants will be asked the following questions:

Their real or alias name with their age.

- Why did you go to the judiciary? Please give a summary of your case.
- Did you go to the courts knowing there is a corrupt system operating?
- How was the quality of the provided services of the judiciary? Did you feel that it was due to the high volumes of cases that your case was not being dealt with fairly?

- Do you think that the judge or the court personnel, due to their personal interests, or the interests of the opposing party, or the prosecutor, did not act impartiality? Please explain.
- If you were aware of this, why did you not report this to the inspection authorities?
- Have you tried to win a case in court, attempted to be released from punishment, or made efforts to create personal interests for court employees or the judges? Did you pay bribes directly, or through any other means? Please explain.
- Did the judge of the court or the employees or people representing on his behalf, ask you to create personal interests for him?
- If you were asked to do so, why did you not report this to the higher authorities?
- Has your attorney represented your case on your behalf? What was your lawyer's reaction to the abuse by the judge or court employees? Has your attorney been informed, or did he have to intervene in this case?
- What was your opinion of the judge, both before and after going to court?
- Why did you not report this corruption to the media?
- If you believe that the judiciary is a corrupt one, what negative effects has it had on your society?

Interview Guide for Interviewing Lawyers

The next category of interviews will be conducted with the following set of questions for the lawyers:

- Is there a background thought in your mind that the Iranian Judiciary is corrupt?
- How was the quality of the service provided by the judiciary? Did you feel that due to the high volume of cases that your client's case would be struck? And was the lack of resources used as an excuse to adjourn the process?
- Have you ever experienced the judge or the court's staff violating their impartiality due to personal interests, the work of the opposing party, or the prosecutor in the case?
- Have you encountered judicial corruption? If so, why did you not report this to the inspection/ investigatory authorities?

- In your opinion, do you think the claim that some lawyers play a role in shaping judicial corruption is correct?
- In your opinion, how much has corruption in the judiciary had a negative impact on the general public's perceptions of the judge and the courts?
- Is the media succeeding as a tool for deterrence in preventing the formation of judicial corruption in Iran? For example, if you are facing legal corruption as a lawyer in Iran, why did you not report this corruption to the media?
- If you agree with the lack of fairness of justice and corruption, how has this impacted negatively on your society?
- Has the requirement for judges to write a detailed judgement and the reasons for issuing its ruling caused corruption itself?
- In your opinion, how effective have lawyers been in expanding or reducing the level of corruption?
- To what extent has "knowing the middleman" played a role in the judiciary?

An Interview Framework (Pre-Revolutionary Era)

There will be an attempt to ask the following questions from individuals, who have had direct experiences during the Pahlavi era:

- Have you ever felt that in the pre-revolutionary period the courts were contaminated with corruption, or put aside their impartiality?
- What was the position of the judges before the revolution? Did a sense of exclusive ranking in society ever exist in the judge's mind?
- Was there a possibility at the time, for example, that a military or security institution, or any authority, had tried to change or influence the opinion of the judge?
- Between 1960 and 1979, what organisations were responsible for combating corruption in Iran? Do you think they were successful at the time?

Awareness and Ethical Framework

Points to Consider for Selecting Interviewees

The author faced several restrictions for choosing interviewees for this research. On the one hand, utmost care needed to be used to prevent harming the participants in the interview. On the other hand, finding reliable interviewees was a very difficult task.

Therefore, extra delicacy was adopted in choosing interviewees.

In this research, several Iranian lawyers introduced the author to several of their clients. With the assurance that these lawyers gave to the interviewees, the author had the opportunity to ask the interviewees to participate in this research, and answer the questions with honesty and transparency.

All interviews were conducted in Persian. When interviewing people living in Iran, for security reasons, the interviews were not recorded; however, notes have been taken. But during interviews with participants outside the country, after obtaining their permission, their voices were recorded. Transcripts of interviews are exhibited in chapter 10 (section 5).

Observing Ethical Principles

In order to achieve objectivity, it is desirable for researchers to first clearly express their values and assumptions, and then try to minimise the effects of these values or assumptions (Myrdal, 1969). Hence the author wishes to confirm that he had the following beliefs before doing this research: (a) The author believed that the Iranian judiciary was severely corrupt, and there was no system against corruption; (b) The author believed that the lack of separation of religion from state plays an important role in the spread of that corruption.

Despite these assumptions, attempts have been made to conduct the research with impartiality. Mental preparations were made in readiness to accept the results of this research, even if they showed that there was no corruption in the judiciary.

Informed Consent of the Interviewees

The author was aware of the usual ethics throughout this research, and the following principles have been considered in this research:

- Respect of the rights of interviewees.
- Minimising adverse impacts of this research.
- Being treated fairly during research and refraining from harming others.

Moreover, since the author of this research is based in the UK, it was obligatory to apply the Data Protection Act 1998 and take utmost care of the personal information of the interviewees.

The ethical principles of academic research in preventing and avoiding harm to the privacy of individuals are very much emphasised. Therefore, to increase the security of witnesses living in Iran, they were asked to choose aliases instead of using their real names.

Coding and Content Analysis

Mayring (2000) defined qualitative content analysis as "an approach of empirical, methodological controlled analysis of texts within their context of communication, following content analytic rules and step by step models, without rash quantification" (Mayring, 2000, p. 2).

Qualitative content analysis was a practical method for this dissertation and allowed me to consider the context in which the data was collected. Furthermore, as Mayring (2007) suggested, I was able to consider the theoretical background of this research.

For interpreting collected data, Mayring (2014) introduced three fundamental methods: summary, explication, and structuring, and he described them as follows:

- Summary: The object of the analysis is to reduce the material in such a way that the essential contents remain, in order to create through abstraction a comprehensive overview of the base material which is nevertheless still an image of it.
- Explication: The object of the analysis is to provide additional material on individual doubtful text components (terms, sentences . . .) with a view to increasing understanding, explaining, and interpreting the particular passage of text.
- Structuring: The object of the analysis is to filter out particular aspects of the material, to give a cross-section through the material according to predetermined ordering criteria, or to assess the material according to certain criteria (p. 66). I interviewed 28 interviewees, and collected a large amount of data. In order to assess this data, the structuring method was used. Moreover, the categories, coding rule, and category system were developed, which will now be outlined below:
- The categories: Marying (2014) suggests that the categories "are deduced from theory, from other studies [or] from previous research" (p.97); therefore, especial attention was paid to the "independence of judiciary" and "judge status" in Iran. By defining the categories in a clear way, it was easy to determine which text belongs to which category. All categories were

created by taking into account previous research and theoretical aspects. Kohlbacher (2005) described this method as "deductive category application" (p. 14).
- Coding rules: The coding rules allowed me to assign text to the appropriate category unambiguously.
- Samples for each category: After defining categories, then the "coding rules" and "samples" were developed. Samples helped me to exemplify the character of each category.
- Category systems: The category systems were developed by employing a theory-guided procedure. As Mayring (2007) suggested, coding the data by using the category system meant I was able to construct my analysis step by step, which increased the reliability and credibility of this research.

By following the above steps, I was able to analyse collected data by following the rules in a systematic manner. Furthermore, I took the following steps:

- In order to have analysable contents, transcripts of all interviews were produced.
- Coding rules and the categories were developed.
- By reviewing the transcripts, I double checked the categories and coding rules.
- All statements were quoted directly.
- After coding transcripts, in Chapter 6, I analysed the data.
- The coding agenda and category system are available in chapter 10 (sections 10-1 and 10-2).

In addition to this, for analysing data, I considered the following suggestion from Mayring (2003) which he suggested as follows:

1. Transparency should be given to determine how unprocessed data is used in this research. This is further elaborated on.
2. The framework of the interview must be presented in a transparent manner.
3. He also recommended that the research question and research background should be mentioned. This topic is explained in Chapters 2, 3, and 4.
4. The subject category used to analyse the data also needs to be provided, and is presented in chapter 10 of the appendix section of this category.
5. Qualitative data analysis software (ATLAS.ti) was used to code the interview transcripts.

References

Bryman, A. (2008). *Social research methods.* Oxford and New York: Oxford University Press.

Hariri, N. (2000). *Ravesh hay asaasy pashoesh*, [research methods]. Tehran: Azad University Publication.

Kohlbacher, F. (2005). The use of qualitative content analysis in case study research [89 paragraphs]. *Forum Qualitative Sozialforschung/ Forum: Qualitative Social Research, 7*(1), Art. 21, http://nbn-resolving.de/urn:nbn:de:0114-fqs0601211.

Mayring, P. (2000). Qualitative content analysis. *Forum: Qualitative Social Research, 1*(2), 105–114. Retrieved from: http://www.qualitative-research.net/index.php/fqs/article/view/1089/2386 (accessed 31-03-2016).

Mayring, P. (2007) '*Qualitative Inhaltsanalyse*' [Qualitative Content Analysis]. In Uwe Flick, Ernst von Kardorff, & Ines Steinke (Eds.), *Qualitative Forschung – Ein Handbuch.* Reinbek: Rowohlt Taschenbuch Verlag GmbH, (Quoted from another research).

Mayring, P.(2014). *Qualitative content analysis: Theoretical foundation, basic procedures and software solution.* Klagenfurt, 2014. Retrieved from: https://goo.gl/Ll428y (accessed 31-03-2016).

Patton, M. Q. (2015). *Qualitative research & evaluation methods: Integrating theory and practice* (4th ed.). Los Angeles: SAGE.

Patton, Q. (2002). *Qualitative research and evaluation methods* (3rd ed.). Thousand Oaks, CA: Sage Publications.

Powell, R. R. (2006). Evaluation research: An overview. *Library Trends, 55*(1), 102–120.

Silverman, D. (2006). *Interpreting qualitative data: Methods for analyzing talk, text and interaction.* London: SAGE.

Silverman, D. (2014). *Interpreting qualitative data.* Los Angeles: SAGE.

Situngkir, H. (2011). *The Structural Dynamics of Corruption-Artificial Society Approach.* Bandung Fe Institute. retrieved from: https://arxiv.org/ftp/nlin/papers/0403/0403042.pdf

Strauss, A., & Corbin, J. (1990). *Basics of qualitative research: Grounded theory procedures and techniques.* Newbury Park, London, New Delhi: Sage Publications, Inc.

5 Data Analysis

In this chapter, the results of the interviews will be analysed based on previous studies into corruption. A detailed description of the category system is presented in Appendix. The most important points that these witnesses have given to their interviews are mentioned in Appendix.

Introducing Interviewees

A total of 28 interviewees were interviewed by the author during this research. A detailed interview was carried out with seven lawyers, two journalists, a former member of parliament, two judges and fourteen witnesses who had direct experience of judicial corruption. This research presents a clear picture of the judiciary. A list of interviewees is displayed in the following table:

Table 5.1: List of interviewees. Source: Author.

Code	Name		Age	Sex	Occupation	Whereabouts
	Nader. S	P	43	M	Trader	Iran
	Shervin Toloei	P	27	M	Businessman	Iran
	Shohreh Sajadi	P	25	F	Unemployed	Iran
	Mahmood Zomordian	P	29	M	Unemployed	Iran
	Mohsen Delavar	P	47	M	Physician	Iran
	Shideh Saboori	P	34	F	Housewife	Iran
	Nik Ahang Kousar	R	47	M	Journalist	USA (living in exile)
	Mehri Jafari	R	35	F	Lawyer in Iran, solicitor in the UK	UK (living in exile)
	Behnam Daraee Zadeh	R	39	M	Lawyer in Iran	Canada (living in exile)
	Houshang Boozari	R	65	M	Researcher	Canada (living in exile)
	Shima Tavakol	P	37	F	Lawyer in Iran	Iran
	Hossein Tavana	P	40		Trader	Iran
	A Alef. (Nosrati)	P	42	M	Lawyer in Iran	Iran
	Behzad Bahrami	R	39	M	Legal officer	Turkey ((living in exile)
	Farzad Azizi	R	43	M	Restaurateur in Iran	Sweden (living in exile)
	Reza Zoghi	R	38	M	Student in Iran, now refugee, living in exile	Turkey (living in exile)
	Mansour Osanloo	R	56	m	Head of trade union	USA (living in exile)
	Amir Iraei	R	50	M	Colonel in army and physician	Norway (living in exile)
	Naghi Mahmoodi	R	40	M	Lawyer in Iran	Germany (living in exile)
	Mohammed Fatemi	P	63	M	Retired judge Hujjat al-Islam,	Iran
	Shirin Ebadi	R	69	F	Nobel Peace Prize Laureate, and Judge and lawyer	UK (living in exile)

Table 5.1: *Continued*

Code	Name		Age	Sex	Occupation	Whereabouts
	Karim Lahijo	R	78	M	Lawyer, former president of the International Federation for Human Rights	France (living in exile)
	Manuchehre Fazel	R	75	M	Journalist	Germany (living in exile)
	Jalil Sadeghi	P	71	M	Lawyer	Iran
	Vahid Shirazi	P	54	M	Engineer	USA
	Mostafa Niazi	P	60	M	Hujjat al-Islam	Iran
	Hasan Yousefi Eshkevari	R	66	M	Former member of Parliament, and Hujjat al-Islam	Germany (living in exile)
	Mohsen Kadivar	R	57	M	Hujjat al-Islam, philosopher and professor of Islamic Studies	USA (living in exile)

R/P: Real name/ pseudonym

Data Analysis

Public Perception of the Islamic Judiciary

In order to understand judicial corruption, it is important to evaluate public perception about the judiciary, because public perception is an important factor for judges or court staff to define themselves. If judges or court staff see themselves as a respectable part of society, they are less likely to commit corrupt acts.

Furthermore, if ordinary citizens see the judiciary as a corrupt organisation, corruption will become a normal thing for them, and therefore it is less likely for them to react to corruption. On the other hand, if they think the judiciary is corrupt, it is more likely for them to engage in corruption and try to bribe judges or court staff to secure their own rights. In fact, if in public perception, the judiciary is a corrupt organisation, then the "opportunity" for corruption will increase. It should be noted that opportunity is an important factor for the occurrence of any crime (Kohen & Falson, 1979). Therefore, in this research, special attention was paid to public perception. In this section, interviewees share their experience:

D 1: Interviewee No. 1

> I had never heard anything about the corruption of the court until I reached the point whereby I got involved and witnessed it first-hand . . .

D 4: Interviewee No. 4

> I was arrested in the Green Movement protest [2009]. I was arrested on the day of Ashoora when I was swearing at the Supreme Leader . . .. The first couple of weeks I was tortured . . . They took me to the Revolutionary Courts. And the first thing I said was I was tortured . . .. The judge said "good". . . The next time, I was tortured even more by the interrogator . . .

D 5: Interviewee No. 5

> . . . It is so evident that the courts and the police are all corrupt . . .

D 6: Interviewee No. 6

> . . . it was the first time I was attending the court . . . Prior to visiting the court for my divorce matter, I was warned by a friend of mine to be cautious, as they [the judge or court's staff], will look at me as prey . . .

D 7: Interviewee No. 7

> . . . therefore, they would also rely on paying bribes in order to relieve themselves of the situations they are in . . . Getting employed with the judicial system has become a tool and a pattern to become reach quick . . .

D 7: Interviewee No. 7

> In another instance, a drug smuggler was executed despite paying bribes since he had rendered the payments to the wrong person

D 7: Interviewee No. 7

> Some judges play an important role in dividing confiscated properties, and this is another source of income for them. Setâd-e Ejrây-ye Farmân-e Emâm [the Executive Headquarters of Imam's Directive] is worth $90 Billion [so you can see the extent

D 8: Interviewee No. 8

> . . . I witnessed many cases in both civil and criminal matters indicating a lack of impartiality and sometimes a judge's prejudicialness to the parties or the subject of the case . . . Sometimes it could easily have the title of deviation and corruption in the judiciary, in a systematic way and not by accident . . .

D 9: Interviewee No. 9

> . . . I personally see judicial corruption as part of an organised corruption within the Islamic system, and what is imperative is that the judiciary is supposed to be people's representative in protecting the general public's rights . . . Prior to becoming a lawyer, I always had the mental assumption that the judiciary is corrupt in the Iranian system . . .

D 11: Interviewee No. 11

> . . . Corruption in the judiciary is a fact and there is no need for the presupposition of the mind. If people who have lived in Iran would have had a tangible experience of such corruptions . . .

D 12: Interviewee No. 12

> I had heard before that the court system is based on offering bribes, but I had never imagined the extent to which the corruption was . . .

D 13: Interviewee No. 13

> In relation to judicial corruption, the answer is that yes . . . there exists a pre-existing mental background . . .

D 16: Interviewee No. 16

> I knew from the outset and before I had any encounters of the system that the judiciary is a corrupt and unjust system in Iran . . .

D 17: Interviewee No. 17

> Another crime was the formation of a mafia network by prison officials, a judicial affiliate of the judiciary . . . These people created a network and every time the families of prisoners arrived to visit, pretending that they were taxi drivers, they

would pick their family up, mainly women ... They would abduct women and force them into the sex trafficking business ... One of them which was called "Green House" leaked ...

D 19: Interviewee No. 19

Before I began to work as a lawyer, I found that the justice system in Iran was suffering from corruption.

D 20: Interviewee No. 20

... I agree that citizens come to court with this background in their head that the court is corrupt, and they think the more you are prepared to pay bribes the more likely you will win in courts ...

D 21: Interviewee No. 21

The public trust in the judiciary has completely disappeared. Of course.

D 25: Interviewee No. 25

Before leaving for Iran, everyone had warned me that Iran is nothing but a place of corruption and robbing from one another's pocket ...

D 26: Interviewee No. 26

I had previously referred to the judiciary as a witness and saw that the court was not impartial.

D 27: Interviewee No. 27

I was familiar with its functions and how corrupt it is ...

D 27: Interviewee No. 27

There is no reputation for the judiciary and the judges ...

The results of interviews conducted:

- The most important aspect of any judiciary is its credibility. Because of corruption, the judiciary in Iran has no credibility, and ordinary citizens see it as a corrupt institution.

- Damage to public perception and the loss of credibility itself caused the spread of corruption. In current legal culture in Iran, paying a bribe to the judge or court staff is not a shameful act.
- Ordinary people think it is easy to pay bribes, and it is not difficult to facilitate such a corrupt act.

The Effects of Corruption on the Credibility of the Judiciary

If citizens trusted the court prior to dealing with it, and go on to witness corrupt acts during the proceeding, they are bound to lose their trust in the judicial system, and this could be the primary basis for encouraging them to commit a similar corruption.

In this section the interviewees will examine the judiciary and the role of this attitude in perpetuating this phenomenon.

D 1: Interviewee No. 1

> Do you not think that the court system is already aware of its employees' pattern of operation?

D 3: Interviewee No. 3

> The first time I had to visit the court was for my husband and I witnessed how he had bribed the court . . .

D 5: Interviewee No. 5

> . . . In my opinion, the judge and all employees are like collective bandits.

D 6: Interviewee No. 6

> . . . Most affairs are run based on bribery in Iran . . . You can even bribe the judge.

D 7: Interviewee No. 7

> I have experienced corruption within the judiciary; taking advantage of their discretions or using their links undermines their impartiality . . .

D 8: Interviewee No. 8

> We see that in such an injustice system [unjust system], where there is a total lack of public trust and confidence, the majority of people attempt to rely on some sort of other means to get their problems tackled.

D 9: Interviewee No. 9

> You always wonder in your mind if this case will go through its proper legal process. There will be corruption in most departments of the judiciary from a simple soldier who presents warrants right through to the Supreme Court judge. Everyone who deals with the judiciary witnesses such corruption daily . . .

D 11: Interviewee No. 11

> . . . Corruption in the judiciary is a fact and there is no need for the presupposition of the mind. If people who have lived in Iran would have had a tangible experience of such corruptions . . . When you witness corruption, you would inevitably tell your friends or neighbours. When you see no one is taking any actions against such corruptions taking place in courts, then the majority of people will lose hope and faith in the judiciary . . .

D 12: Interviewee No. 12

> I had never been involved with the judicial system and I hope I will never have any encounters with them. I had heard before that the court system is based on offering bribes, but I had never imagined the extent to which the corruption was . . .

D 14: Interviewee No. 14

> but after I attended the courts myself this perception of mine got worse . . .

D 15: Interviewee No. 15

> I had seen judicial corruptions before referring to the judiciary. Due to a large number of cases I have witnessed a decrease on the quality of how the judiciary operates . . . I have seen judges not acting impartially . . .

D 15: Interviewee No. 15

> This system of judicial corruption has been a cause for a distribution of poverty, discrimination, and infringement of rights.

D 17: Interviewee No. 17

> I was arrested on December 2004, and after this illegal arrest, which was more than 7 months and 23 days in solitary confinement, I was tortured. When an

intelligence officer or an IRGC officer in section 2 (a) allows himself as a representative of the law, to beat prisoners, to strip them naked or threatens to rape prisoner's wives and children, I call it judicial corruption . . . The law enforcement department of the judiciary is where corruption is bigger and the power pyramid in the judiciary is so that the more corrupt you are you are placed in a higher position . . .

D 18: Interviewee No. 18

] I knew of the judicial corruption before I got to experience it first-hand. They would violate any justice just to protect their own personal or collective interests.

D 19: Interviewee No. 19

I started studying law in order to become a judge. However, after witnessing such judicial corruptions I changed my mind . . .

D 20: Interviewee No. 20

Partially this is caused by my own colleague's wrongdoings . . . Of course, factors such as low incomes of judges and the lack of regulatory body over their operations have all been contributory to this problem . . . it is a shame that this corruption has expanded so much to an extent where the first thing ordinary people will look for as soon as they enter any judicial department is what middleman they should look for . . .

D 21: Interviewee No. 21

This corruption is not specific to the judiciary and covers all the public sector. But people do not expect a system which itself is responsible for fighting corruption to be contaminated with corruption.

D 22: Interviewee No. 22

The loss of hope and faith in the judiciary of ordinary people is more evident in recent years and refers to the judiciary as a factor in the implementation of government policies . . . The law enforcement court of judges and its officials are appointed by one of the clerics appointed by the leader and head of the judiciary . . .

26: Interviewee No. 26

> Until the time I was called for an allegation, I was not aware of the extent of corruption. Please note, I never had any issues with the courts until I got accused and was taken to the clerical court.

D 28: Interviewee No. 28

> Until and before I had any dealings with the judiciary, I had a little knowledge about the instability and the chaos in the system . . .

The results of interviews conducted:

- This judicial corruption encourages people to engage in corrupt acts.
- Judicial corruption has an adverse impact on legal culture.
- In the above interviews, it is easy to see how the rule of law in Iran is influenced by judicial corruption. It is noteworthy that Sen (2000) has particularly emphasised that without the existence of rule of law we cannot see the formation of a free market economy.

The Role of the Media in Combatting Corruption in Iran (and Its Effectiveness)

Robertson (2007) claimed that for countering judicial corruption, the free media should be able and willing to monitor the judiciary (to expose any corruption). In this section, the role of journalists and the media in countering judicial corruption in Iran will be reviewed :

D 1: Interviewee No. 1

> Of course, the media cannot disclose any corruption running through the legal system.

D 4: Interviewee No. 4

> Even if I reported it to the media, they would not be able to publish it . . .. On the other hand, if I liaise with foreign media, they would easily accuse me of espionage . . .

D 7: Interviewee No. 7

> Some media are accused of financial and political corruption in Iran . . . So, to protect their interests, they will have no choice but to turn a blind eye on judicial corruption . . . On the other hand, if the media is not affiliated, the smallest criticism of the judiciary will lead to the closure of the newspaper . . . Overseas media also highlight judicial corruption or its ineffectiveness for the sake of political reasons . . .

D 9: Interviewee No. 9

> In order to examine the role of the media, it should be noted that censorship happens all throughout Iran. We have few researchers and journalist, for whom there is no financial security. On the other hand, disclosing corruption is considered a security issue, and anyone who discloses corruption knows that he has put himself at risk . . .

D 11: Interviewee No. 11

> You may rarely find a newspaper who would dare criticise the functioning of the judiciary.

D 12: Interviewee No. 12

> The media in Iran would not risk to publish news about corruption in judiciary . . .

D 13: Interviewee No. 13

> Except for social media no other official media has been successful in this regard. Broadcasting such incidents are only possible through social media and any other way will face severe clashes on the part of the government . . .

D 18: Interviewee No. 18

> The media is not in a position or has the courage to publicize such incidents as they will have to face serious consequences . . .

D 20: Interviewee No. 20

> If any newspaper or media publish news about judicial corruption, the government thinks that newspaper tried to question the legitimacy of the government

> ... Subsequently, there will be a severe confrontation with the manager of the newspaper or the publishing author ...

D 21: Interviewee No. 21

> There is no freedom to expose corruption ... Mr. Yashar Salehi is an example of being jailed in the municipality due to the disclosure of corruption ... At least there exists no freedom after you have expressed your opinion [or report corruption]. Hence the first course of action for the head of the press is to render censorship before it reaches the Ministry of Intelligence ...

D 21: Interviewee No. 21

> ... For example, Mr. Bahman Omoue was imprisoned for six years after writing an economic paper ...

D 22: Interviewee No. 22

> Lack of media freedom is a typical example of the current state of corruption in the municipality of Tehran, where the reporters who have reported any corruptions have been imprisoned. Instead of investigating the reported crimes, journalists are jailed. When a reporter does not have security from the government, and if they want to exercise their duties in rendition of corruption, they will be imprisoned under such conditions, as corruption becomes of an intrinsic nature ...

The results of interviews conducted:

- Reporters without Borders ranked Iran 170 out of 180 countries in the World Press Freedom Index (Reporters Without Borders, 2017).
- The media plays an important role in reducing judicial corruption. Lack of freedom for the press in Iran contributed to the creation of judicial corruption and its continuation.
- Ordinary citizens have lost their trust in the judiciary because of censorship in Iran, and they believe that the press doesn't report any judicial corruption only because of a lack of freedom of the press. This perception decreases people's trust in the judiciary.

Public Perception of the Disciplinary Court for the Judges

International conventions about combating crime (i.e. corruption) or recommendation from Transparency International emphasised the need for the existence of an inspection office to oversee judges.

In the Iranian judiciary, the Disciplinary Court for the Judges oversees judges. Now, it is important to understand whether ordinary citizens trust this court or not.

In the following, interviewees shared their opinions:

D 1: Interviewee No. 1

> It is true that I could complain that a bribe was demanded of me by the court employees, but I avoided making a complaint as there was a likelihood, I could create additional troubles for myself . . ..

D 3: Interviewee No. 3

> I would never have gone to complain about the judge. It would be total madness to do so, as all judges are united and affiliated . . . If I made a complaint, they would execute my brother . . .

D 4: Interviewee No. 4

> For as long as I am in Iran, I would not dare to report such an incident [make a complaint against a judge]. . . Otherwise I would be going back in jail . . ..

D 4: Interviewee No. 4

> I underwent severe torture, of course I was unable to complain about the judge.

D 5: Interviewee No. 5

> For sure there is a regulatory or disciplinary body, but do they operate properly, no! . . .

D 6: Interviewee No. 6

> I would never dare to make a complaint about the judge's conduct . . . Firstly no one would chastise the judge or his conduct, secondly, suppose I had made a complaint about the judge, the next judge who would have to attend to my complaint would penalise me even more for making an allegation against his peer colleague . . .

D 7: Interviewee No. 7

I was aware of the existence of disciplinary court, but I did not go to the disciplinary court for Judge Mortazavi's illegal conduct, because it would have made my case worse . . . In that court, several cases against judge Mortazavi were open, including rape and financial corruption, but that court refused to hear those cases . . .

D 8: Interviewee No. 8

I personally pursued some cases at the disciplinary Court of Judges, and I believe that even in the most corrupt systems, failure to report corruption will result in reducing the cost of corruption for those sitting in the courtrooms . . .

D 8: Interviewee No. 8

The outcome of my experiences has been that the judge was forced to explain himself and answer questions, and sometimes I had a hope that the court's verdict could have been reversed . . .

D 9: Interviewee No. 9

I have not been to the disciplinary Tribunal court for the judiciary, however I am aware that this regulatory/supervisory body is not separated from the overall structure of the entire judiciary, and corruption is widespread, hence the outcome of such regulatory body can be easily assumed . . .

D 11: Interviewee No. 11

I did not report this corruption because complaint against judges and the Revolutionary Court could have severe consequences for my client or myself . . .

D 12: Interviewee No. 12

When I told my attorney that I was going to lodge a complaint against the judge he was very pessimistic about the outcome of such complaints . . .

D 14: Interviewee No. 14

For example, I encountered a situation where the judge of the second branch of the appeal court, Mr Rahimi, was hunting without permission . . .. I reported it to the authorities to take actions against him. They contacted me and warned me to mind my own business and stay out of trouble . . ..

D 15: Interviewee No. 15

I was aware of judge's disciplinary court. When I consult with several lawyers, I was told there would not be any benefits to drawing attention to the judge's disciplinary courts . . . There is no point in making a complaint about judicial members who are bribe takers. You would be considered lucky, if after complaining about any members of the judiciary you are not held liable or accused of any offences at the judicial Discipline Tribunal. T . . . his would only cost money and an enormous amount of stress with time which is wasted over an injustice . . .

D 18: Interviewee No. 18

I have never been or intended to associate with the judge's disciplinary tribunal, as it can jeopardise the accused situation.

D 19: Interviewee No. 19

There have been instances where reporting judges bribe-taking has had legal consequences, however if the judge is close to the regime, it will be very hard to have any complaints lodged against them, or that it would be very unlikely for them to face dismissals or any kind of consequences . . .

D 20: Interviewee No. 20

. . . judges are examined and observed via so many filtering systems. It would be shameful for the regime or government of the time to convict a judge with a crime such as corruption. So, if a judge commits an offence, it will not be disclosed to anyone . . .

D 21: Interviewee No. 21

One cannot expect fair and lawful conduct from the Disciplinary Court for judges. I myself made a complaint on few occasions but there were not any effective results.

D 22: Interviewee No. 22

. . . The example of ineffectiveness of the [current] disciplinary court for judges is the case of Mortazavi . . .. The complaint which was lodged against him for murdering Zahra Kazemi, a Canadian journalist and photographer, did not have any satisfactory outcome . . .

D 26: Interviewee No. 26

My tenant and I got into some disagreement, for which he lodged a complaint to the court. As soon as they saw me in my clerical clothes I was treated in a respectable manner while the judge spoke rudely to my tenant. I got so upset for the judge's behaviour and could not resist warning him.

D 27: Interviewee No. 27

Mr Asghari was the Minister of Justice during the time I was an MP, yet he claimed he was not the Minister of Justice but a simple courier . . . there was a lack of supervisory regulation on the judiciary]

D 28: Interviewee No. 28

. . . Some Mujtaihds as Seyed Hossein Gomi, Seyed Kazim Shariatmadari, Shekh Bahaee Mahallati have all opposed the operational system of the revolutionary courts . . .

The results of interviews conducted:

- Most ordinary citizens are aware of the Disciplinary Court for the Judges; however, they consider it as another corrupt court, therefore they would not normally report any judge's misconduct to this Court.

Abusing Judicial Power for Private Gains

Bribery is an obvious case of judicial corruption, although judicial corruption is not limited to paying or receiving bribes.

In this section, interviewees share their experiences about abusing power in the Courts:

D 2: Interviewee No. 2

Because of the threats of imprisonment, the manager agreed to sort out the cheque without any further delays . . . If I had not treated this matter in the way I did I would have had to wait for a few years

D 3: Interviewee No. 3

> On one occasion I went to visit the judge to request for a transfer, and that was when he gave me a SIM card [for mobile]. He said he would call me later on that number. He did call and asked if we could have a temporary marriage [Nikah mut'ah . . .] He did not say anything directly that he would help my brother or not . . . He almost implied if I did accept his offer then he would be willing to help me release my brother . . . I was in the temporary marriage for three months until he issued a five-year prison sentence rather than execution or life imprisonment.

D 5: Interviewee No. 5

> He asked for five million Tooman to terminate the case. Otherwise the judge would issue lashing punishments. I was convinced he was acting on behalf of the court employees . . .. Within a few hours we gave him the money he had asked for. Turns out the court had announced the case set aside due to insufficient evidence

D 6: Interviewee No. 6

> . . . when I won my divorce rights and entitlements, the judge was treating me very graciously . . . Apparently if I had not agreed to the 10% then my chances of claiming even half my legal rights would have been curtailed . . .

D 7: Interviewee No. 7

> In relation to my own court case, judge Mortazavi did not act with impartiality . . . He would personally call me with threats . . . He never respected the position of being a judge and relevant conduct . . .. He was an interrogator as well as decision maker for my future . . .. He told me because I had described officers (who work for the Ministry of Intelligence) as brothers of prophet Yusuf [who killed their brother] my punishment was execution or a life sentence . . . He then sent my file to Qum Seminary [to get permission for execution]. . .

D 8: Interviewee No. 8

> For example, a judge let his personal views to intervene in the case, in that civil case, as soon as the judge found out that my client had an affair outside of marriage, he relied on excuses and despite my client being the claimant the judge detained him on the basis of infringing the court order . . . In one instance, I was representing my client who was facing execution . . .. It was during that proceeding I was told by a duty judge at the Revolutionary Court it was in my client's

interest if I had resigned from the case, so that another lawyer will be allocated from the court itself. It appeared they had financial ties with that lawyer, so I did resign from the case for my client's sake . . .

D 10: Interviewee No. 10

I was still being tortured for another five months after the $3 million was paid in Tohid Prison and in solitary confinement due to a non-payment of $2 million from their initial requested ransom. Eventually, I succeeded in convincing Gholam Hossein Mohseni Ajeee [Gholam-Hossein Mohseni-Eje'i], a deputy at the time of the Islamic Revolutionary Prosecutor's Office in the ministry of Intelligence, to be on a temporary release . . . 5 months later and after paying a further 250,000 Dollars to Mr Mohseni Eje[Gholam-Hossein Mohseni-Eje'i], he accepts to release my passport and issued a permit to leave the country in July 1994. I left the country.

D 11: Interviewee No. 11

Within close vicinity to where he used to live. Unfortunately, the intelligence officer was aware of the gay sexual orientation, according to my client, he was seeking to file a case against him. My client always was cautious of his actions. He had even threatened my client directly to file a case against him . . . One day they arrested him for drug trafficking and found some opium in his car despite tests showing that he was not addicted, nor did he have a background in drug trafficking or any similar grounds. Most importantly his social status was such that no such accusations would have been believable. He had a simple life and lived based on his salaries. I took his case and became his lawyer . . . The officer in charge of his file literally told me that if I wanted my client to get rescued, I should have resigned from the case and one of their lawyers should have taken over. He meant, such lawyers who are accustomed to bribery and making deals behind closed doors should be appointed for this case . . . the judge also knew that my client was not involved in any drug smuggling, and evidently was against my client . . .

D 12: Interviewee No. 12

My attorney also told me that he had paid the court to have the court support and suggested to accept half of the money [and settle my claim] In the court trial my client told the judge that he was literally telling witnesses what to say . . .. In the end the verdict was given against me

D 13: Interviewee No. 13

I did not encounter bribing the judge in my own caseloads; however, I have heard of them in other cases . . .

D 14: Interviewee No. 14

Several corruptions that I had witnessed first-hand was at the office of Ayatollah Elmo Lhoda. He has a seminary in Tehran. Mr Nowrouzi, his secretary, was involved in a court case over lands which were worth several billion Toman. The manner in which their interventions takes place is to demand illegally a great portion of the land [or property] in order for them to offer their assistance via their close ties to other judges or officials . . . And the head of this reformist party was a Sheikh called Zare-Foomani. He is also a newspaper owner under the same name . . .. Mr Niri is one of his close friends and always offered his influence in facilitating the running of cases in the Supreme Court.

D 15: Interviewee No. 15

Despite the accumulation of documents and evidence including reports from the police and their confessions, the judge decided in their favour to acquit the accused . . . The deputy prosecutor and even the lawyers were all surprised at how the judge acquitted the defendants without trial . . . In our own family case, I witnessed corruptive judicial process when we had to retrieve our land, the deed of which belonged to my father and was confiscated post revolution by the government who had taken over our land . . . We paid a bribe to a judge at the time via a middle person. We had no choice but pay about one million toman in 1370, which was a significant amount of money at the time, for which my family had to undergo a lot of pressure and distress to get this sum together . . . In the end, only one third of the land was returned to us and two thirds of it remained in possession of the council . . . He was charged with drug trafficking at a minor level. The judge for that case had taken a bribe to overturn the decision

D 16: Interviewee No. 16

I had not committed any crime; however, I was arrested [during a demonstration in 2008] A prosecutor attended the place of custody where we were kept. There were about four hundred of us, each one of us were arrested at different areas or regions in different ways . . .. One would have thought that not all 400 people that were arrested had committed similar crimes . . . The persecutor gave each of us a pre-typed paper with five offences on it that we had to agree and sign. Five offences which could have had consequences such as the death penalty or be considered as a Moharebe [enemy of god]. We all had the same pre- written crimes on these papers . . . We were forced to sign these papers, because if we didn't, they would lash and torture us to stop resisting and ultimately, they would make us sign the alleged committed crimes . . .

D 16: Interviewee No. 16

The prosecutor, the judge, and other members of the court violated the impartiality for their personal and collective interests, and to be able to maintain the power, they manage to suppress officials who are supposed to represent the law in public favour

D 17: Interviewee No. 17

All this time my case was in the revolutionary prosecutor's office based on Moallem Street and was supervised by a person called Judge Fallahi . . .. He was the deputy of Judge Mortazavi . . . Every two months I was taken to him . . . he threatened to place me in a solitary cell if I did not write, sign, and agree to the extent of confession to the offences I had never committed . . . The same judge had issued many unfair and ungrounded summons. Later certain corrupted financial activities of his regarding illegal land ownerships came to light

D 18: Interviewee No. 18

After a while, they took me to court No 5 of the law enforcements. The same judge who had taken a bribe [from me] previously made an official statement: you must sign this confession and based on the medical documentation that my family had presented to the court; I would be released on bail until the actual hearing date . . . The same judge said that I would have been freed at this stage if I had paid a lump sum to him . . . and at the next stage I could be encountering a 15 to 20-year sentence . . .

D 19: Interviewee No. 19

I witnessed corruption in the judiciary, bribe taking and bribery, although I never had to do it myself . . .

D 20: Interviewee No. 20

. . . We have had cases, where the judge had attended appellant's homes and had managed to rape her just because he knew she was alone, he [the judge] was then sent to another city [as judge] just to avoid the spread of the news.

D 25: Interviewee No. 25

> After a few months we were called to attend a court hearing. When we entered the court room Mr Malikpour also attended very briefly. He was respected in a special manner by the judge. He then asked the judge if someone had called them from another office. With a positive reply he reassured us that there was nothing to worry about any more . . . The judge told me in the presence of everyone else that he had been ordered to reserve my rights . . . My lawyer and Mr Malikpour had arranged this hearing just to give me the reassurance that everything is going according to plan in my favour . . .

D 27: Interviewee No. 27

> These courts have the discretionary powers to refer to Shari'a law. They had taken a non-clerical individual to the Special Clerical Courts due to being in charge of a tabloid belonging to a clergyman . . .

D 28: Interviewee No. 28

> For instance, some of Khalkhali's sentences did not have any written sentences . . . In 12/04/1359 he had sentenced 24 people in less than 10 hours in Shiraz, of which 12 individuals were given a death sentence . . .

The results of interviews conducted:

- Judicial corruption in Iran is not limited to bribery and receiving/paying money. Sometimes, judges, for sexual favours, undermine or "sell" their judgement.
- Intelligence services have influence on judges, and they can exercise control. Even if they are not paying any bribe, their behaviour can still be identified as judicial corruption.

Justification of Judicial Corruption by Judges or Court Staff

To analyse any crime, it is important to understand how criminals justify their behaviours.

For white-collar crime, this rationalisation helps criminals to justify their actions for themselves or for a third party, and will allow them to commit crime without feeling any shame (Brytting, Minogue & Morino, 2011).

A retired judge who participated in this interview shared his opinion about this matter as following:

D 20: Interviewee No. 20

> Some of my colleagues imagine that it is their right or entitlement to receive bribes . . . Besides the situation that judges are in a better position financially today, between 1980 to 2000, judges were on very low salaries . . . This became a norm among judges to get involved in bribery so that they can run their personal lives more smoothly . . . The general perception was that judges should have a high moral benchmark with a clear conscience and impartiality to be able to secure the best interests of the society, however due to their low incomes they had difficulties managing their lives. Therefore, they started adopting this mode of earning money via bribes to give them security long term.

Judges never considered this illegal demand of money as bribes; instead, they would rename it as the "cash part of the court costs". . .

The results of interviews conducted:

- Judges or court staff justify their actions with excuses like "everybody does it".
- Institutional Culture plays a major role in the creation of judicial corruption in Iran. This corruption has become a "norm" in the judiciary.

Trigger – Who Initiated the Bribery Process

It is important to understand how the receiver and payer will trust each other to pay and receive the bribe. If in legal culture, paying a bribe to a judge can be seen as taboo, then this process will not start easily.

In this section, interviewees share their experiences about how they engaged in bribery.

D 1: Interviewee No. 1

> One of the court staff stopped me in the corridor and said I should pay two million toman

D 3: Interviewee No. 3

> The first impression you get is that most employees are expecting something from your pocket . . . One of the court personnel even approached me proposing if

I had money, they could speak to the judge . . . On one occasion I went to visit the judge so to request for a transfer, and that was when he gave me a SIM card [for mobile phone].

D 5: Interviewee No. 5

When I visited the court to follow up my case, one of the employees asked for my mobile number . . . He asked for an alternative number in case they could not reach me on the one I was using . . . I gave my wife's number . . .. As soon as we left the court her phone rang . . . It was a man calling on behalf of the head of the court's office . . .

D 6: Interviewee No. 6

. . . As soon as I was called to the judge's room he started telling me about the road traffic on the highway and how he had got tired getting to the court house . . . Immediately after I left the court, I received a call from an unknown caller saying that he could recommend my case to the judge . . . it was obvious that he was directly connected to the judge, as he told me about how the judge complained about the traffic on the highway . . . asked him what did he want?. . . he responded that he could ask the judge to issue a judgement in my favour and order my ex-husband to pay my alimony or what is called "Mehriyeh". . ., however he proposed demanding 10% of the total financial rights of mine . . . He wanted half the sum there and then and the other half after my divorce file was issued in my favour . . .

D 18: Interviewee No. 18

There are middlemen in Iran whose main job is to receive bribes and pay it to the judges . . . My wife had to look for one of these men. He took 40 million toman from my wife as a bribe in 2006.

D 20: Interviewee No. 20

People already recognise which judge to go to with the appropriate acting lawyer, who works closely with the same judge . . . Many lawyers are contaminated with such relationships and many are still with a clear conscience . . .

D 25: Interviewee No. 25

A lawyer was recommended to us in 2005. . . We could claim back a proportion of the land, and the rest of it must be our entitlement for the job we do for you

> to retrieve your land . . . I accepted his offer and set up a meeting with someone called Mr Malikpour, whose wife was a close relative to the supreme Leader . . . He told us to address him by this name, as it was his nickname. We arrived at some mutual agreement over this land and even signed a contract . . .

The results of Interviews conducted:

- In Iran, having the opportunity to commit judicial corruption is an important factor for the creation of this corruption.
- There is no organisation to combat judicial corruption in Iran.
- In the current legal culture, paying or receiving a bribe is not uncommon. Therefore, ordinary people, court staff, or judges can easily start this process. Therefore, everybody has the opportunity to start the bribery process.

Nepotism in the Iranian Judiciary

Judges must be independent and act impartially. If any judge rules according to a recommendation, it will be judicial corruption, even if that judge does not receive any money or benefit directly.

In the meantime, if any judge issues an order or judgement based on their own ideology or personal belief, then they undermine the impartiality of the court.

In this section, interviewees share their experience:

D 2: Interviewee No. 2

> Therefore, I discussed it with one of my peer colleagues, he then spoke to a few of his friends and eventually he managed to introduce someone, who had close connections with The Imam of Friday Prayer in our city . . . The arrangement was for him to force the debtor to pay, and in return he would receive 20% of the value of the cheque . . .. The Imam made a call to a judge he knew . . .. [later in the hearing] The judge threatened the company manager in the presence of all of us . . .

D 14: Interviewee No. 14

> . . . After the uprising in 2008 and the suppression of the people, Mr Ayatollah Vahid Khorasani made a complaint to the Supreme Leader [objecting to how protestors were killed]. When the Supreme Leader visited Qum he left on his arrival, which can be construed as an insulting gesture. This movement meant that he was against the Supreme Leader and as a result Sadegh Larijani, his son of law, was appointed as the head of the judiciary. [to make peace between the Supreme Leader and Ayatollah Vahid Khorasani]

The results of interviews conducted:

- Nepotism is prevalent in the Iranian judiciary.
- It is common practice among judges to issue a judgement based on recommendations from powerful people.
- These traditions undermine the impartially of the Court, and have caused judicial corruption.

The Role of Lawyers in the Creation of Judicial Corruption in Iran

Lawyers play an important role in the creation of judicial corruption. Lawyers can prevent or spread judicial corruption. It should be noted that legal culture dictates to the lawyers how to behave.

In this section, interviewees share their experience:

D 3: Interviewee No. 3

> Initially we had a lawyer, but as soon as I became the judge's temporary wife, the judge said you no longer needed a lawyer . . . My lawyer was not aware of the arrangement between me and the judge.

D 6: Interviewee No. 6

> . . . My lawyer was aware of the situation . . . He refused to continue working on my case as he knew of my agreement with the middleman . . .

D 8: Interviewee No. 8

> . . . Lawyers play an important role in the formation and continuation of corruption . . . I learned of a case where the lawyer who was working in my colleague's office, met the judge of the case in his office, and both decided the verdict of the case together . . . It seems that some attorneys may even believe their participation in judicial corruption is a part of their professional skills . . . the lawyers integrity and independence of the Bar Association gradually is diminished . . . Especially, since legal practitioners licenced by the judiciary began to work as lawyers, and considering they had no training for being professional lawyers . . .

D 9: Interviewee No. 9

> Unfortunately, lawyers are not excluded from this judiciary system. They are all expected to function within such a contaminated judicial structure. The fact is that lawyers are also involved in the reproduction of this corruption . . .

D 11: Interviewee No. 11

> Based on my personal experience, I can say that some lawyers are engaged in the work of a "middle person" in many courts, and this has become a norm in the process . . . Of course, this process is much broader in the Revolutionary Court . . . In principle, the presence of lawyers in the Revolutionary Court is much harder than attending a normal court . . .

D 13: Interviewee No. 13

> It is true that there are unfortunately some lawyers who assist in distributing such corruptions through individuals and intermediaries in the system . . . Unfortunately, this has led people to lose confidence in the judiciary and lawyers, and instead of looking for a legal path through lawyers they look for influential contacts. This could lead to misuse or abuse or fraudulent acts . . . The majority of lawyers do not consider their position from a professional point of view.

D 14: Interviewee No. 14

> These powerful political officials always have a few lawyers to represent cases [where they want to intervene]. . . This means that such [corrupt] individuals are willing to interfere in court cases in return for a lump sum payment from the plaintiff or whomever the court case belongs to . . . there exist female attendees that by offering sexual intercourse to the judges can impact on the direction of the cases. Such female individuals can even function and sway the case in their favour more effectively than professional lawyers.

D 19: Interviewee No. 19

> The breeding ground for judicial corruption in Iran is created by both consultants' associations and the Bar association. Due to the lack of a transparent and just system, lawyers do not always have a fair number of clients, therefore they take up jobs as middle dealers . . .

D 20: Interviewee No. 20

> Unfortunately, lawyers have had a great role in developing such corruptions. If they adhered to their professional conducts instead of acting as middle-men, then the situation would have been much calmer with much less corruption . . . People already recognise which judge to go to with the appropriate acting lawyer, who works closely with the same judge . . . Many lawyers are contaminated with such

> relationships and many are still with clear conscience . . . Nowadays there are fewer lawyers acting with proper and professional conduct and most of them are involved in acts of bribery . . .

D 21: Interviewee No. 21

> Many lawyers incorporate corruption into their advocacy, and by paying bribes they make their positions stronger . . .

D 25: Interviewee No. 25

> A lawyer was recommended to us in 2005. . . We could claim back a proportion of the land, and the rest of it must be our entitlement for the job we do for you to retrieve your land . . . I accepted his offer and set up a meeting with someone called Mr Malikpour, whose wife was a close relative to the Supreme Leader . . . He told us to address him by this name, as it was his nickname. We arrived at some mutual agreement over this land and even signed a contract . . .

The results of interviews conducted:

- Regular checks on lawyers can prevent judicial corruption, and educating them about corruption is an effective method to reduce judicial corruption. As we can see in the above statements, Iranian lawyers have contributed to the creation and spread of judicial corruption.

The Independence of the Iranian Judiciary

A lack of independence for the judiciary will contribute to the creation of judicial corruption. It should be noted that without organisational independence for the judiciary, judges cannot act independently either.

Kar (2012) refers to the Supreme Leader and how he undermines judicial independence. If we review statements from interviewees, we can see a link between a lack of judicial independence and judicial corruption.

In this section, interviewees share their experience:

D 2: Interviewee No. 2

> Therefore, I discussed it with one of my peer colleagues, he then spoke to a few of his friends and eventually he managed to introduce someone, who had close connections with The Imam of Friday Prayer in our city . . . The arrangement was

for him to force the debtor to pay, in return he would receive 20% of the value of the check . . .. The Imam made a call to a judge he knew . . .. [later in the hearing] The judge threatened the company manager in the presence of all of us . . .

D 4: Interviewee No. 4

. . . What was hilarious is that whatever the interrogator ordered, the judge had to do as he was told . . .. The judge was a puppet of the intelligence services

D 10: Interviewee No. 10

In May 1993, when I was visiting Iran, I was kidnapped from my own apartment in Tehran by the officials of the intelligence services [as per instruction of] Mr Hashemi Rafsanjani who was the president of the time . . . the kidnapping took place after a year and a half when the South Pars contracts were signed and there were repeated requests by Mehdi Hashemi Rafsanjani [President's son] and his partner Mehdi Yazdanpanah Yazdi to pay $50 million on bribes, and I had refused to accept to pay such bribes . . . During the first three months of detention in Evin Prison, section 209 and in Touhid Prison for nearly 7 months, and because of my resistance towards brutal torture by the security officials resulted in them getting in contact with my wife. She lived in Rome at the time and they asked for $5 million ransom for my release . . .

D 11: Interviewee No. 11

The revolutionary court considers itself a security institution

D 12: Interviewee No. 12

My attorney also told me that he had paid the court to have the court's support and suggested to accept half of the money [and settle my claim]

D 13: Interviewee No. 13

Due to the high number of cases and the pressure from the top (powerful people or intelligence services or the Supreme Leader or his allies), on court judges and relevant offices and a lack of human resources are all contributory excuses . . .

D 14: Interviewee No. 14

In 2011, I became the director of public relations in the Office of Mr Fallahian, the former Minister of Intelligence Services in Iran. Part of his activities involved "his personal economic activities", which meant that himself and his office officials used the ties they had with the judiciary to influence the cases . . .

D 14: Interviewee No. 14

Several corruptions that I had witnessed first-hand were at the office of Ayatollah Elmo Lhoda. He has a seminary in Tehran. Mr Nowrouzi, his secretary, was involved in a court case over lands which were worth several billion Toman. The manner in which their interventions take place is to demand illegally a great portion of the land [or property] in order for them to offer their assistance via their close ties to other judges or officials. I can refer to the role of Mr Fallahian and Mr Mohseni Ejehi.[Gholam-Hossein Mohseni-Eje'i] Mr. Ejehi has had a special relation and dedication to Mr Fallahian and has been working under his authority for several years in the Ministry of Intelligence . . . In my opinion Mr Ejehi[Gholam-Hossein Mohseni-Eje'i], is the most influential individual in the judiciary . . . Under Mr. Fallahian's recommendation, he would interfere in cases . . . This influence on the judiciary is not limited to a particular mullah or political group . . .

D 16: Interviewee No. 16

I had not committed any crime; however, I was arrested [during a demonstration in 2008] A prosecutor attended the place of custody where we were kept. There were about four hundred of us, each one of us were arrested at different areas or regions in different ways . . .. One would have thought that not all 400 people that were arrested had committed similar crimes . . . The persecutor gave each of us a pre-typed paper with five offences on it that we had to agree and sign. Five offences could have had consequences such as the death penalty or be considered as a Moharebe [enemy of god]. We all had the same pre- written crimes on these papers . . . We were forced to sign these papers, because if we didn't, they would lash and torture us to stop resisting and ultimately, they would make us sign the alleged committed crimes . . .

D 18: Interviewee No. 18

There is no real trial . . . Trials usually lasts about a few minutes and ultimately you are forced to admit to some offences that you had never committed . . .

D 20: Interviewee No. 20

The principle is that if you wish as a judge to progress within the judiciary you are unofficially required to deviate towards corruption . . .. For instance, if a

> judge receives a phone call from another high ranking official, he needs to follow his orders . . .. There are also some judges that will not give into such nonsense, like myself . . .. If a judge abides and adheres to certain allies, they will be given rewards such as opportunities to purchase lands and properties for either one third of the asking price or they are given for free . . .

D 22: Interviewee No. 22

> . . .the judiciary will investigate and prevent the uprising of aggression. For this reason, the pre-requisite for this would be the independence of the judiciary in order to achieve all the above . . .. Unfortunately, there is no such independence in the Republic of Iran. The head of the country and the executive branch is the Supreme Leader, who is not even elected by the people . . .

D 22: Interviewee No. 22

> . . .the Supreme Leader, who is not even elected by the people . . . He sees his legitimacy as divine legitimacy. Hence, he chooses the head of judiciary from the Mujtahids, who agree with his ideology. From the first days of the revolution, when Khomeini chose several people as the prosecutors, I objected to him because of his lack of expertise . . .. You can see the consequences in the existing regime . . . the judiciary has become a means for the implementation of the Supreme Leader's requests . . . which can easily have influence on the judiciary and the judge's powers . . .

D 27: Interviewee No. 27

> It appears that the revolutionary courts are under the umbrella of the IRGC . . . that the Revolutionary courts submit to orders from the security forces . . . Whenever the Special Clerical Courts find it appropriate, they will transfer the case to this court . . . sometimes this is done via the intelligence service or the security forces . . . Mr Larijani explicitly refers to himself as being the soldier of the Supreme Leader.

The results of interviews conducted:

- The above statement shows how attempts by powerful people to influence the judiciary have contributed to the creation of judicial corruption.
- Attempts from the Supreme Leader to influence the judiciary can be compared to making a hole in a dam. Attempts from the Supreme Leader to

influence the judiciary and use it as a tool to suppress his opponents create a breeding ground for judicial corruption.

Personal Independence of Judges

It is important for judges to consider cases based on evidence, and ignore their personal interest. If a judge considers their own personal belief when they want to issue a judgement or order, they would not be independent.

In this section, the relevant parts of statements from interviewees will be reviewed:

D 11: Interviewee No. 11

> . . .the judge also knew that my client was not involved in any drug smuggling, and evidently was against my client . . .

D 14: Interviewee No. 14

> And the head of this reformist party was a Sheikh called Zare-Foomani. He is also a newspaper owner under the same name . . .. Mr Niri is one of his close friends and always offered his influence in facilitating the running of cases in the Supreme Court . . .

D 16: Interviewee No. 16

> The prosecutor, the judge, and other members of the court violated impartiality for their personal and collective interests, to be able to maintain the power, they manage to suppress officials who are supposed to represent the law in public favour

D 19: Interviewee No. 19

> Another important cause of corruption is the selection of judges based on Islamic ideology and how they follow this ideology . . . Instead of relying on knowledge and integrity

D 22: Interviewee No. 22

> . . .the Supreme Leader, who is not even elected by the people . . . He sees his legitimacy as divine legitimacy. Hence, he chooses the head of judiciary from the

> Mujtahids, who agree with his ideology . . . there are two main pre-requisites for judges, the first is their speciality and the second is their independence. In the Islamic Republic, there are no such mercenary standards . . . this does not exist in the law, and no changes have been witnessed in the last three decades . . . The key posts in the past years are in the hands of clerics who have commitment to the Supreme Leader. If one of these clerics or officials do not become corrupted, then there is room for a big surprise . . . These days [after the revolution] the position of judges and judicial remedies have been changed, and people no longer respect the judiciary . . .

The results of interviews conducted:

- The findings of this study show that in Iran, it is common practice for the judges to issue their judgement based on their ideology.
- Furthermore, powerful people or organisations (e.g. the Ministry of Intelligence) can put pressure on judges, or motivate them with money or gifts.

Link between Judicial Corruption and Legal Culture

Legal culture plays an important role in the creation of judicial corruption. In this section, relevant statements from interviewees will be reviewed:

D 2: Interviewee No. 2

> . . .is filled with old wolves, hen/ce you will have to act promptly otherwise you would be crushed under their feet . . .

D 4: Interviewee No. 4

> What was hilarious is that whatever the interrogator ordered, the judge had to do as he was told . . .

D 5: Interviewee No. 5

> . . .It is so evident that the courts and the Police are all corrupt . . .

D 9: Interviewee No. 9

> in relation to the integrity and honourability of judges and the lawyers, such integrity and reputation no longer exist in society and among the general public.

Disclosing various matters relating to corruption cannot do any further damage to the reputation of the judges.

D 11: Interviewee No. 11

The Revolutionary Court is a strange court, not only was I not called for the court order, they did not even allow me to take a copy of the decision. They only allowed me to take notes from the Court's order and determination letter . . . Based on my personal experience, I can say that some lawyers are engaged in the work of a "middle person" in many courts, and this has become a norm in the process . . . of course, this process is much broader in the Revolutionary Court . . . in principle, the presence of lawyers in the Revolutionary Court is much harder than attending a normal court . . . Hence it is very difficult to differentiate between criminals and non-criminals. If someone has a criminal record, he may not necessarily be a bad person, and there is the likelihood that he could have been victimised of wrongful decisions . . .

D 13: Interviewee No. 13

The majority of lawyers do not consider their position from a professional point of view.

D 14: Interviewee No. 14

When the prosecutors or inspecting officer sees that the accused will eventually be released by paying a bribe or by paying minor fines, he will no longer be interested in carrying out his duties properly . . .

D 14: Interviewee No. 14

These powerful political officials always have a few lawyers to represent cases [that they want to intervene in]. . .this means that such [corrupt] individuals are willing to interfere in court cases in return for a lump sum payment from the plaintiff or whomever the court case belongs to . . .

D 15: Interviewee No. 15

. . .judges do not have any shame in using their personal tastes in dealing with cases

D 16: Interviewee No. 16

> . . .in relation to judicial corruption I must emphasise that members of the public have lost faith due to their awareness of what is truly going on via social media and social networking . . .

D 18: Interviewee No. 18

> There is no real trial . . .. Trials usually last about a few minutes and ultimately you are forced to admit to some offences that you have never committed . . .

D 19: Interviewee No. 19

> I myself saw that judges carried their prayers in such filthy and disgraceful manners and there is no observation on their dress code . . .

D 20: Interviewee No. 20

> Some of my colleagues imagine that it is their right or entitlement to receive bribes . . .. Besides the situation that judges are in a better position financially today, between 1980 to 2000, judges were on very low salaries . . . this became a norm among judges to get involved in bribery so that they can run their personal lives more smoothly . . . I do not wish to justify the wrongful acts of my colleagues . . .. Mentioning of this issue only means how the act of bribery came to encompass the whole society . . . Judges never considered this illegal demand of money as bribes, instead they would rename it that it as the "cash part of the court costs". . .Nowadays there are fewer lawyers acting with proper and professional conduct and most of them are involved in acts of bribery . . .

D 21: Interviewee No. 21

> Because of this corruption, people try to resolve their differences outside the court, otherwise if they are forced to go to court then obviously, they will have no choice but utilise bribery to win the case in their favour . . .

D 22: Interviewee No. 22

> The identity of the judge should be clear, but in Iran, many judges are sitting on the bench using their nicknames . . .

D 25: Interviewee No. 25

> A lawyer was recommended to us in 2005. . .We could claim back a proportion of the land, and the rest of it must be our entitlement for the job we do for you to retrieve your land . . . I accepted his offer and set up a meeting with someone called Mr. Malikpour, whose wife was a close relative to the Supreme Leader . . . He told us to address him by this name, as it was his nickname. We arrived at some mutual agreement over this land and even signed a contract . . .

D 27: Interviewee No. 27

> This corrupt act was minimal . . . Instead it has become the common norm, in the judiciary as well as with legal officers.

The results of interviews conducted:

- The findings of this study show that the legal culture in Iran is damaged, and bribery has become an accepted norm to deal with the judiciary. Everybody knows that when they are going to deal with the judiciary, they must prepare themselves to pay a bribe.
- This kind of corruption is identified as institutionalised corruption, and citizens accept this corruption as the norm and deal with it as a part of an informal social contract.
- Some of the harsh laws in Iran (like compulsory hijab) are not accepted by the majority of citizens; therefore, they break that law, and when they are dealing with the consequences of their unlawful acts, they have to pay bribes to avoid jail or the lash. As a result, paying or receiving bribes to avoid these kinds of sentences becomes normal, and is less shameful.
- In general, paying or receiving a bribe is not a shameful act anymore.

Judicial Corruption before the Islamic Revolution in 1979

It is important to ask: is it possible to create a non-corrupt judiciary in Iran? Or does the legal culture of the country not allow for the creation of such a judiciary?

Scholars claim that before the revolution, the court in Iran was semi-independent, although the Shah undermined the independence of the judiciary on a few occasions (Bahraeini, Nayyeri & Sheeran, 2014).

No studies could be found on judicial corruption before the Islamic revolution; therefore in this section, this subject will be addressed.

Comparing Judicial Corruption in Iran Before and After the Revolution. In this section, interviewees share their experience:

D 19: Interviewee No. 19

> Also, the number of corrupt judges were rare . . .

D 21: Interviewee No. 21

> In comparison to the previous judiciary settings during the time of Shah, I can say the judiciary system [in Shah era] was much fairer . . .. As I mentioned before, political claims and slander were not referred to the judiciary . . . And the judiciary only looked into civil and family matters.

D 24: Interviewee No. 24

> . . .Regarding the question of paying bribes before the revolution, the existence of judicial corruption was rare and paying or receiving bribes would not have occurred in one's mind . . .

D 28: Interviewee No. 28

> If we compare the two judicial systems of the Shah regime and the one under the current regime, the standards of rules and regulations of the current judiciary is much lower than the ones in the previous regime . . .

Judicial Corruption before the Islamic Revolution. In this section, interviewees share their experience:

D 19: Interviewee No. 19

> Before the revolution, significant attention was given to judges' status. And, if there was any misconduct they would have been charged with some punishments . . . Also, the number of corrupt judges were rare

D 21: Interviewee No. 21

> In comparison to the previous judiciary settings during the time of Shah, I can say the judiciary system [in Shah era] was much fairer . . .. As I mentioned before, political claims and slander were not referred to the judiciary . . . And the judiciary only looked into civil and family matters.

D 22: Interviewee No. 22

> It might have been corruption in the judiciary in one particular case, but this was exceptional . . . The judiciary is nowhere comparable with the past in terms of expertise and ethical aspects . . .

D 28: Interviewee No. 28

> Before the revolution, there was an independence to the judiciary, therefore political cases were not sent to the judiciary . . .

Public Perception about Judges before the Islamic Revolution. In this section, interviewees share their experience:

D 19: Interviewee No. 19

> Before the revolution, significant attention was given to judges' status. And if there was any misconduct they would have been charged with some punishments . . .

D 21: Interviewee No. 21

> Under such circumstances, courts were more transparent compared to the existing judicial system . . . Of course this does not mean that there was no corruption taking place under the previous regime . . . They used to have more respect and there was a more fair and just system. Judges should have been a graduate from law school. And they had to attend the Ministry of Justice examination . . . They then had to undertake a training course for six months . . . They were required to sit again for the same exams after their training was over . . . If they had not enough knowledge, they would not have qualified to sit as a judge . . . Judges used to earn a higher salary compared to other court members . . . All these were contributory factors for the judges to have a more respected social status in the society . . .

D 22: Interviewee No. 22

> A number of student officers attended Law School to obtain relevant training for the military courts. The only difference between these students and the rest of the students were that they were not required to sit for the necessary exams after completing four years at the law school in order to be qualified as judges in marshal courts . . . At that time [Shah era], people looked at judges with special respect, and they could also condemn the judiciary

D 23: Interviewee No. 23

> The existence of corruption in the pre-revolutionary period was very small and it was considered an exception . . . Judges had a special status in society and their characters were more respectful . . .

D 24: Interviewee No. 24

> The training system of judges was very clear with disciplines, hence there was no possibility of acts of bribery . . . Regarding the respect for judges, they used to be admired by people, their literacy and educational background was much higher than us lawyers . . .. They used to possess a lot of integrity, for example you would not find them dressed in inappropriate clothing

Independence of the Court before the Islamic Revolution. In this section, interviewees share their experience:

D 21: Interviewee No. 21

> Before the revolution there was still corruption and the norm of using contacts to facilitate the running of cases, but it was on a limited scale . . .

D 22: Interviewee No. 22

> [In the Shah era] After the coup which took place in 1953 and the passage of the Security Police Act, political matters would get referred to the military tribunal. Until a few months before the revolution, ordinary lawyers were not permitted to attend the Iranian military tribunals . . .. But a few months before the revolution some changes took place and I was among the very first lawyers who could attend military tribunals.

D 23: Interviewee No. 23

> With regards to interference of security agencies or powerful organisations . . . not everything was ideal.

D 24: Interviewee No. 24

> . . .Except for exceptional circumstances, exercising influence over the judiciary was unlikely and far from one's mind.

D 27: Interviewee No. 27

> . . .I remember what Ahmad Seyed Javadi used to tell me when he was an MP during the first term of the House, that there was a more independent judicial system during the Shah regime, and that . . . Shah was well aware that the judicial system including the judges were not obedient to him . . . Hence they would refer the cases to the Army Prosecutor's Office . . .

D 28: Interviewee No. 28

> Before the revolution, there was an independence to the judiciary, therefore political cases were not sent to the judiciary . . .

The Existence of the Disciplinary Court of Judges before the Islamic Revolution. In this section, interviewees share their experience:

D 21: Interviewee No. 21

> The judicial Disciplinary Tribunal existed in the past regime. The nature of a wrongdoing undertaken by any judge would have been comprehensively investigated, as the judges had to act with much more discipline and adherence to stringent rules . . .

D 22: Interviewee No. 22

> They had opportunities to take their case further on to high courts if they had any complaints against a judge's misconduct.

D 23: Interviewee No. 23

> . . .the supervisory body of the judiciary existed, but due to the rare instance of corruption few cases were referred there. They acted with transparency and their functioning was more successful . . .

D 24: Interviewee No. 24

> The judiciary disciplinary tribunal was also very prominent at that time, and everyone was aware of their precision and attention to detail of everything that goes wrong . . .

The results of carried out interviews:

- Before the revolution and after WWII, there was a non-corrupt judiciary in Iran. Before the revolution, the legal culture in Iran would not tolerate a corrupt judiciary.

Judicial Corruption in the Special Clerical Court

In this section, we will review parts of interviews with people who had some experience with this special court.

D 22: Interviewee No. 22

> The key posts in the past years are in the hands of clerics who have commitment to the Supreme Leader. If some of these clerics or officials do not become corrupted, then there is room for a big surprise . . .

D 26: Interviewee No. 26

> Until the time I was called for an allegation, I was not aware of the extent of corruption. Please note, I never had any issues with the courts until I got accused and was taken to the clerical court . . . In the year 1993, sometime after Khamenei was appointed as the supreme leader, I raised my dissatisfaction about tarnishing appropriate authority in one of the meetings. I was arrested and taken to the Special Court for the Clergy immediately after the meeting . . . I was tortured and beaten so that my nose got fractured . . . My turban dropped on the floor. I told them I was arrested during the Shah period too, but no one had managed to beat my turban off . . . I never saw that person again . . . all they intended was to give me warnings to take my word back about what I had said in the meeting. I resisted and never gave in. I was imprisoned and stripped of my clothes . . . The Special Court for the clergy has become a tool of abuse for Mr Khamenei. As soon as there are signs that do not agree with his line of practice, he punishes them through this court . . . Out of fear of being prosecuted or accused of some offences, no one dare speak anything against his wishes . . . how Khamenei mistreats us clergy men we never experienced from the time of Shah. This court is unconstitutional and against morals.

D 27: Interviewee No. 27

> The Special Clerical Court was established in 1980 in Qum. It had the main role of attending to clerical crimes . . . they thought that if the clerics were tried

in ordinary courts, it would bring shame to Islam ... Mr Montazeri [Deputy of Khominei] was the supporter and the founder of these courts. But he started opposing such courts after the approval of the constitution ... For some time people heard less of such courts until 1986-1987 when people started hearing more of these courts for Mehdi Hashemi's trial ... For some time, the Clergy Court did not have any rules or regulations in place ... The main branch [of the Clergy Court] is in Moghadas Ardebili in Tehran ... Two confiscated buildings are at the possession of this court. The first is the Prosecutor's office and the other is the court. This court deals with all types of crimes and allegations. It will suffice if someone has attended the clergy school for a short period of time, then he will acquire the title of clergyman ... The functions of this court are as follows: inquisition and suppression of the opposing parties or individuals to the religious leader or to the current regime ... For instance, suppressing the followers of Ayattolah Shariatmadari or traditional clergymen or opponents against other clergymen ... In my case it was a death sentence but then this verdict was quashed to seven years imprisonment ... While I was serving my sentence a number of these clerics were brought to the same prison ... There were a few of them that were in prison for political opinions and the rest had committed crimes such as forgery ...

D 28: Interviewee No. 28

...They wanted me to defend myself. I was not going to do anything without my lawyer I replied. I was then detained. I was given a long list of lawyers to choose from as my legal representative. I then realised that they were all their own officers. I opposed to their list but in response they said I had to choose from their list and that who belonged to the special clerical court ... The persecutor of the Clergy Court told me you are going to prison because you criticised the Supreme Leader ...

The results of interviews conducted:

- This is an illegal court, and even the current constituent does not allow the creation of this court.
- This court will hear cases in closed chambers, does not allow defendants to choose their own lawyer, and refuses to hand over its written judgement to the defendants.
- The Supreme Leader uses this court as a tool to punish any clergyman who refuses to comply with his orders or who criticises the Supreme Leader.
- This Court is allowed to ignore the law.

The Principle of "The Knowledge of The Judge"

In this section, interviewees share their experience:

D 13: Interviewee No. 13

> Of course, the judge's impartiality is undermined in criminal cases more than civil cases . . . because in criminal cases, the judge can rely on his personal knowledge . . . Ultimately the general public have lost faith and confidence in the judiciary . . . In civil matters, based on evidence and documentation the judge is expected to reach its verdict. However, in criminal matters, considering the new law, it has expanded the judges' discretions, some judges if not most tend to abuse this allocated discretion and despite submitted evidence or defence by lawyers, judges will make their decisions arbitrarily . . . In criminal affairs, the judge sees himself as the representative of the government and God. Therefore, the laws in place and appropriate procedures are all ignored.

Text Cloud

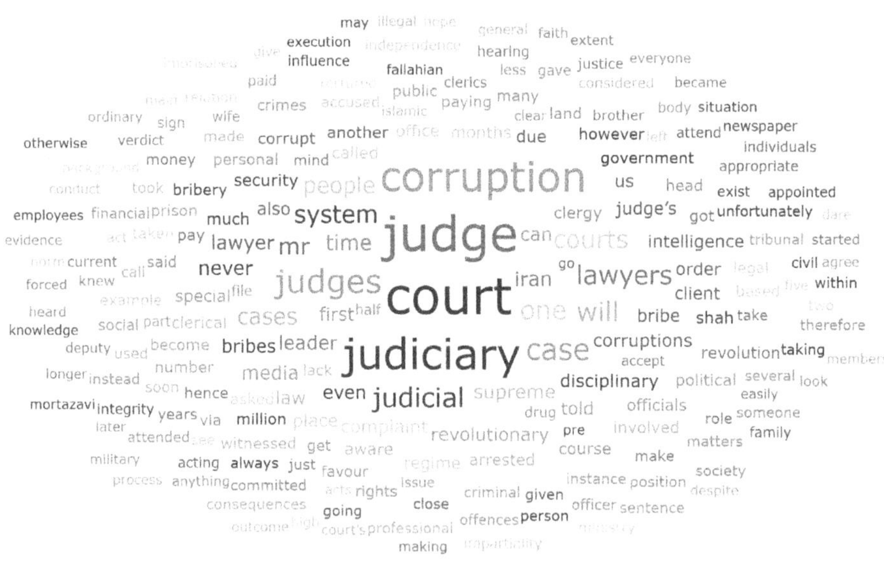

Figure 5.1: Text cloud (based on interviews). Source: Author.

References

Bahraeini, R., Nayyeri, M., & Sheeran, S. (2014). *Electoral process in Iran: Analysis of political participation and Iran's compliance with international human rights obligations.* University of Essex. https://www.essex.ac.uk/hri/documents/electoral-process-in-iran.pdf

Brytting, T., Minogue, R., & Morino, V. (2011). *The anatomy of fraud and corruption.* [electronic resource]: Organizational causes and remedies. Farnham, Surrey, England; Burlington, VT: Gower.

Cohen, L., & Felson, M. (1979). Social change and crime rate trends: A routine activity approach. *American Sociological Review, 44*. doi:10.2307/2094589.

Kar, M. (2012). *Who are the judges in the Islamic Republic of Iran.* London: Legatum Institute.

Robertson, G. (2006). *Crimes against humanity: The struggle for global justice* (3rd ed.). London: Penguin.

Robertson, G. (2007). The media and judicial corruption. In D. Rodriguez & L. Ehrich (Eds.), *Global corruption report 2007.* Cambridge: Cambridge University Press.

Robertson, G. (2014). *Judicial independence: Some recent problems.* International Bar Association's Human Rights Institute (Ibahri); Thematic Papers No 4.

Sen, A. (2000). *'What Is the Role of Legal and Judicial Reform In The Development Process?'* Speech delivered at the World Bank Conference on Legal and Judicial Reform. http://www1.worldbank.org/publicsector/legal/legalandjudicail.pdf (accessed 04/01/2016).

6

Comparison and Assessment

Shortcomings and Advantages of Comparative Approaches

Scholars claim that a comparative approach should be used to better understand the judicial system and provide suggestions for reform in the judiciary (Cole, George F., Frankowski, Stanislaw, Gertz & Marc, 1987). In fact, the comparison of judicial systems helps to abandon the existing cultural frameworks or "self-sealing cultural logics" (Nelken, 2010, p 11), and have a better understanding of the judicial systems. However, the researcher might face problems when making comparisons. For example, a body of research might deal with the judiciary in other countries like a "tourist" with only a marginal understanding of the culture and the host country. In this way the researcher may be unable to have an in-depth understanding, or may have a lack of mastery of the language in the country in which it intends to compare (Zedner, 1995).

In this research, in order to achieve a better understanding of judicial corruption in Iran, the judiciary has been compared with that of developing countries, including China; and with developed countries' judicial systems such as England and Wales.

Comparative Approach (Iran, England, and Wales)

The UK judicial system and its complexities are one of the oldest and most transparent judicial systems in the world. The transparency in the UK, which results from citizens' free access to information, gives permission to every citizen to freely access its organisations, activities, and events.

The following points are considered when comparing the performance of these two regulatory systems:

- There is evidence of widespread corruption in Iran's judiciary.
- In contrast the British judicial system is very reliable.
- The disciplinary system is independent in the United Kingdom and acts in a completely transparent manner, while being pragmatic. The function of the organisation is such that the attendees will have trust from the beginning. Being treated with respect and transparency in responsiveness and providing information is one of those important issues.
- In Iran, the disciplinary court for the judges acts in a non-transparent manner, and most importantly, the way in which its officials are elected means it has no judicial independence.

In 2015, the Global Justice Project examined the indicators of the rule of law in different countries throughout the world, and has published it worldwide, which will be used for this project. There are eight components of the law that are considered in assessing the rule of law. The following two elements can be considered for the assessment of the courts and corruption within it.

- The Quality of the Civil Courts – Is this court accessible to all and can ordinary people pay court fees? Is the court free from corruption and discrimination? Do the authorities have the power to influence and exercise power in courts? Is the judicial process a transparent one over a period of time?
- Quality of Criminal Courts – The criminal courts will be judged on the basis of the following measures: that their ability to deal successfully with criminal cases is independent and free of discrimination and immune from corruption. Also, that the courts are protected from the influence of the owners of powers.

After comparing the results of the research findings and comparing the judiciary of Iran with the judicial organisation of England and Wales the following points are highlighted:

- In Iran, the quality of services provided and citizen's access to justice in civil courts garnered only 55% while the British were given a score of 75%.
- The quality of service provisions and access of citizens to the state in the criminal courts of Iran received a score of 43% while the UK was awarded 76%.

Now, if we take a look at the World Bank Index, the results will be similar (the score awarded is between 1 and 100):

- Iran's Anti-Corruption index in 2015 ranked 16th out of 100, but the UK stood at 96th Place.
- Iran's Rule of Law index ranked 30 out of 100, but the UK had 94 out of 100 (Kaufmann, Kraay & Mastruzzi, 2010) (Figure 6.1).

Comparison of Iran and China's Judiciary Systems

In China, people from different parts of the judicial system are referred to as "Political-legal cadres", and this is where over two hundred thousand judges deal with more than six million cases a year (Bergstein, 2006, p.81). In the absence of a jury, judges have full authority over their decisions. In the structure of the Supreme Court, there is a body called "the Central Political Legal Committee", a political organisation, which runs the Chinese judicial system (Eric, 2010). The courts in China are dependent on regional administration due to the need to help them fund the courts. In China, the Supreme Court sometimes appears as a legislative body (Eric, 2010).

In China, there are no accurate statistics on judicial corruption; it is also not clear how many judges are prosecuted due to corruption, which indicates that the judicial system in China is not transparent. Judicial corruption has become common practice, and it is not uncommon for a lawyer to invite the judge for dinner and offer a bribe. In certain circumstances, politicians can influence the courts' decisions. In other words, they can not only influence the process during the trial, but also after the issuance of a ruling; they can set aside that ruling, and any attempt to create an independent judiciary will face opposition from the ruling party. In China, the independence of the judiciary means that judges must be independent of the parties and not separate from the communist party (Ip, 2008).

Li (2012) examines judicial corruption in China and states that corruption is institutionalised in the structure of China's judicial system. He mentions the Supreme People's Court has repeatedly announced various campaigns to fight corruption, and during these campaigns several judges were forced to retire or were punished. Furthermore, other significant measures such as the decentralisation of courts and the creation of inspection officers were carried out. However, despite serious measures, corruption has continued to survive and even expand. Li (2012) believed insufficient judge's salary, lack of financial resources for the courts, and the lack of necessary judicial education, including non-independence of the judges without any accountabilities for their actions are some reasons for such corruption. He believes that the structure of the judiciary in China and the decision-making process in the courts at all levels of the judicial system provide the breeding ground for the formation of corruption. The scholar states that the judicial process in China has been designed in such a way as to ensure the control of all affairs by the ruling party, and the ruling party is above the law. Such a process has had the influence of politicians on the court and provides the right atmosphere for corrupt judges to use this mechanism to commit corruption.

In conclusion and according to Li's findings, one can summarise that communist party officials in the regions, and different parts of the province, are considered as the head of the judicial organisation of that area, and they can influence the courts. In fact, these powers are given to the judges in order to welcome communist party officials to have influence over cases. Extensive exercise and influences have led to the creation of a corrupt court in China. One can conclude that the main problem of the Chinese judicial system is the lack of independence, which has led to corruption.

When investigating judicial corruption, indicators of the rule of law and the control of corruption in this country should be considered. In the World Bank report, these figures are as follows (the score awarded is between 1 and 100):

- Rule of law: 39.90
- Control of Corruption: 48.80 (Kaufmann, Kraay & Mastruzzi, 2010)

Comparison of the findings of the Global Justice Foundation report shows that there are many resemblances between Iran and China in terms of the quality and purity of civil and criminal courts. The Annual Report of the Foundation for International Justice on the Rule of Law reported (World Justice Project, 2015):

- In Iran, the quality of services provided and citizen's access to justice in civil courts garnered only 55% while China were given a score of 52%.
- The quality of service provisions and access of citizens to the state in the criminal courts of Iran received a score of 43% while the UK was awarded 52%.

The World Bank Law enforcement and anti-corruption indicators provide a similar picture of the situation in Iran and China. This is shown in the chart below (the score awarded is between 1 and 100):

The volume of corruption in China is much less than in Iran; hence, one can examine many similarities in the causes and ways of forming corruption:

- One of the most important reasons for judicial corruption in China and Iran is the lack of independence of the judicial system and the lack of independence of judges in personal terms.
- In China, a judge will be considered independent if they have no prior relation to any of the parties of the case; however, any judge in China must have full commitment to the Communist party; therefore, the judge still can be under the influence of the Communist party (Li, 2012). In fact, in China, it is mandatory that judges believe in the Communist Party and have full commitment to this political party.
- One can observe similar conditions in Iran, and the judge must have full commitment to the orders of the "Guardianship of the Islamic Jurist". The independence of the judge does not mean that he should be independent of the official ideology of the government. In fact, we see a strong attachment of judges to the official ideology of the Islamic regime.

Figure 6.1: The rule of law index (Iran and China). Adopted from "*The Worldwide Governance Indicators: Methodology and Analytical Issues.* By Kaufmann, Kraay,& Mastruzzi (2010).

	I.R. IRAN	China
Rule of Law	17.31	39.9
Control of Corruption	31.73	48.8

- It is worth mentioning that the bulk of executive bodies of the country are governed by the Supreme Leader. In Iran, law enforcement agencies (including the police and intelligence agencies) and the Armed Forces are operating under the administration of the Supreme Leader.
- There exists no organisational independence of the courts in China. Li's findings reveal that the courts in China are under the absolute control of the Chinese Communist Party. On the other hand, the law is just one instrument of regulation that the law enforcers can interpret or manipulate, and the Communist party is superior overall.
- There exists a similar situation in Iran where the leader has absolute sovereignty in the courts. The findings of this study indicate that the Iranian judiciary has no organisational independence.
- Both in China and in Iran, the judiciary system is not independent and has become a tool to ensure the ruler's survival.
- In both countries, those who are affiliated with the official ideology have manipulated the power in a way that does not permit other political activists to criticise them.
- There are other similarities between China and Iran. The selection of judges and all high-ranking officials are appointed based on their proximity to such ideology. We also see that security officials or political officials easily influence the courts or the judiciary.
- In both countries, the lack of media freedom in reporting corruption or criticising its government has led to the spread of corruption. Such a lack of trust has caused significant damage to the legal culture. There seems to be a direct link between the collapse of the legal culture of society and the lack of freedom of expression.
- In both countries, the judiciary systems are astonishingly under the influence of the leading political group and in fact lack any inherent autonomy.

Assessing the Judiciary Based on International Transparency Standards

Based on collected data, it is now possible to evaluate corruption in the Iranian judiciary. International Transparency has developed a "toolkit" to identify the variables that are effective in judicial corruption cases.

In this section, based on the findings of this research and the analysis of available data, these variables are examined.

Safeguards for the Protection of Judicial Independence

- Institutional independence: The Supreme Leader appoints the head of the judiciary; therefore, there is no institutional independence for the judiciary in Iran. Independence of the judiciary is not recognised in Iran. In fact, the Supreme Leader can be seen as a part of the executive branch because law enforcement and the military are part of his administration. Ultimately it is the Supreme Leader who determines the head of the judiciary.
- Individual independence: The findings of this research shows the judge in Iran can be influenced by the Supreme Leader and his administration, various intelligence services, and powerful clergymen; and receiving bribes is a common practice in Iran.
- Immunity: The judges in Iran legally enjoy immunity.
- Integrity: It is a common practice in Iran for judges to demand bribes. Judges are aware that the public do not respect the judiciary, and they don't try to uphold the dignity of the judicial office.

Good Working Conditions for Judges.

- The judge's pensions are fair compared to other employees, but it does not meet the standards of living in Iran and the relative poverty line. It is natural that this causes corruption among judges because they are not financially secure.
- In Iran, the judges do not have job security, and the head of the judiciary can easily expel them.

Appointment of Judges

- There is no clear trend for selecting judges in Iran. Selection of judges is carried out in regard to taste and choice and not based on the efficiency and knowledge of individuals.
- The process of appointment and promotion for judges in Iran is not objective and transparent. For the head of the judiciary, it is possible to promote the judges who are obedient enough to the Supreme Leader.
- It is not clear how members of the appointments body are selected. In Iran, such individuals are not appointed with transparency. The Supreme Leader and his assigned person, the head of the judiciary, have exclusive and uncontrolled autonomy in this matter.

- Judicial appointments or promotions of judges are not based on merit, competence, or integrity. The most important factors for appointment or promotion, are how committed candidates are to the supreme leader. The selection criteria for judges in Iran are subjective.
- In Iran, appointment decisions are not documented.
- The appointment of judges in Iran is not transparent, and although the legislature and the executive cannot influence the selection of the judge, the Supreme Leader can. The principles of choosing judges are complex, as a small number of judges have enormous power. In Iran, there is a corrupt way to choose judges, and from the very beginning, attempts are made to select judges without independency. The outcomes of their actions are evidently shown. The judiciary has become a tool for the implementation of the supreme leader's spirituality. The head of the judiciary is responsible to the judges and can influence their powers.

Accountability

- There is an appellate structure of court systems in Iran for ordinary cases; however, there is no clear appellate structure for Clergy Courts or Revolutionary Courts.
- Grounds for appeal are well defined in Iranian law.
- Judges in Iran are not required to justify their decisions. Judges don't give reasons for their judicial decisions. In fact, Revolutionary Court and Clergy Courts refuse to hand down their judgement.
- There are no objective criteria to determine the placement of judges in particular court locations.
- Case assignment is not objective or transparent.
- Court staff and judges can postpone the hearing and court process as much as they please.
- Judges usually have adequate time to hear cases and prepare judgements.
- There are no performance-monitoring measures in the judiciary in Iran.
- There is no financial accountability in the Iranian judiciary. In 2016, the media reported that part of the judiciary budget (more than IRR 250 billion) was deposited into the personal account belonging to the head of the judiciary (Radiofarda, 2016).
- No detailed information such as budget and how resources are allocated to the selection of judges are available to the Iranian citizens.

- There is a code of conduct for judges in Iran. However, that code of conduct is not compatible with the "Bangalore Principles on Judicial Conduct".
- The findings of this research show judges rarely facing any consequences for misconduct or corruption. Disciplinary Court (a body who receives complaints) is not independent.

Transparency and Resources

- Iranian citizens have access to some information about some parts of the judiciary. However, members of the public have no access to information about the Revolutionary Court or Clergy Court. Iranian courts do not publish their decisions, and give no reason for their judicial orders. Judges are allowed to rely on Shari'a law, which is not clear; therefore, there is no legal certainty in Iran.
- In Iran, the judges are provided with education. However, most of the legal material is about Islamic law. There is no education about corruption for judges.
- Judges in Iran have adequate access to legislation, cases, court procedures, case notes, and records of judgements, and are kept up-to-date on legal developments.
- In Iran, the authority of the court is respected by the government. However, the Supreme Leader and his administration in some cases interfere with the court process. For example, in 2016, when a prominent Iranian Qur'an reciter who was close to the Supreme Leader was accused of raping a 19-year-old child, a deputy of the Supreme Leader ordered the court to close the case (Radiofarda, 2016).

Political Activities of the Judges

- In Iran, all of the judges are required to have full commitment to the Supreme Leader. They are required to show their support.
- The Supreme Leader in Iran is not appointed by a fair and free election. Therefore, he is not an independent person, and he gets involved in many political issues. Judges are required to follow and support him. This procedure has undermined the independence and credibility of the Judges.

Relationship between other Branches and the Judiciary

- Despite the fact that the president is known to be the protector of the constitution, and the Committee no 90 of the Parliament has a great deal of discretion to oversee the work of the judiciary, this executive branch and the legislative branch refrain from monitoring the work of the judiciary. The reason being is that the judiciary is the subset of the Supreme Leader.

Appellate Structure of Court System

- In the special Clerical Court, for which there is little information about its structure, the possibility of appeals is also difficult and is granted only with the consent of the court's chief.
- There is no transparent process in the Revolutionary Court, and the revision of the sentences is not easily possible.
- In most courts, the structure of the court is clear, and the possibility of appeal in some cases is available.

Transparency in Court and Giving Reasons for Judicial Order

- In all courts the workflow of the cases is not transparent. The judge does not write what the workflow was and how it was based on the ruling, which has ultimately led to the lack of transparency of the court's functionality. It is only the tribunal in the country that mentions the workflow of the cases and any ordinary courts do not state any step-by-step process of the case. Most importantly, no court verdicts will be officially published.
- The Revolutionary Court considers itself a court of law and does not allow perpetrators or their lawyers to receive their verdicts. They are only allowed to attend the court room and take note of the verdict.
- In summing up, it can be said that the Iranian courts do not act transparently, and the judges are not obliged to mention the file's workflow and the details of the case and its reasons for issuing the verdict.

References

Bergstein, C. F., Gill, B., Lardy, N. R., & Mitchell, D. (2006). *China: The balance sheet, Public Affairs,* New York, p. 69.

Cole, G. F., Frankowski, S., & Gertz, M. G. (1987). *Major criminal justice systems: A comparative survey.* Beverly Hills, CA: Sage.

Eric, C. (2010). The Supreme Court and the making of public policy in contemporary China. *The Michigan Journal of Public Affairs, 7,* Spring 2010. The University of Michigan. Can be retrieved at: http://mjpa.umich.edu/files/2014/06/2010-Ip-ChinaSupremeCourt.pdf

Ip, E. C. (2008). Judicial corruption and its threats, to National Governance in China. *JOAAG, 3*(1). joaag.com/uploads/8_IpFinal.pdf

Kaufmann, D., Aart, K., & Lobatón, P. (1999). *Governance matters.* World Bank, retrieved from: https://goo.gl/h3Fs7V; (accessed 31-03-2016).

Kaufmann, D., & Kraay, A. (2008). *Governance indicators: Where are we, where should we be going?* Oxford University Press. doi:10.1093/wbro/lkm012.

Kaufmann, D., Kraay, A., & Mastruzzi, M. (2006). *Measuring corruption: Myths and realities.* The World Bank.

Kaufmann, D., Kraay, A., & Mastruzzi, M. (2009). *Governance matters VIII.* The World Bank Development Research Group Macroeconomics and Growth Team.

Kaufmann, D., Kraay, A., & Mastruzzi, M. (2010). *The worldwide governance indicators: Methodology and analytical issues.* World Bank Policy Research Working Paper No. 5430.

Kaufmann, D., Kraay, A., & Zoido-Lobato´n, P. (1999). *"Aggregating Governance Indicators."* Policy Research Working Paper 2195. Washington, DC: World Bank.

Li, L. (2012). The 'Production' of corruption in China's courts: Judicial politics and decision making in a one-party state. *Law & Social Inquiry, 37*(4), 848–877. doi:10.1111/j.1747-4469.2012.01285.x.

Nelken, D. (2010). *Comparative criminal justice: Making sense of difference.* London: SAGE Publications Ltd.

Nelken, D. (2014). Thinking about legal culture. *Asian Journal of Law and Society, 1*(2), 255–274.

World Justice Project. (2016). Rule of Law Index 2016. Available at: https://worldjusticeproject.org/sites/default/files/documents/RoLI_Final-Digital_0.pdf

Zedner, L. (1995). Comparative research in criminal justice. In L. Noaks, M. Levi, & M. Maguire (Eds.), *Contemporary issues in criminology* (pp. 8–25). Cardiff: University of Wales Press.

7 Conclusion

In this section we will summarise the results of the research team.

Summary of Findings

According to the interviews, it can be concluded that Iran's judicial system is corrupt, and this corruption is also widespread. The Supreme leader has laid the cornerstone of judicial corruption in Iran by using it as a means to suppress critics or opponents. For the judiciary to be able to act as a suppressive organisation, previous and current supreme leaders have taken the following steps:

- There has been a poor structure designed for the judiciary with no personal independence for the judges or organisational independence for the judiciary.
- Secondly, the disciplinary court has been disarmed in its ability to combat corruption.
- And thirdly, the freedom of the press has been restricted.

The former World Bank's General Counsel, Shihata, claimed: "Systems can corrupt people as much as, if not more than, people are capable of corrupting systems" (The World Bank, 1997, p. 20). Under normal circumstances, individuals or firms, including some financial agencies, opt to pay bribes to achieve reductions in costs (Joang, 2010). The situation with Iran's judiciary is different. In fact, in many cases, judges force citizens to pay bribes.

The following points can be cited as the main findings of the research:

1. The judiciary and the courts are designed in such a way that the leader or his associates can use the courts as a tool to suppress critics and opponents. Therefore, the judiciary and the courts are not independent in Iran. Lack of independence for the judges and the judicial system has created a breeding ground for the spread of judicial corruption. The influence of the Supreme Leader on the judiciary is the most important factor in this corruption.
2. Judges do not have personal independence. Their thoughts and ideologies are involved in the administration of the court and the issuance of the verdicts. Furthermore, some organisations and powerful authorities have many means to influence the judges.
3. Journalists and the media are confronted with being barred from reporting judicial corruption.
4. The legal culture is severely damaged in the society, and the judiciary has lost its reputation; therefore, judges have had to face a diminution of their legal supremacy.
5. Judges are elected by a particular class with certain ideologies, having a special commitment to the current regime, and since this system does not have a popular legitimacy, the judges do not hold a special place in their society. In addition, judges in the community do not get respect for themselves.
6. The recently recruited judges witness corrupt acts of more senior judges on a daily basis. In such situations, they are also encouraged to behave in the same way, and as Kourchekian (2007) argues, judges behave like other judges.
7. Citizens of Iranian society do not consider the courts to have integrity and credibility, and as a result, paying bribes to judges of the court including the court personnel is not considered to be a disgraceful practice. On the other hand, ordinary people, or the court staff, including judges, have no fear and are unashamed of receiving bribes.

8. The Iranian citizens do not trust the judiciary and consider it to be a corrupt system.
9. Citizens face widespread corruption when they go to the judiciary; hence, this reduces the public confidence in it. The less public confidence in the judiciary the more there will be opportunity for the occurrence of corruption.
10. Some lawyers have also contributed to the spread of judicial corruption. These lawyers do not prevent corruption, but play a role in expanding this corruption and use it as a tool.
11. In Iran, the media do not act as a weapon to fight corruption, and the media industry is reluctant to disclose this corruption due to a lack of freedom of speech and job security.
12. Due to the lack of independence of the disciplinary court, citizens of Iran have no confidence in this organisation. As a result, this regulatory system lacks efficiency.
13. The judicial corruption in Iran has become common practice and an unwritten part of the social contract in Iran.
14. It can be concluded that corruption has been institutionalised in Iran.
15. Scholars claim that there is a reverse relationship between women holding high ranking positions within the government and managerial positions and the expansion of corruption (Swamy, Knack, Lee & Azfar, 2001). Meanwhile, the role of being a judge is dedicated to men, and women are not allowed to hold judicial positions.
16. The creation of an illegal court called the Special Court for the Clergy has caused the judiciary to be seriously damaged. In fact, this illegal entity serves as a tool for suppressing clerical judges.
17. Judges are not required to state reasons for issuing verdicts.
18. The judge's knowledge "Elme-Ghazi" as one of the grounds for issuing a verdict is one of the most important reasons for the occurrence of judicial corruption. In fact, judges have the opportunity to issue an order without reference to evidence arbitrarily.

Examination of Corruption in the Judicial System

According to the research carried out, this section will examine the widespread corruption of the judiciary.

Investigating the Independence of the Judiciary as an Institution

Previous studies and the findings of this study clearly indicate that there is a direct correlation between the level of judicial corruption and judicial independence. It can be argued that the most important tool for assessing the level of corruption in a judicial system in any country is its independence (Vagut & Gutman, 2015).

The findings of this research indicate that the Iranian judiciary is not an independent system. The following points are used to prove this claim. The head of the judiciary is appointed by the Supreme Leader. However, the legitimacy of the Supreme Leader itself is questionable. The Iranian people do not play a role in having the Supreme Leader elected, and the leader is not accountable towards the Iranian public (Cress, Kent, Nayyeri, 2014). The lack of oversight on the leader is to the extent that the head of the judiciary makes an official declaration that there is no supervision over the actions of the Supreme Leader. Asre-Iran (2014, p.1) states, "In the constitution we do not have anything called supervising the Supreme Leader".

It should be borne in mind that the Supreme Leader, as an unelected person or entity, will appoint the head of the judiciary. A large portion of the Iranian economy, and all of the law enforcement agencies and army operate under the administration of the Supreme Leader and they are at his disposal; Institutions such as the following are under the supervision of the Supreme Leader: the army, Islamic Revolutionary Guard Corps, Sāzmān-e Basij-e Mostaz'afin, National Radio and Television Institution and the Imams of the Friday Prayer.

According to Article 158 of the constitution, the head of the judiciary, who is appointed by the leader, has the authority to appoint and dismiss judges. Here it can be seen that the judiciary (who are under the control of the Supreme Leader) are supposed to hear crimes or disputes in society. While other institutions are under the control of the Supreme Leader and hold a large part of the economy, and all the while there is no oversight on the actions and leadership of the Supreme Leader. In such situations, the formation of an impartial judiciary is very unlikely. The departments under the supervision of the Supreme Leader are all involved in economic activities, or individuals who have close affiliations with the Supreme Leader. As a result, the leader or the institutions under his leadership are all collectively party to a dispute, and in such circumstances the court cannot act independently.

The European Commission for Democracy recommends that judges be appointed by judicial council, and ultimately this commission should have the power to dismiss and appoint judges. According to the recommendations of the

Commission, it is desirable for the members of the Judicial Council to be composed of the following individuals:

- The majority of them should be among the judges of the judicial system
- A minority from this council will be elected by parliament

This commission does not recommend that judges be elected by parliamentarians because members of parliament may use their influence later. It should be noted that in the above research, most of the judicial systems in the named countries are transparent and clear, and therefore the proposed council is likely to be a non-corrupt and transparent one. Hence, the implementation of this recommendation to the Iranian judiciary may not be feasible and another way should be sought. For example, lawyers with a history of transparency can be used to create this judicial council.

In the above-mentioned matter, the importance of removing and appointing judges for the creation of a non-corrupt judiciary can be seen. It should be recalled that in the judiciary of Iran, the power to dismiss judges is given to the head of the judiciary, who is appointed by the Supreme Leader. Even though the leader has not been elected by the citizens, they have not come to power via free elections or a fair and just system.

One of the most important issues in the Iranian system is that the head of the judiciary and judges are appointed by the Supreme Leader. Consequently, Iran's judiciary as an institution and judges as individuals are not independent in any way. There is no transparency in dismissing or appointing the judges. Only the ones who have close affiliations to the Supreme Leader are selected.

The judiciary in Iran is not independent, and it functions as a subordinate entity of the Supreme Leader. This is why Hashemi Sharoodi is convinced that the judiciary is part of the Supreme Leader's administration, and meant he had a right to refuse the request of parliamentarians to inspect the official judiciary.

The judiciary, as an institution that needs to regulate justice in society, has become a playing card in political engagements. For example, Behzad Bahrami, the head of public relations at the office of Fallahian, said the following in an interview with the author (Ali Fallahian is a politician and cleric. He is a Member of the Assembly of Experts and former Minister of Intelligence of Iran):
D 14: Interviewee No. 14

> . . .as for the appointment of Mr Sadeq Larijani as head of the judiciary, I must say first Mr Fallahian was supposed to be appointed to the post of President.

> He even said there were consultations relating to changes and replacements. But after the events and the repression of the people in the 1989 protest, Mr Vahid Khorasani, complained to the Supreme Leader. When the Supreme Leader was paying a visit to Qum, he left Qum, which was a strong gesture of opposition. In order to keep him quiet and as Mr Larijani is his son in law, he was assigned as the head of the judiciary.

Examination of the Independence of the Judges

When assessing judicial corruption, the independence of judges is of particular importance. The findings of this study indicate that Iran's judges have very little personal independence. The independence of judges means that judges are immune from any influence, and that they can reach a level of perfection and integrity that does not interfere with their ideology while they are hearing or issuing a judgement. This means they are able to make a judgement only on the basis of the facts in the case (Cameron, 2009; Chemerinsky, 1989).

The relevant laws and regulations about the appointment of judges in Iran state that they must be male, as well as believe in Islam and in the current regime. Meanwhile, the findings of this study indicate that security institutions are involved in choosing judges as part of the appointment process. This is to ensure the unconditional conviction of the candidate to the ideology of the religious clergy, and to ensure that he prioritises the interests of the ruling system.

This is where we are seeing the arbitrary selection of judges, and practically the law of necessity for the belief in the fundamental ideologies of the current regime as a condition for the appointment of judges. On the other hand, we see that one of the most fundamental principles for promoting judges is the proximity of their attitude to the government.

Influence of the Supreme Leader on the Judiciary

At the outset, it is noteworthy to reconsider the problem of corruption in China. Research carried out by Ip (2008) shows that judicial independence does not have its own normal meaning. The aforementioned researcher believes that any attempts to create a fundamental reform in the Chinese judiciary will face opposition from the ruling party. In China, the independence of the judiciary merely means that judges must be independent of the parties, but they are not independent of the Communist Party. The study found that the cause of the formation and corruption of justice in China is the same lack of independence, and emphasises that the ruling party in China is the most important barrier to fight against judicial corruption in China. Now we will look at the ideology governing the Islamic Republic:

- When appointing judges in Iran one of the essential conditions for their appointment is their belief in Velayat-e-Faqih and the Islamic Republic's system.
- If the conditions of Iran and China are compared, one can see that the conditions are quite similar. In Iran, the judges' independence does not mean independence from the supreme jurisprudent, and he is strongly influenced by this theory including the Supreme Leader and his associates.
- On the other hand, the leader of the Islamic Republic is not accountable and is not actually chosen in a democratic manner.
- The organisational independence of the judiciary is now going to be examined, and it can be seen that this organisational independence is practically absent in Iran. This organisation is somewhat a sub-organisation affiliated with the Supreme Leader and under his influence (Kar, 2012).
- Judges' ideology is strongly influenced by the theory of velayat-e-faqih (the Governance of the Jurist), a theory that is highly aggressive and allows them to misuse their position as a judge to protect the Islamic Republic. In fact, this theory and belief has led to the elimination of personal independence of the judges.

Supervision of the Executive and the Legislature

In Article 133 of the previous constitution of the Islamic Republic, the President had a duty and power to regulate the relationship between the three powers. However, in the amendment of the constitution in 1988, this power was taken away from the presidency. Therefore, there is no monitoring of the judiciary by the executive branch. Yousefi Eshkoori, the former MP, said in an interview with the author:

D 27: Interviewee No. 27

> . . .my statement stands as a statement that: Mr Asghari was the Minister of Justice during my first term as an MP. He told me that he was in fact not a minister but a carrier in the judiciary and had no discretion . . .

Article 90 of the constitution allows the parliament to ask questions and demand answers from the judiciary. However, despite this principle, parliamentarians have not yet exercised their authority to oversee the work of the judiciary. It

should be noted that scholars claim that the legislative branch is not independent, and MPs are not elected in a democratic process. The Guardian Council monitors the electoral process. Furthermore, The Guardian Council eliminates any candidate who has no full commitment to the Supreme Leader (Cress et al., 2014). One of the interviewees, who is a journalist, stated:
D 7: Interviewee No. 7

> MPs in Iran never disclose any matters regarding judicial corruption as they are well aware of their own corruption being on the verge of disclosure.

It can be argued that the very fact that the members of parliament were handpicked by the Supreme Leader (or his agents) means he has eliminated all of his opponents from positions of power. Therefore, the parliament itself has no capacity or power to oversee the work of the judiciary, considering the Supreme Leader appoints the head of it. When investigating corruption in the judiciary and the behaviour of parliamentarians, it is possible to consider the spread of corruption from one institution to another. By examining the reports of the parliament to the judiciary, and comparing that report with the findings of this study, it can be concluded that these MPs only superficially attempted to investigate the judiciary, while in fact turning a blind eye to the widespread corruption within the judiciary.

The Effects of Corruption in the Judiciary on the Other Branches of Government

The judiciary is the most important means of preventing corruption in the executive and the legislative branch. The executive branch in Iran suffers from rampant corruption. According to International Transparency, Iran rates 130 among other countries (Transparency international, 2015). It is evident that in such a situation, while the judiciary suffers from widespread corruption, it is natural that there is no proper supervision on the executive branch too. In fact, the more there is corruption in the judiciary, the more corruption will be created in the executive and the legislative branches.

Supervision of the Media on the Judiciary

Reporters without Borders (2014) has ranked media freedom in different countries, and Iran was graded 173 out of 179 ranks. One of the interviewees, who is a journalist, shared his experience with judicial corruption, he stated:

D 7: Interviewee No. 7

> In some of the media, they are involved in financial and political corruptions, and to protect their interests they have no choice but to ignore the issue of corruption in the judiciary. On the other hand, even if the media publish the smallest criticism of the judiciary, it will lead to the closure of the newspaper. This is a forcing power of the judiciary on media. Overseas media, also in the form of political issues, deal with corruption in the judiciary or its ineffectiveness.

The precise monitoring of the media and their freedom in reporting offenders including judges or court employees is an effective tool that can prevent corruption. Many scholars are of the opinion that the media plays a significant role in ensuring the transparency and existence of non-corrupt courts of the judicial system (Robertson, 2007). Due to a lack of freedom of the press in Iran there cannot be such an observatory system on the judiciary. Many citizens in Iran have claimed and witnessed that the media does not have such leverage or autonomy to be exploring corruption in the judiciary. The basic belief of journalists is that due to a widespread level of judicial corruption throughout the whole system, the authorities are taking advantage of their discretions and powers to suppress opposing media. Disclosure of judicial corruption by journalists is considered to be a violation of national security and would lead to legal consequences against them.

A lack of investigative journalists in Iran has also been a significant factor in failures to highlight corruptions in the judiciary. Robertson (2007) rightly claimed that due to the complexity of judicial corruption it would be necessary to have journalists who possess a legal background to enable them to investigate the surrounding issues relating to judicial corruptions.

Legal Culture Governing the Iranian Society

The outcome of the research carried out showed that if in public opinion, corruption in society is widespread, then it will be more likely for ordinary people to engage in corruption (Fehr, and Fischbacher, 2005).

The legal culture governing Iranian society has played a very important role in the spread of judicial corruption. The existence of laws that are in clear opposition to the human rights of citizens (e.g. freedom of dress codes), and the desires of a significant portion of society have created a situation where breaking the law has become a common trend, and is not shameful. One interviewee explained how he paid bribes to avoid incurring penalties for drinking. It is easy to observe how the law itself generates corruption. When a citizen evaluates the law as unfair and inhuman, they will feel no shame in paying a bribe in order to avoid inhumane punishments. In fact, having inhumane and unfair law, which is against the "general will", can undermine the very rule of law.

The widespread corruption in the judiciary, and the lack of monitoring of judges or employees and the court have led to a loss of public confidence. The procedure for appointing judges is one of the most important reasons for the damage of the culture of law. Judges in Iran are completely selective and based mainly on their affiliation and loyalty to the Supreme Leader. It is natural that this default caused the community to lose its trust. Due to the above-mentioned factors, people's views of judges are doubtful. Therefore, judges do not carry a respected position in society. As a result:

- Judges do not consider themselves obliged to comply with high standards of behaviour.
- Rent seekers and deceitful individuals easily and readily opt for paying bribes.

The Contamination of Courts and the Judiciary with Politics and Lack of Impartiality

The interviewees described how courts engaged in politics. Mohsen Kadivar, clergyman, who was a vocal critic of the Supreme Leader, stated:

D 28: Interviewee No. 28

> . . .the judiciary has practically become a tool in hand of the Supreme Leader . . .

Furthermore, Yousefi Eshkavari, former member of the Iranian Parliament, said the following regarding the Special Clerical Court:

D 27: Interviewee No. 27

> . . .the functions of this court are as follows: inquisition and suppression of the opposing parties or individuals to the religious leader or to the current regime . . .

The judiciary is not a bias free system and is used as a means of repressing political activists and journalists:

- The Supreme Leader only allows the people close to the ideology of the Islamic regime to be appointed as a judge.

- On the other hand, to ensure that this judiciary can do anything that is needed to fulfil the demands of the Supreme Leader, there is no effective method for the proper monitoring of judges
- The Supreme Leader and his associates want to have this option to put pressure on any judge and to manipulate any case in any way they wish; therefore, they designed the disciplinary court in a way to allow the Supreme Leader to use it as tool to punish any judge. Instead of being a monitoring tool to ensure the transparency and purity of the judiciary, the disciplinary court itself has become a factor to undermine the independence of judges and works as a pressure point, which has led to corruption.
- Corruption in Iran, therefore, is very similar to the corruption in China, as the influence of the ruling party on China's courts is the main cause of the spread of corruption in the country.

Overall, it can be argued that the Iranian judiciary is designed in such a way that the Supreme Leader can suppress opposition to the regime via the judiciary, and this itself has led to the creation of corruption.

The Role of Lawyers

The findings of the research carried out by Tesoonga and Dia (2007) show the need to maintain the independence of the Bar Association and to provide the necessary training. The findings of this study indicate that some lawyers have an active role in the spread of judicial corruption.

Inefficiency and Corruption in the Court of Disciplinary for Judges

One of the interviewees, who had spent time in jail in Iran for defending the rights of labour in an interview, said the following:

D 15: Interviewee No. 15

> I was aware of the judge's Disciplinary Court. When I consulted with several lawyers, I was told there would not be any benefits to drawing attention to the judge's Disciplinary Courts. . . .there is no point in making a complaint about judicial members who are bribe takers. You would be considered lucky, if after complaining about any members of the judiciary, you are not be held liable or being accused of any offences at the judicial Discipline Tribunal. T . . .his would only cost money and an enormous amount of stress with time which is wasted over an injustice. . . .

Most of the witnesses who were interviewed have expressed even less trust in the Disciplinary Court for judges. In fact, right from the start there was no initial confidence in this regulatory system, and the system's inability to combat corruption has corroborated this lack of trust. Perhaps the best version is from a recently retired judge in Iran who described the functioning of the regulatory system, as the following:

D 20: Interviewee No. 20

> . . .judges are examined and observed via so many filtering systems. It would be shameful for the regime or government of the time to convict a judge with a crime such as corruption. So, if a judge commits an offence, it will not be disclosed to anyone. . . .there are a lot of corruption cases, but you don't hear about them all . . .and one should not think that there is no supervision at all . . .we have had cases, where the judge had attended an appellant's home and had managed to rape her just because he knew she was alone, he [the judge] was then sent to another city [as judge] just to avoid the spread of the news.

The Disciplinary Court for judges has virtually become a means of forcing judges to be submissive to the Supreme Leader and his associates.

The Disciplinary Court for judges should be independent as a court. However, the head of the judiciary (which is appointed by the Supreme Leader) has the power to appoint or change the judge of the Disciplinary Court.

How Is Judicial Corruption Generated?

In Chapter 2 and the review of the studies, it has been pointed out that judicial independence and accountability must complement each other.

Freedom of the media is an important factor in reducing judicial corruption (Robertson, 2007). The Supreme Leader of the Islamic Republic has played an important role in creating restrictions on the media. For example, the judiciary (which functions under his supervision) shouts down the free media and newspapers on a regular basis. The Islamic Republic's 6th legislature in 1999, however, proposed a bill to give more freedom to the press. Unfortunately, the Supreme Leader personally intervened, and did not permit the parliament to consider the bill (Roozonline 2000).

Considering the above points, one can conclude that the Supreme Leader is the main reason for the emergence of judicial corruption in Iran. By exercising influence over the judiciary, the Supreme Leader and the head of his judiciary have created a breeding ground for judicial corruption. They use their power to manipulate the process of appointment of the judges, and choose only those individuals who have a closer ideology to themselves.

The Supreme Leader and the head of his judiciary started the process for the creation of judicial corruption when they undermined the independent judiciary. By doing so, they introduced judicial corruption as an "informal social contract" to the society.

Cultivation of Corruption in the Judiciary

The lack of judicial independence at both a fundamental level (for the whole judiciary as an organisation) and at a personal level for the judges has contributed to the creation of such corruptions. The judiciary is under the influence of the leader and security forces or influential clerics can easily press the judges.

Judges are allowed to use their personal knowledge (Elme-Ghazi) in issuing orders or judgements. Furthermore, the ideology of the judges influences them when issuing judgements, and this has led to their lack of independence.

The lack of transparency in the process of issuing judgements is another main drawback of the Iranian judiciary, because:

- During the issuance of the verdict, judges do not mention their reasoning, and in the verdict, the workflow of the case, as well as the reasons for issuing the sentences, are not mentioned.
- Sentences issued by the judiciary are not available to the public.
- Given the above, public opinion cannot judge the performance of the judges.

The free media as one of the most imperative factors in preventing judicial corruption does not exist in Iran. And diaspora journalists have also paid very little attention to this issue.

Current anti-corruption laws in Iran are very old. It's imperative that the laws on anti-corruption are dynamic and updated.

The authorities of the judiciary refrain from accepting the existence of judicial corruption, and therefore they will take no action to combat it. For example, the deputy head of the judiciary officially announced, "According to the inspection agency, 72% of the people are satisfied with the functioning of the judiciary, of which 36% are very pleased." (Isna, 2015)

Corruption in the judiciary acts like a vicious circle. Given the above, the following graphs illustrate the formation and increase in corruption (Figure 7.1):

Figure 7.1: Formation and increase in judicial corruption in Iran. Source: Author.

Understanding Judicial Corruption in Iran Using the Broken Window Theory

In order to understand the judicial corruption in Iran, it is necessary to pay attention to the broken window theory. This opinion was presented by Wilson and Kelling (1982). These scholars argued that small crimes will lead to more serious crimes and antisocial behaviour. It is argued that the failure to deal with trivial crimes creates the feeling that social control is less dominant.

The fact is that there is no system in the Iranian judiciary to effectively deal with minor crimes of judges or court personnel. The head of the judiciary in Tehran explicitly states that the judges ask female clients for sexual favours: It can be seen how crimes such as attempted sexual abuse are immune from prosecution. In such situations, it can be argued according to the broken window theory that this itself leads to the formation of judicial corruption on the wider spectrum.

The Consequences of Judicial Corruption on Society

Klitgaard (2006) argues that systematic corruption eliminates incentives, it weakens the foundations of the government, and villainous individuals will possess power and unlawful wealth. The corruption of the judiciary has taken over all parts of the government. Nobel Peace Prize Laureate, Shirin Ebadi, stated:

D 21: Interviewee No. 21

> "...such corruption has contaminated the body of society, the symbol of democracy and the independence of the judiciary."

Legal Corruption and Human Rights Violations

Corruption has caused the human rights of Iranian citizens to be violated, including the following rights:

- The right to fair trial (Universal Declaration of Human Rights and Article IV of the International Covenant on Civil and Political Rights).
- The right to non-discrimination against the equality of citizens and the right to benefit from the law (International Covenant on Civil and Political Rights).

Spread of Corruption and Its Reproduction

By comparing judicial corruption in China and Iran, it can be concluded that corruption in countries governed by totalitarian regimes will have an adverse impact on society. In the following, some of the impacts of judicial corruption in Iran will be reviewed:

- Judicial corruption in Iran has contributed to the restriction of the media
- Judicial corruption undermines the rule of law in Iran

As the findings of this research have demonstrated, judicial corruption in Iran has reduced public confidence in the courts. On the other hand, the consequences of the corruption mentioned above will lead to an increase in judicial corruption because when the media and the press are not free, they cannot monitor the judiciary thus cannot expose any corrupt actions or steps taken by the judiciary. This can ultimately lead to further corruption.

When the rule of law decreases in society, the chances of all citizens being treated equally in the eyes of the law is reduced, and ordinary citizens will attempt to "buy judgement" and influence the courts by bribery. The spread of such a situation will lead to an increase in judicial corruption.

By reducing public confidence in the judicial system, citizens will not respect the courts or the judges, and are likely to buy justice via bribes. This trend can increase the spread of judicial corruption.

This cycle of production and reproduction of corruption in the judiciary creates a dangerous sequence for the corruption to expand to a wider spectrum. In fact, corruption in Iran's judicial system has a positive feedback and strengthens itself.

One of the interviewees (a former MP) claimed that in the first years of the revolution, as a parliamentarian at the time, receiving bribes by judges was much less frequent than in recent years. It is important to note that even in the first years of the revolution there was no judicial independence in place. It can be seen how judicial corruption is developed and increased by the passing of time.

This cycle of production and reproduction is depicted in the following image (Figure 7.2):

Figure 7.2: Production and reproduction of judicial corruption in Iran. Source: Author.

Judicial Corruption and Media Freedom

Dutta and Roy (2016) investigate the links between corruption and media freedom in different countries. Their findings show when media freedom is accompanied by citizen's freedom it will inevitably lead to a reduction in corruption.

Judicial corruption reduces the freedom of the media, and there is no freedom of expression in Iran. The findings of this study indicate that the judiciary has become a tool to restrict the media. In conclusion, judicial corruption in Iran has caused the media to be restricted in disseminating corruption in other government departments too.

A Formula on Corruption

In this section, the views of Klitgaard's formula are reviewed. It is important to study this formula despite many years since its first presentation, as many researchers are still trying to understand corruption on the basis of it.

Corruption = monopoly + discretion – accountability (Klitgaard, 1988)

According to the findings of this study, this formula can be expanded, as several main contributing factors have not been highlighted in the formation of corruption. As was shown in the previous sections, the legal culture has played a very important role in the rise and formation of corruption in Iran. On the other hand, the lack of freedom of the media was another important factor in spreading judicial corruption. Freedom of the media is also a very important factor in fighting corruption. Therefore, the above-mentioned formula can be expanded as follows (the legal culture can be a negative or a positive factor):

C = Cu x (M + D – A – F)

Corruption= Culture x (monopoly plus discretion minus accountability minus freedom of press).

Based on the findings of this research, we can construct a new formula for assessing corruption in the judiciary:

C = LC x (M + D – JI– F)

Corruption= Legal culture x (monopoly plus discretion minus Judicial independence minus accountability minus freedom of press).

Now according to this new formula, we will measure corruption in Iran:

1. The legal culture of society is severely damaged by the spread of corruption.
2. Judges in Iran can operate based on the judge's knowledge; in fact, they have infinite freedom to act. On the other hand, the Disciplinary Court for the judges is also inefficient and incapable of operating effectively.

3. There is no organisational independence in the judiciary.
4. Judges have no personal independence.
5. Judges in Iran are not accountable. They are not required to write down the workflow and the reasons for issuing their verdict.
6. The Disciplinary Court for the judges is also far too corrupt.
7. In Iran, there is no media freedom to publish news related to Judicial Corruption.

If we enter these points in the above formula, we can see the depth and cause of the current corruption in the judiciary.

The Spread of Corruption from the Judiciary to Other Sectors

In Figure 7.3, attempts have been made to explain how cancerous corruption is.

Categories of Corruption in the Judiciary

Corruption in the judiciary should be considered as institutional corruption, as an influential external power can affect the functioning of the judiciary. This external factor is the influence of the Supreme Leader. Such influence is predictable and has removed the judiciary from its organisational goal. The influence of such an external factor is consistent with the definition Lisseng (2013) has given.

Future: Improving Conditions in the Judiciary

List of Suggested Solutions for Improvement

The Iranian judiciary is a very corrupt system with a reproductive ripple effect and is one of the most important factors in the emergence and perpetuation of corruptions in other institutions of society. Hough (2013) rightly argued that one can combat corruption in one part of the government if there is a culture of accountability and transparency in society. Therefore, to create a clean judicial system, a change in the culture of society is a necessary requirement. Given the above issues, the following recommendations are in place in order to reduce corruption in the judiciary:

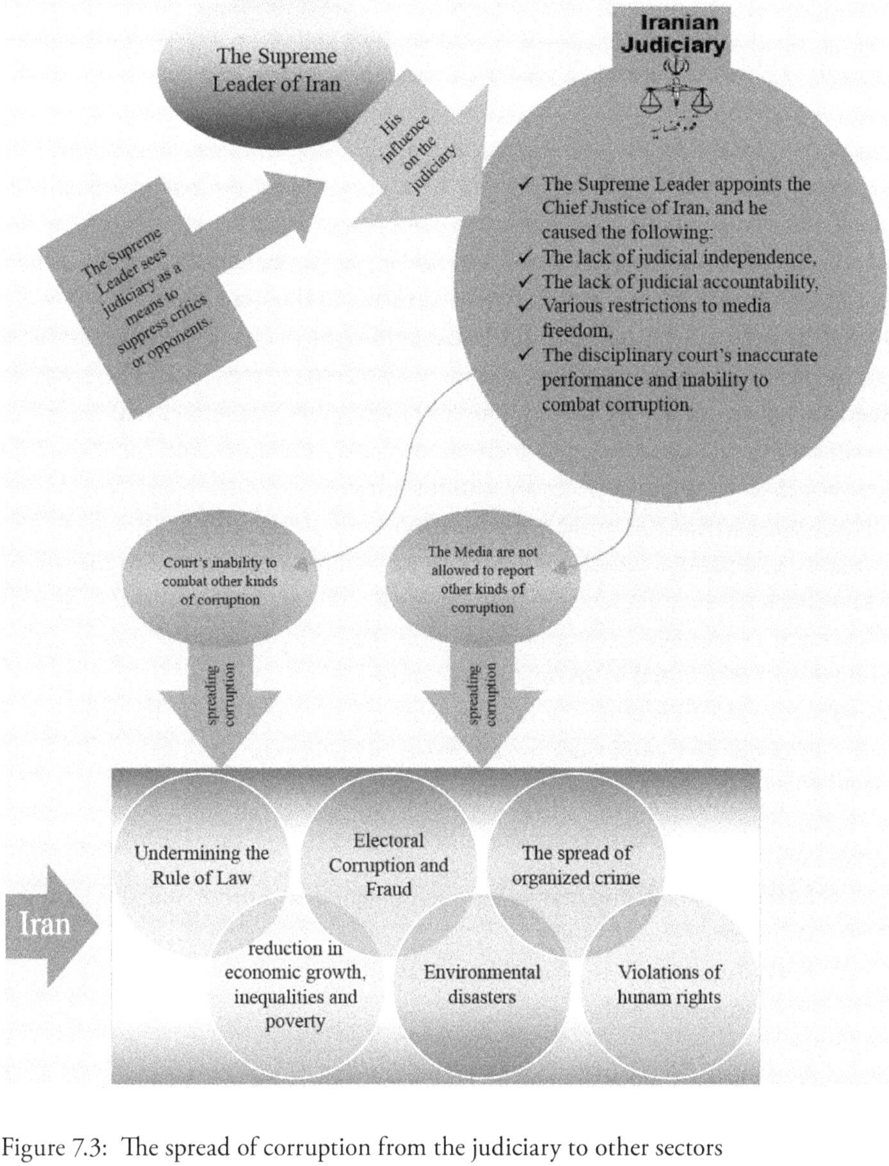

Figure 7.3: The spread of corruption from the judiciary to other sectors

Judicial Independence. The most imperative problem of the judiciary is the lack of independence. This branch should become independent of the institutions of the Supreme Leader or other institutions of power in Iran. A judicial council should be created to run the judiciary in Iran and administer justice; and the judges should be appointed by a council from which the majority of the members of the council should be elected from the judiciary. However, because of the selective appointment policy of judges, those who are now employed as judges are dependent on a particular group; they have a certain ideology, and the choice of the Judiciary Council from them is not a solution.

Judicial Appointment Process. The judge's appointment process will have to be changed, and these appointments will be made only on the basis of qualifications and competencies. The following conditions should be eliminated for the appointment of judges: gender discrimination, (judges being males only), adherence to the jurisprudence of the Islamic Republic of Iran and being born in wedlock. The process of promotion for judges will need to change completely to be on the basis of their hard efforts and merits. Necessary steps should be taken to increase salaries to ensure that employees of the court and judges will enjoy the minimum standards of living by increasing salaries. All judges and court employees should be required to swear an oath for justice.

The Special Clerical Court. The Special Clerical Court should be dissolved. The existence of a parallel judicial system with its own judiciary has led to the spread of corruption in the judiciary. Many judges in Iran are clergy, and this Special Court acts as leverage to control them; thus, the independence of judges is disturbed and interrupted in an organised manner.

Employees of the Judiciary. The current legal culture, as well as the presence of corrupt judges and employees in the courts, will increase the likelihood of the new judges and employees to fall into corruption. The following solutions can be considered:

- Early retirement and compulsory retirement of all current employees of the judiciary
- Recruitment and the provision of training to lawyers who were not previously involved in the judiciary

Training. Necessary steps should be taken to train judges and court personnel that their own ideologies should not interfere with the judicial process.

Freedom of the press. Freedom of the media to ensure the publication of news regarding the judicial system and corruption in this system must be guaranteed. Whistle-blowers who report judicial corruption should be protected. Their security should be guaranteed if they report corruption, with a clear and transparent law in place to protect the safety and security of those disclosing such corruption.

Passing new laws. Judges must state their reasoning when issuing an order or judgement on every individual case. Also, all judgement passed in the Iranian court should be freely accessible to everyone. Given the widespread corruption in Iran that stems from the roots of the judicial system, one will need to facilitate the possibilities of overseeing parliament administration including the executive branch. Of course, parliament and the executive branch should be elected during a free and fair election. Otherwise, the transfer of supervisory power to an unelected system will cause the parliament and the executive branch to exercise its power to corrupt the judiciary.

Disciplinary Court. A completely independent system should replace the current Disciplinary Court for the Judges, and this new system will need to gain public confidence and trust with its transparent functioning. The establishment of a special judicial court against corruption is another effective measure.

Lawyers. On top of ensuring the independence of the Bar Association, anti-corruption training courses will need to be provided for lawyers. An efficient regulatory system should also be in place at the Bar Association to combat corruption.

NGO. An Independent non-governmental organisation also needs to be created for combating and reporting judicial corruption.

Reduction of Corruption via Routine Activity Approach

Based on the Routine Activity Approach (Cohen & Felson, 1979) for corruption to occur there has to be the following three factors: the offender is determined to commit a crime; there is an unguarded target; and no existence of any deterrent factor to stop the offender. Now, we should consider the following points in order to devise ways to reduce corruption:

- To reduce the motivation among judges, they need to enjoy financial security. Furthermore, the judiciary must have an effective programme to familiarise judges with the consequences of judicial corruption.
- Provide a situation whereby citizens are given reassurance that courts' performance is just and fair. Education should also be provided that in order to have access to legal services they will not be required to pay bribes.
- A transparent and independent regulatory body should be created. The media should be empowered to report corruption-related news so that deterrence can be strengthened.

Proposed Future Research

Other researchers are encouraged to investigate the following:

1. The Special Court for the clergy is shrouded in secrecy, and there is a need for academic research to take place. This court is an effective instrument of the government to control the clerics who oppose the government.
2. Is money laundering and the existence of an informal economy contributing to the spread of judicial insecurity in Iran? Does this informal and macroeconomic economy cause the proliferation of judicial corruption?
3. The consequences and effects of corruption in Iran on social capital.
4. Judicial review plays a very important role in creating good governance for the promotion of human rights. In Iran, this task has been delegated to the Administrative Justice Court and some institutional organisations. It is necessary to consider the role and ineffectiveness of the Iranian Administrative Justice Court in reaching the desired criteria of good governance, and that which one should be considered.
5. Judicial corruption is a barrier against the formation of democracy in Iran.
6. The role of corruption in the judiciary and the spread of organised crime in Iran.
7. The lack of legal certainty in the country's law and regulations and its adverse effects on the rule of law in Iran.
8. Review the World Bank's proposals for judicial reform and the implementation of these reforms in Iran.
9. The consequences of referring to religious laws in Iranian laws.
10. Corruption in the Revolutionary Courts and during the handling of drug-related cases.
11. Linkage between judicial corruption in Iran and its role in spreading organised crime in Iran.

References

Ahmadi, N. (2015, 3 June). *Ghoveh Ghazaei dar gozar tarikh* [History of Iranian judiciary]. Isna. https://bit.ly/35elobh

Cameron, E. (2009). *The need for the independence of the judiciary and the legal profession'*. Ankara, Turkey.

Chemerinsky, E. (1989). Ideology, judicial selection and judicial ethics. 2 *Georgetown Journal of Legal Ethics* 643–664 (1989). Available at: http://scholarship.law.duke.edu/cgi/viewcontent.cgi?article=2145&context=faculty_scholarship (accessed 31-03-2016).

Cress, R., Kent, C., & Nayyeri, M. (2014). *Rule of law in Iran.* University of Essex, retrieved from: https://www.essex.ac.uk/hri/documents/rule-of-law-in-iran.pdf (accessed 31-03-2016).

Dutta, N., & Roy, S. (2016). The interactive impact of press freedom and media reach on corruption. *Economic Modelling*, 58227-236. doi:10.1016/j.econmod.2016.05.008.

Fehr, E., & Fischbacher, U. (2005). The economics of strong reciprocity. In H. Gintis, S. Bowles, R. Boyd, & E. Fehr (Eds.), *Moral sentiments and material interests. The foundations for cooperation in economic life* (pp. 151–193). Cambridge: MIT Press.

Ghazi, F. (2014). *In favor of Shahroodi: Details of the transaction.* Roozonline, (accessed 31-03-2016). Retrieved from: http://www.roozonline.com/persian/news/newsitem/article/-2d3930d4ee.html

Hough, D. (2013). *Corruption, anti-corruption and governance.* Basingstoke: Palgrave Macmillan.

Ip, E. C. (2008). Judicial corruption and its threats, to National Governance in China. *JOAAG, 3*(1). joaag.com/uploads/8_IpFinal.pdf

Kar, M. (2012). *Who are the judges in the Islamic Republic of Iran.* London: Legatum Institute.

Kurkchiyan, M. (2007). *Judicial corruption in the context of legal culture.* In D. Rodriguez & L. Ehrich (Eds.), *Global corruption report 2007.* Cambridge: Cambridge University Press.

Lessig, L. (2013). Foreword: "*Institutional corruption*" defined. *Journal of Law, Medicine and Ethics, 41*(3), 553–555. doi:10.1111/jlme.12063.

Swamy, A., Knack, S., Lee, Y., & Azfar, O. (2001). Gender and corruption. *Journal of Development Economics*, 6425–55. doi:10.1016/S0304-3878(00)00123-1.

Voigt, S., & Gutmann, J. (2015). On the wrong side of the law – Causes and consequences of a corrupt judiciary. *International Review of Law & Economics*, 43156–166. doi:10.1016/j.irle.2014.04.005.

Appendix

Coding Agenda

No	Category	Variables	Definition of the Category	Examples from the Interviews	Coding Rules
2	Category no 2-Public perception about Iranian judiciary:	▪ Perception about the judiciary, ▪ Perception about judges, ▪ potential bribery.	In their perception, how do ordinary citizens see the judiciary? In their opinion, is it possible to pay bribes? Should anybody try to commit bribery?	Interviewee No. 1: I had never heard anything about the corruption of the court until I reached the point whereby, I got involved and witnessed it first-hand.	Their personal opinion will not be considered.
3	Category no 3-The effects of corruption on the credibility of the judiciary (and trust of citizens):	▪ Change in perception after witnessing corruption.	This part will try to gather information about the impact of judicial corruption on the credibility of the courts.	Interviewee No. 1: Do you not think that the court system is already aware of its employees' pattern of operation.	Only impacts of personal experience will be assessed.
4	Category no 4-Role of media to combat corruption in Iran:	▪ Reporting judicial corruption by the media. ▪ Media's refusal to report judicial corruption	Impacts of the media and their role to combat judicial corruption will be reviewed.	Interviewee No. 1: Of course, the media cannot disclose any corruption running through the legal system.	Any incident about reporting judicial corruption on social media will be included.

No	Category	Variables	Definition of the Category	Examples from the Interviews	Coding Rules
5	Category no 5-Public perception about The Disciplinary Court of Judges:	▪ The public's trust in The Disciplinary Court of Judges:	This category will gather information about why people would not report judicial corruption to The Disciplinary Court of Judges.	Interviewee No. 5: For sure there is a regulatory or disciplinary body but do they operate properly, no! [. . .]	In this section, any information, even personal opinion will be considered.
6	Category no 6-Abusing judicial power for private gain:	▪ Receiving any private gain by judge or third party	Any abuse of judicial power by any judge to secure private gain for himself or anybody else.	Interviewee No. 6: [. . .] when I won my divorce rights and entitlements, the judge was treating me very graciously. [. . .] Apparently if I had not agreed to the 10% then my chances of claiming even half my legal rights would have been curtailed. [. . .]	In this section, any private gain, bribery, gift, or even sexual services will be considered.
7	Category no 7-Justification of judicial corruption by judges or court staff:	▪ Any attempt to justify corruption	This category will attempt to gather information about how judges or court staff try to justify their wrongdoings.	Interviewee No. 20: This became a norm among judges to get involved in bribery so that they can run their personal lives more smoothly [. . .]	Including orders from the Supreme Leader and his associates.

No	Category	Variables	Definition of the Category	Examples from the Interviews	Coding Rules
No	Category	Variables	Definition of the Category	Examples from the Interviews	Coding Rules
8	Category no 8-Who initiated the bribery process:	▪ Direct or indirect requests or bribes or private gain.	This category will try to gather information to understand who starts these criminal acts.	Interviewee No. 1: One of the court staff stopped me in the corridor and said I should pay two million toman	Including the role of third parties
9	Category no 9-Nepotism in the Iranian judiciary:	▪ Interfering with the appointment of the judges. ▪ Appointment of friends or family in judiciary	Any information about judicial appointment will be gathered in this section.	Interviewee No. 2: The Imam made a call to a judge he knew [. . .].	Any indication of influence on Judicial appointment to appoint a friend or family in any part of Judiciary.
10	Category no 10-Role of lawyers in the creation of judicial corruption in Iran	▪ Paying bribes, ▪ Receiving bribes, ▪ Reaction to bribery,	The role of lawyers in Iran in the creation of corruption will be examined.	Interviewee No. 6: [. . .] My lawyer was aware of the situation. [. . .] He refused to continue working on my case as he knew of my agreement with the middleman [. . .]	Any attempt from lawyers to pay/receive bribes, or their attempt to report corruption.

No	Category	Variables	Definition of the Category	Examples from the Interviews	Coding Rules
11	Category no 11-The independence of the Iranian judiciary:	▪ Interfering with judicial appointment, ▪ Interfering with judicial removal.	This category will try to assess if the judiciary as an organisation is immune from any external and political pressures.	Interviewee No. 11: The revolutionary court considers itself as a security institution.	Any attempt to undermine the independence of judiciary.
12	Category no 12-Personal independence of the judges:	▪ Any attempt to influence a judge by any powerful person or organisation; ▪ Any attempt by a judge to use their own ideology to issue a judgement.	This category will focus on the judge's behaviour to assess for issuing a ruling that is immune from any influence, either political or governmental influence or personal ideologies.	Interviewee No. 11: [. . .] the judge also knew that my client was not involved in any drug smuggling, and evidently was against my client. [. . .]	Any attempt to undermine independence of judge.
13	Category no 13-Linkage between judicial corruption and legal culture:	▪ Status of the judges, ▪ Seeing the courts as a sacred place, ▪ Lawyers opinion about importance of their jobs.	This category will assess public perception, such as how citizens see or consider paying or receiving bribes (bad or good). Furthermore, it will try to investigate judicial corruption in a local context.	Interviewee No. 5: [. . .] It is so evident that the courts and the Police are all corrupt [. . .]	This category will be limited to impacts of public perception on legal culture.

No	Category	Variables	Definition of the Category	Examples from the Interviews	Coding Rules
No	Category	Variables	Definition of the Category	Examples from the Interviews	Coding Rules
15	Category no 15- Judicial corruption in Clergy Courts:	▪ Any information about the Clergy Court	This category will try to gather information about the Clergy Court.	Interviewee No. 22: The key posts in the past years are in the hands of clerics who have commitment to the Supreme Leader. If one of these clerics or officials do not become corrupted, then there is room for a big surprise [. . .]	Considering a lack of data about this court: Any information about the Clergy Court will be mentioned in this category.
16	Category no 16- Comparing judicial corruption in Iran before and after the revolution:	▪ Comparison between the judiciary before and after revolution.	This category will focus on comparisons.		This category will be limited to comparisons only.
17	Category no 17- Judicial corruption before the revolution	▪ Any information about judicial corruption before revolution	This category will try to gather information about the existence of judicial corruption before revolution.	Interviewee No. 28: Before the revolution, there was an independence to the judiciary, therefore political cases were not sent to the judiciary [. . .]	No comparison, only incidents of judicial corruption.

No	Category	Variables	Definition of the Category	Examples from the Interviews	Coding Rules
18	Category no 18- Public perception about judges before the revolution:	▪ Status of the Judge, ▪ Their dress code, ▪ Their salary,	This category will try to provide a clear picture of judge status before revolution	Interviewee No. 19: Before the revolution, significant attention was given to judges' status. And if there were any misconducts they would have been charged with some punishments [. . .]	In this section, any information about public perception about the judges will be considered.
19	Category no 19- Independence of the Court before the revolution:	▪ External factors (political pressure) on judges.	This category will try to assess the possibility of the creation of indepen-dence in the judiciary in Iranian society	Interviewee No. 21: Before the revolution there were still corruptions and the norm of using contacts to facilitate the running of cases, but it was on a lim-ited scale [. . .]	Information about JI after revolution 1979 will not be considered in this section,
20	Category no 20- The existence of the Disciplinary Court of Judges before the revolution	▪ Any Information about the Disciplinary Court of Judges.	This category will try to show whether is possible to have an independent Disciplinary Court of Judges.	Interviewee No. 22: They had opportunities to take their case further on to high courts if they had any complaints against a judge's misconduct.	In this section, any information, even comparison with disciplinary court after rev-olution will be considered.

No	Category	Variables	Definition of the Category	Examples from the Interviews	Coding Rules
No	Category	Variables	Definition of the Category	Examples from the Interviews	Coding Rules
21	Category no 21- The judge's knowledge (Elme- Ghazi)	▪ Any information on the judge's knowledge.	This part will try to gather information about how judges can issue judicial orders arbitrarily.	Interviewee No. 13: Of course, judge's impartiality is undermined in criminal cases more than civil cases. [. . .] Because in criminal cases, the judge can rely on his personal knowledge [. . .] Ultimately the general public have lost faith and confidence in the judiciary [. . .]	Any direct information about the judge's knowledge.

Category System

ID	Interviewee Number	Quotation	Category Number/ Category	Reference
1:1	Interviewee No. 1	I had never heard anything about the corruption of the court until I reached the point whereby, I got involved and witnessed it first-hand	2-Public perception about Iranian judiciary:	86–223
1:2	Interviewee No. 1	One of the court staff stopped me in the corridor and said I should pay two million toman	8-who initiated the bribery process:	441–529
1:3	Interviewee No. 1	other party has paid bribes	6-Abusing judicial power for private gain:	630–658
1:4	Interviewee No. 1	It is true that I could complain that a bribe was demanded of me by the court employees, but I avoided making a complaint as there was a likelihood, I could create additional troubles for myself [. . .].	5-Public perception about The Disciplinary Court of Judges:	1164–1361
1:5	Interviewee No. 1	Do you not think that the court system is already aware of its employees' pattern of operation	3-The effects of corruption on the credibility of the judiciary (and trust of citizens):	1414–1508
1:6	Interviewee No. 1	Of course, the media cannot disclose any corruption running through the legal system.	4-Role of media to combat corruption in Iran (and their effectiveness):	1515–1598

ID	Interviewee Number	Quotation	Category Number/ Category	Reference
2:1	Interviewee No. 2	Therefore, I discussed it with one of my peer colleagues, he then spoke to a few of his friends and eventually he managed to introduce someone, who had close connections with The Imam of Friday Prayer in our city.[. . .] The arrangement was for him to force the debtor to pay, in return he would receive 20% of value of the check [. . .]. The Imam made a call to a judge he knew [. . .]. [later in the hearing] The judge threatened the company manager in the presence of all of us [. . .]	11-The independence of the Iranian judiciary: 9-Nepotism in the Iranian judiciary:	430–899
2:2	Interviewee No. 2	Because of the threats of imprisonment the manager accepted to sort out the cheque without any further delays. [. . .] If I had not treated this matter in the way I did I would have had to wait for a few years	6-Abusing judicial power for private gain:	901–1104
2:3	Interviewee No. 2	[. . .] is filled with old wolves, hence you will have to act promptly otherwise you would be crushed under their feet[. . .]	13-Linkage between judicial corruption and legal culture:	1343–1455
3:1	Interviewee No. 3	The first time I had to visit the court was for my husband and I witnessed how he had bribed the court	3-The effects of corruption on the credibility of the judiciary (and trust of citizens):	448–550
3:2	Interviewee No. 3	The first impression you would get is that most employees are expecting something from your pocket or your handbag	8-who initiated the bribery process:	774–886

ID	Interviewee Number	Quotation	Category Number/ Category	Reference
3:3	Interviewee No. 3	One of the court personnel even approached me proposing if I had money they could speak to the judge	8-who initiated the bribery process:	944–1042
3:4	Interviewee No. 3	On one occasion I went to visit the judge so to request for a transfer, and that was when he gave me a SIM card [for mobile]. He said he would call me later on that number. He did call and asked if we could have a temporary marriage [Nikah mut'ah . . .] He did not say anything directly that he would help my brother or not [. . .] He almost implied if I did accept his offer then he would be willing to help me release my brother. [. . .] I was in the temporary marriage for three months until he issued a five-year prison sentence rather than execution or life imprisonment. [. . .]	6-Abusing judicial power for private gain:	1047–1613
3:5	Interviewee No. 3	On one occasion I went to visit the judge so to request for a transfer, and that was when he gave me a SIM card [for mobile].	8-who initiated the bribery process:	1048–1173
3:6	Interviewee No. 3	I would never have gone to complain about the judge. It would be total madness to do so, as all judges are united and affiliated. [. . .] if I made a complaint, they would execute my brother	5-Public perception about The Disciplinary Court of Judges:	1877–2064
3:7	Interviewee No. 3	Initially we had a lawyer, but as soon as I became the judge's temporary wife, the judge said you no longer needed a lawyer [. . .] My lawyer was not aware of the arrangement between me and the judge.	10-Role of lawyers in the creation of judicial corruption in Iran:	2067–2263

ID	Interviewee Number	Quotation	Category Number/ Category	Reference
4:1	Interviewee No. 4	I was arrested in the Green Movement protest [2009]. I was arrested on the day of Ashoora when I was swearing at the Supreme Leader [. . .]. The first couple of weeks I was tortured. [. . .] They took me to the Revolutionary Courts. And the first thing I said was I was tortured[. . .]. The judge said "good" [. . .] The next time I was tortured even more by the interrogator	2-Public perception about Iranian judiciary:	67–421
4:2	Interviewee No. 4	[. . .] What was hilarious is that whatever the interrogator ordered, the judge had to do as he was told[. . .]. The judge was a puppet of the intelligence services	11-The independence of the Iranian judiciary:	423–578
4:3	Interviewee No. 4	What was hilarious is that whatever the interrogator ordered, the judge had to do as he was told	13-Linkage between judicial corruption and legal culture:	427–524
4:4	Interviewee No. 4	For as long as I am in Iran I would not dare to report such an incident [make a complaint against a judge] [. . .]. Otherwise I would be going back in jail	5-Public perception about The Disciplinary Court of Judges:	582–734
4:5	Interviewee No. 4	Even if I reported it to the media they would not be able to publish it [. . .]. On the other hand if I liaise with foreign media they would easily accuse me of espionage [. . .]	4-Role of media to combat corruption in Iran (and their effectiveness):	735–903
4:6	Interviewee No. 4	I underwent some severe torturing, of course I was unable to complain about the judge. [. . .]	5-Public perception about The Disciplinary Court of Judges:	927–1018

ID	Interviewee Number	Quotation	Category Number/ Category	Reference
5:1	Interviewee No. 5	[. . .] It is so evident that the courts and the police are all corrupt	2-Public perception about Iranian judiciary:	333–399
5:2	Interviewee No. 5	[. . .] It is so evident that the courts and the police are all corrupt	13-Linkage between judicial corruption and legal culture:	333–403
5:3	Interviewee No. 5	When I visited the court to follow up my case, one of the employees asked for my mobile number [. . .] He asked for an alternative number in case they could not reach me on the one I was using [. . .]. I gave my wife's number[. . .]. As soon as we left the court her phone rang [. . .] It was a man calling on behalf of the head of the court's office [. . .]	8-who initiated the bribery process:	479–810
5:4	Interviewee No. 5	He asked for five million Tooman to terminate the case. Otherwise the judge would issue lashing punishments.	6-Abusing judicial power for private gain:	871–979
5:5	Interviewee No. 5	He asked for five million Tooman to terminate the case. Otherwise the judge would issue lashing punishments. I was convinced he was acting on behalf of the court employees [. . .]. Within a few hours we gave him the money he had asked for. The court had announced the case set aside due to insufficient evidence	6-Abusing judicial power for private gain:	871–1177

ID	Interviewee Number	Quotation	Category Number/ Category	Reference
5:6	Interviewee No. 5	[. . .] in my opinion, the judge and all employees are like collective bandits.	3-The effects of corruption on the credibility of the judiciary (and trust of citizens):	1267–1342
5:7	Interviewee No. 5	For sure there is a regulatory or disciplinary body but do they operate properly, no! [. . .]	5-Public perception about The Disciplinary Court of Judges:	1397–1487
6:1	Interviewee No. 6	[. . .] it was the first time I was attending the court. [. . .] prior to visiting the court for my divorce matter, I was warned by a friend of mine to be cautious, as they [the judge or court's staff], will look at me as prey	2-Public perception about Iranian judiciary:	64–284
6:2	Interviewee No. 6	[. . .] As soon as I was called to the judge's room he started telling me about the road traffic on the highway and that he got tired getting to the court house [. . .] Immediately after I left the court, I received a call from an unknown caller saying that he could recommend my case to the judge [. . .] it was obvious that he was directly connected to the judge, as he told me about how the judge complained about traffic on the highway	8-who initiated the bribery process:	612–1029

ID	Interviewee Number	Quotation	Category Number/ Category	Reference
6:3	Interviewee No. 6	I asked him what he wanted [. . .] he responded that he could ask the judge to issue a judgement in my favour and order my ex-husband to pay my alimony or what is called "Mehriyeh" [. . .], however he proposed to be demanding 10% of the total financial rights of mine. [. . .] he wanted half the sum there and then and the other half after my divorce file was issued in my favour.	8-who initiated the bribery process:	1032–1400
6:4	Interviewee No. 6	[. . .] when I won my divorce rights and entitlements, the judge was treating me very graciously. [. . .] Apparently if I had not agreed to the 10% then my chances of claiming even half my legal rights would have been curtailed. [. . .]	6-Abusing judicial power for private gain:	1721–1944
6:5	Interviewee No. 6	[. . .] my lawyer was aware of the situation. [. . .] he refused to continue working on my case as he knew of my agreement with the middleman	10-Role of lawyers in the creation of judicial corruption in Iran:	1942–2078
6:6	Interviewee No. 6	I would never dare to make a complaint about the judge's conduct [. . .]. Firstly no one would chastise the judge or his conduct, secondly, suppose I had made a complaint about the judge, the next judge who would have to attend to my complaint would penalise me even more for making an allegation against his peer colleague.	5-Public perception about The Disciplinary Court of Judges:	2081–2403

ID	Interviewee Number	Quotation	Category Number/ Category	Reference
6:7	Interviewee No. 6	[. . .] most affairs are run based on bribery in Iran. [. . .] you can even bribe the judge.	3-The effects of corruption on the credibility of the judiciary (and trust of citizens):	2514–2595
7:1	Interviewee No. 7	I have experienced corruption within the judiciary, taking advantage of their discretions or using their links undermines their impartiality [. . .]	3-The effects of corruption on the credibility of the judiciary (and trust of citizens):	35–178
7:2	Interviewee No. 7	[. . .] therefore, they would also rely on paying bribes in order to relieve themselves of the situations they are in [..]. Getting employed with the judicial system has become a tool and a pattern to become reach quick [. . .]	2-Public perception about Iranian judiciary:	288–502
7:3	Interviewee No. 7	In another instance, a drug smuggler was executed despite paying bribes since he had rendered the payments to the wrong person	2-Public perception about Iranian judiciary:	756–883
7:4	Interviewee No. 7	In relation to my own court case, judge Mortazavi did not act with impartiality [. . .]. He would personally call me with threats [. . .]. He never respected the position of being a judge [. . .]. He was an interrogator as well as decision maker for my future [. . .]. He told me because I had described officers (who work for ministry of intelligence) as brother of prophet Yousof [who killed their brother] my punishment was execution or life sentence [. . .]. He then sent my file to Qum Seminary [to get permission for execution] [. . .]	6-Abusing judicial power for private gain:	1139–1672

ID	Interviewee Number	Quotation	Category Number/ Category	Reference
7:5	Interviewee No. 7	Some judges play an important role in dividing confiscated properties, and this is another source of income for them. Setâd-e Ejrây-ye Farmân-e Emâm [the Executive Headquarters of Imam's Directive] is worth $90 Billion so you can see the extent	2-Public perception about Iranian judiciary:	2367–2611
7:6	Interviewee No. 7	Some media are accused of financial and political corruption in Iran [. . .]. So, to protect their interests, they will have no choice but to turn a blind eye on judicial corruption [. . .]. On the other hand, if the media is not affiliated, the smallest criticism of the judiciary will lead to the closure of the newspaper [. . .]. Overseas media also highlight judicial corruption or its ineffectiveness for the sake of political reasons [. . .]	4-Role of media to combat corruption in Iran (and their effectiveness):	2615–3041
7:7	Interviewee No. 7	I was aware of the existence of disciplinary court, but I did not go to the disciplinary court for Judge Mortazavi's illegal conduct, because it would have made my case worse. [. . .] In that court, several cases against judge Mortazavi were open, including rape and financial corruption, but that court refused to hear those cases [. . .]	5-Public perception about The Disciplinary Court of Judges:	3232–3563
8:1	Interviewee No. 8	[. . .] I witnessed many cases in both civil and criminal matters indicating a lack of impartiality and sometimes a judge's prejudicialness to the parties or the subject of the case [. . .]. Sometimes it could easily have the title of deviation and corruption in the judiciary, in a systematic way and not by accident.	2-Public perception about Iranian judiciary:	280–588

ID	Interviewee Number	Quotation	Category Number/ Category	Reference
8:2	Interviewee No. 8	For example, a judge let his personal views intervene in the case, in that civil case, as soon as the judge found out that my client had an affair outside marriage, he relied on excuses and despite my client being the claimant the judge detained him on the basis of infringing the court order	6-Abusing judicial power for private gain:	595–889
8:3	Interviewee No. 8	I personally pursued some cases at the disciplinary Court of judges, and I believe that even in the most corrupt systems, failure to report corruption will result in reducing the cost of corruption for those sitting in the courtrooms.	5-Public perception about The Disciplinary Court of Judges:	895–1134
8:4	Interviewee No. 8	The outcome of my experiences has been that the judge was forced to explain himself and answering questions, and sometimes I had a hope that the court's verdict could have been reversed [. . .]	5-Public perception about The Disciplinary Court of Judges:	1134–1323
8:5	Interviewee No. 8	[. . .] lawyers play an important role in the formation and continuation of corruption. [. . .] I learned of a case that the lawyer who was working in my colleague's office, met the judge of the case in his office, and both had decided the verdict of the case together [. . .	10-Role of lawyers in the creation of judicial corruption in Iran:	1423–1686
8:6	Interviewee No. 8	It seems that some attorneys may even believe their participation in judicial corruption as a part of their professional skills [. . .] the lawyers integrity and independence of the Bar Association gradually is diminished [. . .] especially, since legal practitioners licenced by judiciary began to work as lawyers, and considering they had no training for being professional lawyers [. . .]	10-Role of lawyers in the creation of judicial corruption in Iran:	1689–2066

ID	Interviewee Number	Quotation	Category Number/ Category	Reference
8:7	Interviewee No. 8	We see that in such an injustice system where there is total lack of public trust and confidence, the majority of people attempt to rely on some sort of means to get their problems tackled.	3-The effects of corruption on the credibility of the judiciary (and trust of citizens):	2069–2249
8:8	Interviewee No. 8	courts that are held for political and social regards, or the Special Clerical Courts, on the type of judicial corruption	3-The effects of corruption on the credibility of the judiciary (and trust of citizens):	2590–2710
8:9	Interviewee No. 8	In one instance, I was representing my client who was facing execution [. . .]. It was during those proceedings I was told by a duty judge at the Revolutionary Court it was in my client's interest if I resigned from the case, so that another lawyer will be allocated from the court itself. It appeared they had financial ties with that lawyer, so I did resign from the case for my client's sake.	6-Abusing judicial power for private gain:	2862–3261
9:1	Interviewee No. 9	[. . .] I personally see judicial corruption as part of an organised corruption within the Islamic system, and what is imperative is that the judiciary is supposed to be people's representative in protecting the general public's rights. [. . .] prior to becoming a lawyer, I always had the mental assumption that the judiciary was corrupt in the Iranian system.	2-Public perception about Iranian judiciary:	40–397

ID	Interviewee Number	Quotation	Category Number/ Category	Reference
9:2	Interviewee No. 9	You always wonder in your mind if this case will go through its proper legal process. There will be corruption in most departments of the judiciary from a simple soldier who presents warrants right through to the supreme court judge. Everyone who deals with the judiciary witnesses such corruption daily.	3-The effects of corruption on the credibility of the judiciary (and trust of citizens):	731–1038
9:3	Interviewee No. 9	I have not been to the Disciplinary Tribunal Court for the judiciary, however I am aware that this regulatory/supervisory body is not separated from the overall structure of the entire judiciary, and corruption is widespread, hence the outcome of such regulatory body can be easily assumed.	5-Public perception about The Disciplinary Court of Judges:	1039–1339
9:4	Interviewee No. 9	Unfortunately, lawyers are not excluded from this judiciary system. They are all expected to function within such a contaminated judicial structure. The fact is that lawyers are also involved in the reproduction of this corruption.	10-Role of lawyers in the creation of judicial corruption in Iran:	1341–1566
9:5	Interviewee No. 9	In order to examine the role of the media, it should be noted that censorship happens all throughout Iran. We have few researchers and journalists, for which they have no financial security. On the other hand, disclosing corruption is considered a security issue, and anyone who discloses corruption knows that he has put himself at risk.	4-Role of media to combat corruption in Iran (and their effectiveness):	1570–1911

ID	Interviewee Number	Quotation	Category Number/ Category	Reference
9:6	Interviewee No. 9	In relation to the Integrity and honourability of judges and the lawyers, such integrity and reputation no longer exist in society and among the general public. Disclosing various matters relating to corruption cannot do any further damage to the reputation of the judges.	13-Linkage between judicial corruption and legal culture:	1912–2187
10:1	Interviewee No. 10	In May 1993, when I was visiting Iran, I was kidnapped from my own apartment in Tehran by the officials of the intelligence services [as per instruction of Mr Hashemi Rafsanjani who was the president of the time. [. . .] the kidnapping took place after a year and a half when the South Pars contracts were signed and there were repeated requests by Mehdi Hashemi Rafsanjani [President's son] and his partner Mehdi Yazdanpanah Yazdi to pay $50 million on bribes, and I had refused to accept to pay such bribes. [. . .] During the first three months of detention in Evin Prison, section 209 and in Touhid Prison for nearly 7 months, and because of my resistance towards brutal tortures by the security officials resulted in them getting in contact with my wife. She lived in Rome at the time and they asked for $5 million ransom for my release.	11-The independence of the Iranian judiciary:	1100–1938

ID	Interviewee Number	Quotation	Category Number/ Category	Reference
10:2	Interviewee No. 10	I was still being tortured for another five months after the $3 million was paid in Tohid Prison and in solitary confinement due to a non-payment of $2 million from their initial requested ransom. Eventually, I succeeded in convincing Gholam Hossein Mohseni Ajeee, a deputy at the time of the Islamic Revolutionary Prosecutor's Office in the ministry of Intelligence, to be on a temporary release. […] 5 months later and after paying a further 250,000 Dollars to Mr Mohseni Eje, he accepted to release my passport and issued a permit to leave the country in July 1994, I left the country.	6-Abusing judicial power for private gain:	2260–2848
11:1	Interviewee No. 11	Witness No. 11: Ms Shima (Lawyer) […] corruption in the judiciary is a fact and there is no need for the presupposition of the mind. If people whom have lived in Iran would have had a tangible experience of such corruptions. […]	2-Public perception about Iranian judiciary: 3-The effects of corruption on the credibility of the judiciary (and trust of citizens):	0–229

ID	Interviewee Number	Quotation	Category Number/ Category	Reference
11:2	Interviewee No. 11	[. . .] within close vicinity to where he used to live. Unfortunately, the intelligence officer was aware of the gay sexual orientation, according to my client, he was seeking to file a case against him. My client always was cautious of his actions. He had even threatened my client directly to file a case against him. One day they arrested him for drug trafficking and found some opium in his car. Despite testing showing that he was not addicted, and he did not have any background in drug trafficking nor of similar grounds. Most importantly his social status was such that no such accusations would have been believable. He had a simple life and lived based on his salaries. I took his case and became his lawyer[. . .]. The officer in charge of his file literally told me that if I wanted my client to get rescued, I should have resigned from the case and one of their lawyers should have taken over. He meant, such lawyers who are accustomed to bribery and making deals behind closed doors should be appointed for this case.	6-Abusing judicial power for private gain:	742–1767
11:3	Interviewee No. 11	[. . .] the judge also knew that my client was not involved in any drug smuggling, and evidently was against my client. [. . .]	12-Personal independence of the judges: 6-Abusing judicial power for private gain:	2044–2163

ID	Interviewee Number	Quotation	Category Number/ Category	Reference
11:4	Interviewee No. 11	The Revolutionary court is a strange court, not only I was not called for the court order, they did not even allow me to take a copy of the decision. They only allowed me to take notes from the Court's order and determination letter.	13-Linkage between judicial corruption and legal culture:	2165–2401
11:5	Interviewee No. 11	The revolutionary court considers itself as a security institution	11-The independence of the Iranian judiciary:	2403–2468
11:6	Interviewee No. 11	I did not report this corruption because complaint against judges and the Revolutionary Court could have severe consequences for my client or myself. [. . .]	5-Public perception about The Disciplinary Court of Judges:	2559–2712
11:7	Interviewee No. 11	Based on my personal experience, I can say that some lawyers are engaged in the work of a "middle person" in many courts, and this has become a norm in the process. [. . .] of course, this process is much broader in the Revolutionary Court. [. . .] in principle, the presence of lawyers in the Revolutionary Court is much harder than attending a normal court.	10-Role of lawyers in the creation of judicial corruption in Iran: 13-Linkage between judicial corruption and legal culture:	2716–3071
11:8	Interviewee No. 11	When you witness corruption, you would inevitably tell your friends or neighbours. When you see no one is taking any actions against such corruptions taking place in courts, then the majority of people will lose hope and faith in the judiciary.	3-The effects of corruption on the credibility of the judiciary (and trust of citizens):	3074–3318

ID	Interviewee Number	Quotation	Category Number/ Category	Reference
11:9	Interviewee No. 11	Hence it is very difficult to differentiate between criminals and non-criminals. If someone has a criminal record, he may not necessarily be a bad person, and there is a likelihood that he could have been victimised of wrongful decisions.	13-Linkage between judicial corruption and legal culture:	3319–3560
11:10	Interviewee No. 11	You may rarely find a newspaper who would dare criticise the functioning of the judiciary.	4-Role of media to combat corruption in Iran (and their effectiveness):	3562–3652
12:1	Interviewee No. 12	I had never been involved with the judicial system and I hope I will never have any encounters with them.	3-The effects of corruption on the credibility of the judiciary (and trust of citizens):	53–158
12:2	Interviewee No. 12	I had heard before that the court system is based on offering bribes but I had never imagined the extent to which the corruption was.	2-Public perception about Iranian judiciary: 3-The effects of corruption on the credibility of the judiciary (and trust of citizens):	164–301
12:3	Interviewee No. 12	My attorney also told me that he had paid the court to have the court support and suggested to accept half of the money [and settle my claim]	11-The independence of the Iranian judiciary: 6-Abusing judicial power for private gain:	1426–1565

ID	Interviewee Number	Quotation	Category Number/ Category	Reference
12:4	Interviewee No. 12	In the court trial my client told the judge that he was literally telling witnesses what to say [. . .]. In the end the verdict was given against me.	6-Abusing judicial power for private gain:	2023–2170
12:5	Interviewee No. 12	[. . .] then told my attorney that I was going to lodge a complaint against the judge. He was very pessimistic about the outcome of such complaints.	5-Public perception about The Disciplinary Court of Judges:	2174–2319
12:6	Interviewee No. 12	[. . .] media in Iran would not risk publishing news about corruption in the judiciary [. . .]	4-Role of media to combat corruption in Iran (and their effectiveness):	2320–2399
13:1	Interviewee No. 13	In relation to judicial corruption, the answer is that yes [. . .] there exists a pre-existing mental background. [. . .]	2-Public perception about Iranian judiciary:	42–155
13:2	Interviewee No. 13	Due to the high number of cases and the pressure from the top (powerful people or intelligence services or Supreme leader or his allies), on court judges and relevant offices and lack of human resources are all contributory excuses.	11-The independence of the Iranian judiciary:	246–486
13:3	Interviewee No. 13	I did not encounter bribing the judge in my own caseloads; however, I have heard of them in other cases [. . .]	6-Abusing judicial power for private gain:	488–594

ID	Interviewee Number	Quotation	Category Number/ Category	Reference
13:4	Interviewee No. 13	It is true that there are unfortunately some lawyers who assist in distributing such corruptions through individuals and intermediaries in the system [. . .]. Unfortunately, this has led people to lose their confidence in the judiciary and lawyers, and instead of looking for a legal path through lawyers they look for influential contacts. This could lead to misuse or abuse or fraudulent acts.	10-Role of lawyers in the creation of judicial corruption in Iran:	727–1120
13:5	Interviewee No. 13	Aside from social media no other official media has been successful in this regard. Broadcasting such incidents is only possible through social media and any other way will face severe clashes on the part of the government.	4-Role of media to combat corruption in Iran (and their effectiveness):	1123–1354
13:6	Interviewee No. 13	Of course, judge's impartiality is undermined in criminal cases more than civil cases. [. . .] because in criminal cases, the judge can rely on his personal knowledge [. . .]. Ultimately the general public have lost faith and confidence in the judiciary [. . .]	21-The judge's knowledge (Elme- Ghazi)	1355–1602
13:7	Interviewee No. 13	In civil matters, based on evidence and documentations the judge is expected to reach its verdict. However, in criminal matters, considering the new law, it has expanded judges' discretions, some judges if not most tend to abuse this allocated discretion and despite submitted evidence or defences by lawyers, judges will make their decisions arbitrarily. [. . .] In criminal affairs, the judge sees himself as the representative of the government and God. Therefore, the laws in place and appropriate procedures are all ignored.	21-The judge's knowledge (Elme- Ghazi)	1841–2367

ID	Interviewee Number	Quotation	Category Number/ Category	Reference
13:8	Interviewee No. 13	The majority of lawyers do not consider their position from a professional point of view.	10-Role of lawyers in the creation of judicial corruption in Iran: 13-Linkage between judicial corruption and legal culture:	2986–3071
14:1	Interviewee No. 14	In 2011, I became the director of public relations in the Office of Mr Fallahian, the former Minister of intelligence services in Iran. Part of his activities involved "his personal economic activities", which meant that himself and his office officials used their ties they had with the judiciary to influence the cases.	11-The independence of the Iranian judiciary:	410–734
14:2	Interviewee No. 14	Several corruptions that I had witnessed first-hand was at the office of Ayatollah ElmoLhoda. He has a seminary in Tehran. Mr Nowrouzi, his secretary, was involved in a court case over lands which were worth several billion Toman. The manner in which their interventions takes place is to demand illegally a great portion of the land [or property] in order for them to offer their assistance via their close ties to other judges or officials	11-The independence of the Iranian judiciary: 6-Abusing judicial power for private gain:	736–1175
14:3	Interviewee No. 14	When the prosecutors or inspecting officer sees that the accused will eventually be released by paying a bribe or by paying minor fines, he will no longer be interested to carry out his duties properly.	13-Linkage between judicial corruption and legal culture:	1476–1681

ID	Interviewee Number	Quotation	Category Number/ Category	Reference
14:4	Interviewee No. 14	For example, I encountered a situation where the judge of the second branch of the appeal court, Mr Rahimi, was hunting without permission [. . .]. I reported it to the authorities to take actions against him. they contacted me and warned me to mind my own business and stay out of trouble [. . .].	5-Public perception about The Disciplinary Court of Judges:	1683–1974
14:5	Interviewee No. 14	I can refer to the role of Mr Fallahian and Mr Mohseni Ejehi. Mr Ejehi has had a special relation and dedication to Mr Fallahian and has been working under his authority for several years in the Ministry of Intelligence. [. . .] in my opinion Mr Ejehi, is the most influential individual in the judiciary. [. . .]. Under Mr Fallahian's recommendation, he would interfere in cases [. . .]. This influence on the judiciary is not limited to a particular mullah or political group [. . .]	11-The independence of the Iranian judiciary:	2054–2523
14:6	Interviewee No. 14	And the head of this reformist party was a Sheikh called Zare-Foomani. He is also a newspaper owner under the same name [. . .]. Mr Niri is one of his close friends and always offered his influence in facilitating the running of cases in the Supreme Court.	12-Personal independence of the judges: 6-Abusing judicial power for private gain:	2884–3139
14:7	Interviewee No. 14	These powerful political officials always have a few lawyers to represent cases [that they want to intervene in]. [. . .] this means that such [corrupt] individuals are willing to interfere in court cases in return for a lump sum payment from the plaintiff or whomever the court case belongs to. [. . .]	10-Role of lawyers in the creation of judicial corruption in Iran: 13-Linkage between judicial corruption and legal culture:	3142–3436

ID	Interviewee Number	Quotation	Category Number/ Category	Reference
14:8	Interviewee No. 14	but after I attended the courts myself this perception of mine got worse. [. . .]	3-The effects of corruption on the credibility of the judiciary (and trust of citizens):	3509–3587
14:9	Interviewee No. 14	[. . .] there exist female attendees that by offering sexual intercourse to the judges can impact on the direction of the cases. Such female individuals can even function and lead the case to their favour more effectively compared to professional lawyers.	10-Role of lawyers in the creation of judicial corruption in Iran:	3723–3980
14:10	Interviewee No. 14	[. . .] after the uprising in 2008 and suppression of people, Mr Ayatollah Vahid Khorasani made a complaint to the Supreme Leader [objected how protestors were killed] When the Supreme Leader visited Qum he left on his arrival, which can be construed as an insulting gesture. This movement meant that he was against the Supreme Leader and as a result Sadegh Larijani, his son of law, was appointed as the head of the judiciary. [. . .to make peace between the Supreme Leader and Ayatollah vahid khorasani]	9-Nepotism in the Iranian judiciary:	4142–4638
15:1	Interviewee No. 15	I had seen judicial corruptions before referring to the judiciary. Due to a large number of cases, I have witnessed a decrease on the quality of how the judiciary operates. [. . .] I have seen judges not acting impartially [. . .]	3-The effects of corruption on the credibility of the judiciary (and trust of citizens):	262–483

ID	Interviewee Number	Quotation	Category Number/ Category	Reference
15:2	Interviewee No. 15	Despite the accumulation of documents and evidence including reports from the police and their confessions, the judge decided in their favour to acquit the accused. [. . .] the deputy prosecutor and even the lawyers were all surprised at how the judge acquitted the defendants without trial.	6-Abusing judicial power for private gain:	486–773
15:3	Interviewee No. 15	I was aware of the judge's Disciplinary Court. When I consulted with several lawyers, I was told there would not be any benefits to drawing attention to the judge's Disciplinary Courts. [. . .]	5-Public perception about The Disciplinary Court of Judges:	774–954
15:4	Interviewee No. 15	In our own family case, I witnessed corruptive judicial process when we had to retrieve our land, of which the deed belonged to my father and was confiscated post revolution by the government who had taken over our land. [. . .] we paid a bribe to a judge at the time via a middle person. We had no choice but pay about one million toman in 1370, which was a significant amount of money at the time, for which my family had to undergo a lot of pressure and distress to get this sum together. [. . .] in the end, only one third of the land was returned to us and two thirds of it remained in possession of the council.	6-Abusing judicial power for private gain:	955–1566
15:5	Interviewee No. 15	He was charged with drug trafficking at a minor level. The judge for that case had taken a bribe to overturn the decision	6-Abusing judicial power for private gain:	1652–1770

ID	Interviewee Number	Quotation	Category Number/ Category	Reference
15:6	Interviewee No. 15	There is no point in making a complaint about judicial members who are bribe takers. You would be considered lucky, if after complaining about any members of the judiciary you are not held liable or being accused of any offences at the judicial Discipline Tribunal. T [. . .] his would only cost money and an enormous amount of stress with time which is wasted over an injustice.	5-Public perception about The Disciplinary Court of Judges:	2019–2398
15:7	Interviewee No. 15	[. . .] Judges do not have any shame in using their personal tastes in dealing with cases	13-Linkage between judicial corruption and legal culture:	4714–4798
15:8	Interviewee No. 15	This system of judicial corruption has been a cause for a distribution of poverty, discrimination and infringement of rights.	3-The effects of corruption on the credibility of the judiciary (and trust of citizens):	4804–4931
16:1	Interviewee No. 16	I knew from the outset and before I had any encounters with the system that the judiciary is a corrupt and unjust system in Iran.	2-Public perception about Iranian judiciary:	32–163

ID	Interviewee Number	Quotation	Category Number/ Category	Reference
16:2	Interviewee No. 16	I had not committed any crime; however I was arrested [during a demonstration in 2008] A prosecutor attended to the place of custody where we were kept. There were about four hundred of us, each one of us was arrested at different areas or regions in different ways [. . .]. One would have thought that not all 400 people that were arrested had committed similar crimes. [. . .] the persecutor gave each of us a pre-typed paper with five offences in it that we had to agree and sign. Five offences which could have had consequences such as the death penalty or be considered as a Moharebe [enemy of god]. We all had the same pre- written crimes on these papers. [. . .] we were forced to sign these papers, because if we didn't they would lash and torture us to stop resisting and ultimately they would make us sign the alleged committed crimes.	11-The independence of the Iranian judiciary: 6-Abusing judicial power for private gain:	268–1102
16:3	Interviewee No. 16	The prosecutor, the judge, and other members of the court violated the impartiality for their personal and collective interests, and to be able to maintain the power, they manage to suppress officials who are supposed to represent the law in public favour	12-Personal independence of the judges: 6-Abusing judicial power for private gain:	1421–1677
16:4	Interviewee No. 16	[. . .] in relation to judicial corruptions I must emphasise that members of public have lost faith due to their awareness of what is truly going on via social media and social networking.	13-Linkage between judicial corruption and legal culture:	3322–3510

ID	Interviewee Number	Quotation	Category Number/ Category	Reference
17:1	Interviewee No. 17	I was arrested on December 2004, and after this illegal arrest, which was more than 7 months and 23 days in solitary confinement, I was tortured, when an intelligence officer or an IRGC officer in section 2 (a) allows himself as a representative of the law, to beat prisoners, to strip them naked or threats of rape to prisoner's wives and children, I call it judicial corruption.	3-The effects of corruption on the credibility of the judiciary (and trust of citizens):	617–1003
17:2	Interviewee No. 17	All this time my case was in the revolutionary prosecutor's office based on Moallem street and was supervised by a person called judge Fallahi [. . .]. He was the deputy of judge Mortazavi. [. . .] every two months I was taken to him. [. . .] he threatened to place me in a solitary cell if I did not write, sign and agree to the extent of confession to the offences I had never committed [. . .]	6-Abusing judicial power for private gain:	1004–1389
17:3	Interviewee No. 17	The same judge had issued many unfair and ungrounded summons. Later certain corrupted financial activities of his regarding illegal land ownerships came to light.	6-Abusing judicial power for private gain:	1390–1552
17:4	Interviewee No. 17	Another crime was the formation of a mafia network by prison officials, a judicial affiliate of the judiciary [. . .]. These people created a network and every time when the families of prisoners arrived to visit, pretending that they were taxi drivers, they would pick their family up, mainly women [. . .]. They would abduct women and force them into the sex trafficking business. [. . .] one of them which was called "Green House" leaked [. . .]	2-Public perception about Iranian judiciary:	1879–2307

ID	Interviewee Number	Quotation	Category Number/ Category	Reference
17:5	Interviewee No. 17	[. . .] the law enforcement department of the judiciary is where corruption is bigger and the power pyramid in the judiciary is that the more corrupt you are you are placed in a higher position. [. . .]	3-The effects of corruption on the credibility of the judiciary (and trust of citizens):	5704–5904
18:1	Interviewee No. 18	After a while, they took me to court No 5 of the law enforcement. The same judge whom had taken a bribe [from me] previously made an official statement: you must sign this confession and based on the medical documentation that my family had presented to the court; I would be released on bail until the actual hearing date. [. . .] the same judge said that I would be freed at this stage if I had paid a lump sum to him. [. . .] and at the next stage I could be encountering a 15 to 20 year sentence.	6-Abusing judicial power for private gain:	310–808
18:2	Interviewee No. 18	There are middlemen in Iran whose main job is to receive bribes and pay it to the judges [. . .] My wife had to look for one of these men. He took 40 million toman from my wife as a bribe in 2006.	8-who initiated the bribery process:	809–1004
18:3	Interviewee No. 18	There is no real trial [. . .] trials usually last about a few minutes and ultimately you are forced to admit to some offences that you had never committed.	11-The independence of the Iranian judiciary: 13-Linkage between judicial corruption and legal culture:	1006–1163

ID	Interviewee Number	Quotation	Category Number/ Category	Reference
18:4	Interviewee No. 18	I knew of the judicial corruption before I got to experience it first-hand. They would violate any justice just to protect their own personal or collective interests.	3-The effects of corruption on the credibility of the judiciary (and trust of citizens):	1252–1420
18:5	Interviewee No. 18	I have never been or intended to associate with the judge's Disciplinary Tribunal, as it can jeopardise the accused's situation.	5-Public perception about The Disciplinary Court of Judges:	1526–1647
18:6	Interviewee No. 18	The media is not in a position or have the courage to publicise such incidents as they will have to face serious consequences.	4-Role of media to combat corruption in Iran (and their effectiveness):	1649–1779
19:1	Interviewee No. 19	Before I began to work as a lawyer, I found that the justice system in Iran was suffering from corruption.	2-Public perception about Iranian judiciary:	93–198
19:2	Interviewee No. 19	I started studying law in order to become a judge. However, after witnessing such judicial corruptions I changed my mind	3-The effects of corruption on the credibility of the judiciary (and trust of citizens):	200–319
19:3	Interviewee No. 19	[. . .] segments of society in Iran are somehow involved with the judiciary	2-Public perception about Iranian judiciary:	490–560
19:4	Interviewee No. 19	I witnessed corruption in the judiciary, bribe taking and bribery, although I never had to do it myself [. . .]	6-Abusing judicial power for private gain:	805–910

ID	Interviewee Number	Quotation	Category Number/ Category	Reference
19:5	Interviewee No. 19	There have been instances that reporting judges bribe taking has had legal consequences, however if the judge is close to the regime, it will be very hard to have any complaints lodged against them, or that it would be very unlikely for them to face dismissals or any kind of consequences [. . .]	5-Public perception about The Disciplinary Court of Judges:	1025–1316
19:6	Interviewee No. 19	The breeding ground for judicial corruption in Iran is created by both consultants associations and the Bar association.	10-Role of lawyers in the creation of judicial corruption in Iran:	1318–1437
19:7	Interviewee No. 19	Due to a shortage of a transparent and just system, lawyers do not always have a fair number of clients, therefore they take up a job as a middle dealer [. . .]	10-Role of lawyers in the creation of judicial corruption in Iran:	1442–1599
19:8	Interviewee No. 19	Another important cause of corruption is the selection of judges based on Islamic ideology and how they follow this ideology [. . .] Instead of relying on knowledge and integrity	12-Personal independence of the judges:	1601–1779
19:9	Interviewee No. 19	I myself saw that judges carried their prayers in such filthy and disgraceful manners and there is no observation on their dress code [. . .]	13-Linkage between judicial corruption and legal culture:	1787–1924
19:10	Interviewee No. 19	Before the revolution, significant attention was given to judges' status. And if there were any misconducts they would have been charged with some punishments.	17-Judicial corruption before the revolution 18-Public perception about judges before the revolution:	2030–2192

ID	Interviewee Number	Quotation	Category Number/ Category	Reference
19:11	Interviewee No. 19	Also, the number of corrupt judges were rare, [. . .]	16-Comparing judicial corruption in Iran before and after the revolution: 17-Judicial corruption before the revolution	2195–2243
20:1	Interviewee No. 20	[. . .] I agree that citizens come to court with this background in their head that the Court is corrupt, and they think the more you are prepared to pay bribes the more likely you will win in courts	2-Public perception about Iranian judiciary:	46–242
20:2	Interviewee No. 20	Partially this is caused by my own colleague's wrongdoings [. . .]. Of course, factors such as low incomes of judges and the lack of a regulatory body over their operations have all been contributory to this problem. [. . .]	3-The effects of corruption on the credibility of the judiciary (and trust of citizens):	246–460
20:3	Interviewee No. 20	Some of my colleagues imagine that it is their right or entitlement to receive bribes [. . .]. Besides the situation that judges are in a better position financially today, between 1980 to 2000, judges were on very low salaries. [. . .] this became a norm among judges to get involved in bribery so that they can run their personal lives more smoothly [. . .]	13-Linkage between judicial corruption and legal culture: 7-Justification of judicial corruption by judges or court staff:	463–810
20:4	Interviewee No. 20	The general perception was that judges should have a high moral benchmark with clear conscience and impartiality to be able to secure the best interest of the society, however due to their low incomes they had difficulties managing their lives. Therefore, they started adopting this mode of earning money via bribes to give them security long term.	7-Justification of judicial corruption by judges or court staff:	811–1155

ID	Interviewee Number	Quotation	Category Number/ Category	Reference
20:5	Interviewee No. 20	I do not wish to justify the wrongful acts of my colleagues [. . .] mentioning of this issue only means how the act of bribery came to encompass the whole society.	13-Linkage between judicial corruption and legal culture:	1156–1318
20:6	Interviewee No. 20	Judges never considered this illegal demand of money as bribes, instead they would rename it as the "cash part of the court costs".	13-Linkage between judicial corruption and legal culture: 7-Justification of judicial corruption by judges or court staff:	1324–1462
20:7	Interviewee No. 20	[. . .] judges are examined and observed via so many filtering systems. It would be shameful for the regime or government of the time to convict a judge with a crime such as corruption. So, if a judge commits an offence, it will not be disclosed to anyone. [. . .]	5-Public perception about The Disciplinary Court of Judges:	1463–1719
20:8	Interviewee No. 20	[. . .] We have had cases, that the judge had attended an appellant's home and had managed to rape her just because he knew she was alone, he [the judge] was then sent to another city [as judge] just to avoid the spread of the news.	6-Abusing judicial power for private gain:	1857–2084
20:9	Interviewee No. 20	If any newspaper or media publish news about judicial corruption, the government thinks that newspaper tried to question the legitimacy of the government [. . .]. Subsequently, there will be severe confrontation with the manager of the newspaper or the publishing author [. . .]	4-Role of media to combat corruption in Iran (and their effectiveness):	2085–2355

ID	Interviewee Number	Quotation	Category Number/ Category	Reference
20:10	Interviewee No. 20	Unfortunately, lawyers have had a great role in developing such corruptions. If they adhered to their professional conducts instead of acting as a middle-man, then the situation would have been much calmer with much less corruption.	10-Role of lawyers in the creation of judicial corruption in Iran:	2356–2592
20:11	Interviewee No. 20	People already recognise which judge to go to with an appropriate acting lawyer, who works closely with the same judge [. . .]. Many lawyers are contaminated with such relationships and many are still with a clear conscience [. . .]	10-Role of lawyers in the creation of judicial corruption in Iran: 8-who initiated the bribery process:	2594–2812
20:12	Interviewee No. 20	Nowadays there are fewer lawyers acting with proper and professional conduct and most of them are involved in acts of bribery [. . .]	10-Role of lawyers in the creation of judicial corruption in Iran: 13-Linkage between judicial corruption and legal culture:	2814–2944
20:13	Interviewee No. 20	The principle is that if you wish as a judge to progress within the judiciary you are unofficially required to deviate towards corruption [. . .]. For instance, if a judge receives a phone call from another high ranking official, he needs to follow his orders [. . .]. There are also some judges that will not give into such nonsense, like myself [. . .]. If a judge abides and adheres to certain allies, they will be given rewards such as opportunities to purchase lands and properties either one third of the asking price or are given for free [. . .]	11-The independence of the Iranian judiciary:	2945–3481

ID	Interviewee Number	Quotation	Category Number/ Category	Reference
20:14	Interviewee No. 20	It is a shame that this corruption has expanded so much to an extent where the first thing ordinary people will look for as soon as they enter any judicial department is what middleman they should look for [. . .]	3-The effects of corruption on the credibility of the judiciary (and trust of citizens):	3652–3863
21:1	Interviewee No. 21	The public trust in the judiciary has completely disappeared. Of course.	2-Public perception about Iranian judiciary:	57–128
21:2	Interviewee No. 21	This corruption is not specific to the judiciary and covers all the public sectors. But people do not expect a system which itself is responsible for fighting corruption to be contaminated with corruption.	3-The effects of corruption on the credibility of the judiciary (and trust of citizens):	129–336
21:3	Interviewee No. 21	Because of this corruption, people try to resolve their differences outside the court, otherwise if they are forced to go to court then obviously, they will have no choice but via bribery to win the case in their favour [. . .]	13-Linkage between judicial corruption and legal culture:	338–560
21:4	Interviewee No. 21	There is no freedom to expose corruption. [. . .] Mr Yashar Salehi is an example of being jailed in the municipality due to the disclosure of corruption. [. . .] at least there exists no freedom after you have expressed your opinion [or reported corruption]. Hence the first course of action for the head of press is to render censorship before it reaches the Ministry of Intelligence.	4-Role of media to combat corruption in Iran (and their effectiveness):	563–943

ID	Interviewee Number	Quotation	Category Number/ Category	Reference
21:5	Interviewee No. 21	[. . .] for example, Mr Bahman Omoue was imprisoned for six years after writing an economic paper. [. . .]	4-Role of media to combat corruption in Iran (and their effectiveness):	1070–1165
21:6	Interviewee No. 21	One cannot expect fair and lawful conduct from the Disciplinary Court for judges. I myself made a complaint on few occasions but there were not any effective results.	5-Public perception about The Disciplinary Court of Judges:	1359–1525
21:7	Interviewee No. 21	Many lawyers incorporate corruption into their advocacy, and by paying bribe its will make their positions stronger [. . .]	10-Role of lawyers in the creation of judicial corruption in Iran:	1531–1646
21:8	Interviewee No. 21	In comparison to the previous judiciary settings during the time of Shah, I can say the judiciary system [in the Shah era] was much fairer [. . .]. As I mentioned before, political claims and slander were not referred to the judiciary [. . .] and the judiciary only looked into civil and family matters.	16-Comparing judicial corruption in Iran before and after the revolution: 17-Judicial corruption before the revolution	1648–1941
21:9	Interviewee No. 21	Under such circumstances, courts were more transparent compared to the existing judicial system [. . .] of course this does not mean that there were no corruptions taking place under the previous regime.	18-Public perception about judges before the revolution:	1944–2147

ID	Interviewee Number	Quotation	Category Number/ Category	Reference
21:10	Interviewee No. 21	They used to have more respect and there was a more fair and just system. Judges should have been a graduate from law school. And they had to attend the Ministry of Justice examination [. . .]. They then had to undertake a training course for six months [. . .]. They were required to sit again for the same exams after their training was over [. . .] if they had not enough knowledge, they would not have qualified to sit as a judge [. . .]	18-Public perception about judges before the revolution:	2152–2586
21:11	Interviewee No. 21	Judges used to earn higher salaries compared to other court members [. . .]. All these were contributory factors for the judges to have a more respected social status in the society [. . .]	18-Public perception about judges before the revolution:	2587–2766
21:12	Interviewee No. 21	Before the revolution there were still corruptions and the norm of using contacts to facilitate the running of cases, but it was on a limited scale [. . .]	19-Independence of the Court before the revolution:	2768–2919
21:13	Interviewee No. 21	The judicial Disciplinary Tribunal existed in the past regime. The nature of a wrongdoing undertaken by any judge would have been comprehensively investigated, as the judges had to act with much more discipline and adherence to stringent rules.	20- The existence of the Disciplinary Court of Judges before the revolution	3110–3358

ID	Interviewee Number	Quotation	Category Number/ Category	Reference
22:1	Interviewee No. 22	[. . .] The judiciary will investigate and prevent the uprising of aggression. For this reason, the pre-requisite for this would be the independence of the judiciary in order to achieve all the above [. . .]. Unfortunately, there is no such independence in the Republic of Iran. The head of the country and the executive branch is the supreme leader, who is not even elected by the people.	11-The independence of the Iranian judiciary:	449–828
22:2	Interviewee No. 22	The supreme leader, who is not even elected by the people. [. . .] he sees his legitimacy as divine legitimacy. Hence, he chooses the head of judiciary from the Mujtahids, who agree with his ideology.	11-The independence of the Iranian judiciary: 12-Personal independence of the judges:	766–962
22:3	Interviewee No. 22	[. . .] There are two main pre-requisites for judges, the first is their speciality and the second is their independence. In the Islamic Republic, there are no such mercenary standards. [. . .] This does not exist in the law, and no changes have been witnessed in the last three decades.	12-Personal independence of the judges:	964–1246
22:4	Interviewee No. 22	From the first days of the revolution, when Khomeini chose several people as prosecutors, I objected to him because of the lack of expertise [. . ..] You can see the consequences in the existing regime. [. . .] the judiciary has become a means for the implementation of the Supreme Leader's requests [. . .] which can easily have influence on the judiciary and the judge's powers.	11-The independence of the Iranian judiciary:	1249–1617

ID	Interviewee Number	Quotation	Category Number/ Category	Reference
22:5	Interviewee No. 22	The key posts in the past years are in the hands of clerics who have commitment to the supreme leader. If one of these clerics or officials do not become corrupted, then there is room for a big surprise [. . .]	12-Personal independence of the judges: 15-Judicial corruption in Clergy Courts:	1619–1828
22:6	Interviewee No. 22	The loss of hope and faith in the judiciary by ordinary people is more evident in recent years and refers to the judiciary as a factor in the implementation of government policies [. . .]. The law enforcement court of judges and its officials are appointed by one of the clerics appointed by the leader and head of the judiciary.	3-The effects of corruption on the credibility of the judiciary (and trust of citizens):	2031–2359
22:7	Interviewee No. 22	The example of ineffectiveness of [current] disciplinary court for judges is the case of Mortazavi [. . .]. The complaint which was lodged against him for murdering Zahra Kazemi, a Canadian journalist and photographer, did not have any satisfactory outcome [. . .]	5-Public perception about The Disciplinary Court of Judges:	2517–2777
22:8	Interviewee No. 22	The identity of the judge should be clear, but in Iran, many judges are sitting on the bench with their nicknames [. . .]	13-Linkage between judicial corruption and legal culture:	2779–2891
22:9	Interviewee No. 22	These days [after revolution] the position of judges and judicial remedies have been changed, and people no longer respect the judiciary [. . .]	12-Personal independence of the judges:	2893–3033

ID	Interviewee Number	Quotation	Category Number/ Category	Reference
22:10	Interviewee No. 22	Lack of media freedom is a typical example of the current state of corruption in the municipality of Tehran, where the reporters who have reported any corruptions have been imprisoned. Instead of investigating the reported crimes, journalists are jailed. When a reporter does not have security from the government, and if they want to exercise their duties in rendition of corruption, they will be imprisoned under such conditions, as corruption becomes of an intrinsic nature.	4-Role of media to combat corruption in Iran (and their effectiveness):	3034–3516
22:11	Interviewee No. 22	[In the Shah era] After the coup which took place in 1953 and the passage of the Security Police Act, political matters would get referred to the military tribunal. Until a few months before the revolution, ordinary lawyers were not permitted to attend the Iranian military tribunals [. . .]. But a few months before the revolution some changes took place and I was among the very first lawyers who could attend military tribunals.	19-Independence of the Court before the revolution:	3517–3941
22:12	Interviewee No. 22	A number of student officers attended law school to obtain relevant trainings for the military courts. The only difference between these students and the rest of the students were that they were not required to sit for the necessary exams after completing four years at law school in order to be qualified as judges in marshal courts.	18-Public perception about judges before the revolution:	3946–4292
22:13	Interviewee No. 22	It might have been corruption in the judiciary in one particular case, but this was exceptional. [. . .] the judiciary is nowhere comparable with the past in terms of expertise and ethical aspects.	17-Judicial corruption before the revolution	4780–4977

ID	Interviewee Number	Quotation	Category Number/ Category	Reference
22:14	Interviewee No. 22	At that time [Shah era], people looked at judges with special respects, and they could also condemn the judiciary	18-Public perception about judges before the revolution:	4979–5091
22:15	Interviewee No. 22	They had opportunities to take their case further on to high courts if they had any complaints against a judge's misconduct.	20 - The existence of the Disciplinary Court of Judges before the revolution	5148–5271
23:1	Interviewee No. 23	The existence of corruption in the pre-revolutionary period was very small and it was considered as an exception	18-Public perception about judges before the revolution:	37–148
23:2	Interviewee No. 23	[. . .] judges had a special status in society and their characters were more respectful.	18-Public perception about judges before the revolution:	149–239
23:3	Interviewee No. 23	With regards to interference of security agencies or powerful organisations [. . .] not everything was ideal.	19-Independence of the Court before the revolution:	241–346
23:4	Interviewee No. 23	The supervisory body of the judiciary existed, but due to a rare instance of corruption, fewer cases were referred there. They acted with transparency and their functioning was more successful.	20 - The existence of the Disciplinary Court of Judges before the revolution	379–580

ID	Interviewee Number	Quotation	Category Number/ Category	Reference
24:1	Interviewee No. 24	[. . .] regarding the question of paying bribes before the revolution, the existence of judicial corruption was rare and paying or receiving bribes would not have occurred in one's mind [. . .]	16-Comparing judicial corruption in Iran before and after the revolution:	44–227
24:2	Interviewee No. 24	The training system of judges was very clear with discipline, hence there was no possibility of acts of bribery.	18-Public perception about judges before the revolution:	229–345
24:3	Interviewee No. 24	Regarding the respect for judges, they used to be admired by people, their literacy and educational background was much higher than us lawyers [. . .]. They used to possess a lot of integrity, for example you would not find them dressed in appropriate clothing. [. . .]	18-Public perception about judges before the revolution:	347–608
24:4	Interviewee No. 24	. . .] unless in exceptional circumstances, exercising influence over the judiciary was unlikely and far from one's mind.	19-Independence of the Court before the revolution:	724–840
24:5	Interviewee No. 24	The judiciary Disciplinary Tribunal was also very prominent at that time, and everyone was aware of their precision and attention to detail of everything that goes wrong.	20-The existence of the Disciplinary Court of Judges before the revolution	842–1016
25:1	Interviewee No. 25	Before leaving for Iran, everyone had warned me that Iran is nothing but a place of corruption and rubbing from one another's pocket [. . .]	2-Public perception about Iranian judiciary:	827–970

ID	Interviewee Number	Quotation	Category Number/ Category	Reference
25:2	Interviewee No. 25	A lawyer was recommended to us in 2005[. . .]. We could claim back a proportion of the land, and the rest of it must be our entitlement for the job we do for you to retrieve your land [. . .] I accepted his offer and set up a meeting with someone called Mr Malikpour, whose wife was a close relative to the supreme leader [. . .]. He told us to address him by this name, as it was his nickname. We arrived at some mutual agreement over this land and even signed a contract. [. . .]	10-Role of lawyers in the creation of judicial corruption in Iran: 13-Linkage between judicial corruption and legal culture: 8-who initiated the bribery process:	972–1435
25:3	Interviewee No. 25	After a few months we were called to attend a court hearing. When we entered the court room Mr Malikpour also attended very briefly. He was respected in a special manner by the judge. He then asked the judge if someone had called them from another office. With a positive reply he reassured us that there was nothing to worry about any more. [. . .] The judge told me in the presence of everyone else that he had been ordered to reserve my rights. [. . .] my lawyer and Mr Malikpour had arranged this hearing just to give me the reassurance that everything is going according to plan in my favour [. . .]	6-Abusing judicial power for private gain:	1928–2518
26:1	Interviewee No. 26	I had previously referred to the judiciary as a witness and saw that the court were not impartial.	2-Public perception about Iranian judiciary:	60–158

ID	Interviewee Number	Quotation	Category Number/ Category	Reference
26:2	Interviewee No. 26	Until the time I was called for an allegation, I was not aware of the extent of corruption. Please note, I never had any issues with the courts until I got accused and was taken to the clerical court.	15-Judicial corruption in Clergy Courts: 3-The effects of corruption on the credibility of the judiciary (and trust of citizens):	160–360
26:3	Interviewee No. 26	My tenant and I got into some disagreement, for which he lodged a complaint to the court. As soon as they saw me in my clerical clothes I was treated in a respectable manner while the judge spoke rudely to my tenant. I got so upset for the judge's behaviour and could not resist warning him.	5-Public perception about The Disciplinary Court of Judges:	395–686

ID	Interviewee Number	Quotation	Category Number/ Category	Reference
26:4	Interviewee No. 26	In the year 1993, sometime after Khamenei was appointed as the Supreme Leader, I raised my dissatisfaction about tarnishing appropriate authority in one of the meetings. I was arrested and taken to the Special Court for the Clergy immediately after the meeting. [. . .] I was tortured and beaten so my nose got fractured. [. . .] my turban dropped on the floor. I told them I was arrested during the Shah period too but no one had managed to beat my turban off [. . .] I never saw that person again. [. . .] all they intended was to give me warnings to take my word back about what I had said in the meeting. I resisted and never gave in. I was imprisoned and stripped of my clothes. [. . .] The special court for the clergy has become a tool of abuse for Mr Khamenei. As soon as there are signs that do not agree with his line of practice, he punishes them through this court [. . .] out of fear of being prosecuted or accused of some offences no one dare speak anything against his wishes. [. . .] How Khamenei mistreats us clergymen we never experienced from the time of Shah. This court is unconstitutional and against morals. [. . .]	15-Judicial corruption in Clergy Courts:	819–1909
27:1	Interviewee No. 27	I was familiar with its functions and how corrupt it is [. . .]	2-Public perception about Iranian judiciary:	190–249

ID	Interviewee Number	Quotation	Category Number/ Category	Reference
27:2	Interviewee No. 27	This corrupt act was minimal [. . .] instead it has become common norm, in the judiciary as well as legal officer	13-Linkage between judicial corruption and legal culture:	1098–1208
27:3	Interviewee No. 27	[. . .]I remember what Ahmad Seyed Javadi used to tell me when he was an MP during the first term of the House, that there was a more independent judicial system during the Shah regime, and that [. . .] Shah was well aware that the judicial system including the judges were not obedient to him [. . .] Hence they would refer the cases to the Army Prosecutor's Office.	19-Independence of the Court before the revolution:	1212–1572
27:4	Interviewee No. 27	It appears that the revolutionary courts are under the umbrella of the the IRGC [. . .]	11-The independence of the Iranian judiciary:	1575–1658
27:5	Interviewee No. 27	[. . .] that the Revolutionary courts submit to orders from the security forces. [. . .]	11-The independence of the Iranian judiciary:	1675–1753
27:6	Interviewee No. 27	Mr Asghari was the Minister of Justice during the time I was an MP, yet he claimed he was not the Minister of Justice but a simple courier [. . .there was lack of supervisory regulation on the judiciary]	5-Public perception about The Disciplinary Court of Judges:	1954–2157

ID	Interviewee Number	Quotation	Category Number/ Category	Reference
27:7	Interviewee No. 27	The Special Clerical Court was established in 1980 in Qum. It had the main role of attending to clerical crimes. [. . .] they thought that if the clerics were tried in ordinary courts, it would bring shame to Islam [. . .] Mr Montazeri [Deputy of Khominei] was the supporter and the founder of these courts. But he started opposing to such courts after the approval of the constitution [. . .]. For some time people heard less of such courts until 1986–1987 when people started hearing more of these courts for Mehdi Hashemi's trial [. . .] For some time, Clergy court did not have any rules or regulations in place [. . .] The main branch [of Clergy Court] is in Moghadas Ardebili in Tehran [. . .] Two confiscated buildings are at the possession of this court. The first is the Prosecutor's office and the other is the court. This court deals with all types of crimes and allegations. It will suffice if someone has attended the clergy school for a short period of time, then he would acquire the title of clergyman [. . .]	15-Judicial corruption in Clergy Courts:	2158–3161
27:8	Interviewee No. 27	Whenever the Special Clerical Courts find it appropriate they will transfer the case to this court. [. . .] sometimes this is done via the intelligence service or the security forces.	11-The independence of the Iranian judiciary:	3163–3346
27:9	Interviewee No. 27	The functions of this court are as follows: inquisition and suppression of the opposing parties or individuals to the religious leader or to the current regime [. . .]	15-Judicial corruption in Clergy Courts:	3348–3513

ID	Interviewee Number	Quotation	Category Number/ Category	Reference
27:10	Interviewee No. 27	For instance, suppressing the followers of Ayattolah Shariatmadari or traditional clergymen or opponents against other clergymen [. . .]. In my case there was a death sentence but then this verdict was quashed to seven years imprisonment [. . .]. While I was serving my sentence a number of these clerics were brought to the same prison [. . .]. There were a few of them that were in prison for political opinions and the rest had committed crimes such as forgery [. . .]	15-Judicial corruption in Clergy Courts:	3514–3970
27:11	Interviewee No. 27	These courts have the discretionary powers to refer to Sharie law. They had taken a non-clerical individual to the Special Clerical Courts due to being in charge of a tabloid belonging to a clergyman [. . .]	6-Abusing judicial power for private gain:	3971–4175
27:12	Interviewee No. 27	There is no reputation for the judiciary and the judges [. . .]	2-Public perception about Iranian judiciary:	4176–4235
27:13	Interviewee No. 27	[. . .] Mr Larijani explicitly refers to himself as being the soldier of the supreme leader.	11-The independence of the Iranian judiciary:	4418–4508
28:1	Interviewee No. 28	Until and before I had any dealings with the judiciary, I had a little knowledge about the instability and the chaos in the system [. . .]	3-The effects of corruption on the credibility of the judiciary (and trust of citizens):	410–545

ID	Interviewee Number	Quotation	Category Number/ Category	Reference
28:2	Interviewee No. 28	Before the revolution, there was an independence to the judiciary, therefore political cases were not sent to the judiciary. [. . .]	17-Judicial corruption before the revolution 19-Independence of the Court before the revolution:	546–674
28:3	Interviewee No. 28	If we compare the two judicial systems of the Shah regime and the one under the current regime, the standards of rules and regulations of the current judiciary is much lower than the ones in the previous regime [. . .]	16-Comparing judicial corruption in Iran before and after the revolution:	761–975
28:4	Interviewee No. 28	For instance some of Khalkhali's sentences did not have any written sentences [. . .]. In 12/04/1359 he had sentenced 24 people in less than 10 hours in Shiraz, of which 12 individuals were given a death sentence [. . .]	6-Abusing judicial power for private gain:	976–1188
28:5	Interviewee No. 28	[. . .] some Mujtaihds as Seyed Hossein Gomi, Seyed Kazim Shariatmadari, Shekh Bahaee Mahallati had all opposed the operational system of the revolutionary courts [. . .]	5-Public perception about The Disciplinary Court of Judges:	1339–1504
28:6	Interviewee No. 28	[. . .] they wanted me to defend myself. I was not going to do anything without my lawyer I replied. I was then detained. I was given a long list of lawyers to choose one as my legal representative. I then realised that they were all their own officers. I opposed to their list but in response they said I had to choose from their list and that who belonged to the Special Clerical Court. [. . .] the persecutor of the Clergy Court told me you are going to prison because you criticised the Supreme Leader.	15-Judicial corruption in Clergy Courts:	1661–2155

Code Report

Project: Judicial Corruption in Iran
Report created by Mehdi Khosravi
Code Report

○ **10-Role of lawyers in the creation of judicial corruption in Iran:**
17 Quotations:
3:7 Initially we had a lawyer, but as soon as I became the judge's temporary . . . . (2067:2263) - D 3: interviewee No. 3/ 6:5 [. . .] My lawyer was aware of the situation. [. . .] He refused to continue w . . . . (1942:2078) - D 6: interviewee No. 6/ 8:5 [. . .] Lawyers play an important role in the formation and continuation . . . . (1423:1686) D 8: interviewee No. 8/ 8:6 It seems that some attorneys may even believe their participation in j . . . . (1689:2066) - D 8: interviewee No. 8/ 9:4 Unfortunately, lawyers not excluded from this judiciary system. They a . . . . (1341:1566) - D 9: interviewee No. 9/ 11:7 Based on my personal experience, I can say that some lawyers are engag . . . . (2716:3071) - D 11: interviewee No. 11/ 13:4 It is true that there are unfortunately some lawyers who assist in dis . . . . (727:1120) - D 13: interviewee No. 13/ 13:8 Majority of lawyers do not consider their position from a professional . . . . (2986:3071) - D 13: interviewee No. 13/ 14:7 These powerful political officials always have a few lawyers to repre . . . . (3142:3436) - D 14: interviewee No. 14/ 14:9 [. . .] there exist female attendees that by offering sexual intercourse t . . . . (3723:3980) - D 14: interviewee No. 14/ 19:6 The breeding ground for judicial corruption in Iran is created by both . . . . (1318:1437) - D 19: interviewee No. 19/ 19:7 Due to a shortage of a transparent and just system, lawyers do not alw . . . . (1442:1599) - D 19: interviewee No. 19/ 20:10 Unfortunately, lawyers have had a great role in developing such corrup . . . . (2356:2592) - D 20: interviewee No. 20/ 20:11 People already recognise which judge to go to with appropriate acting . . . . (2594:2812) - D 20: interviewee No. 20/ 20:12 Nowadays there are less lawyers acting with proper and professional co . . . . (2814:2944) - D 20: interviewee No. 20/ 21:7 Many lawyers incorporate corruption to their advocacy, and by paying b . . . . (1531:1646) - D 21: interviewee No. 21/ 25:2 A lawyer was recommended to us in 2005[. . .] We could claim back a propor . . . . (972:1435) - D 25: interviewee No. 25

○ **11-The independence of the Iranian judiciary:**
19 Quotations:
2:1 Therefore, I discussed it with one of my peer colleagues, he then spok .... (430:899) - D 2: interviewee No. 2/ 4:2 [. . .] What was hilarious is that whatever the interrogator ordered the j .... (423:578) - D 4: interviewee No. 4/ 10:1 In May 1993, when I was visiting Iran, I was kidnapped from my own apa .... (1100:1938) - D 10: interviewee No. 10/ 11:5 The revolutionary court considers itself as a security institution (2403:2468) - D 11: interviewee No. 11/ 12:3 My attorney also told me that he had paid the court to have the court .... (1426:1565) - D 12: interviewee No. 12/ 13:2. Due to the high number of cases and the pressure from the top (power .... (246:486) - D 13: interviewee No. 13/ 14:1 In 2011, I became the director of public relations in the Office of Mr .... (410:734) - D 14: interviewee No. 14/ 14:2 Several corruptions that I had witnessed first-hand was at the office .... (736:1175) - D 14: interviewee No. 14/ 14:5 I can refer to the role of Mr Fallahian and Mr Mohseni Ejehi. Mr Ejehi .... (2054:2523) - D 14: interviewee No. 14/ 16:2 I had not committed any crime; however I was arrested [during demonst .... (268:1102) - D 16: interviewee No. 16/ 18:3 There is no real trial [. . .]Trials usually lasts about a few minutes and .... (1006:1163) - D 18: interviewee No. 18/ 20:13 The principle is that if you wish as a judge to progress within the ju .... (2945:3481) - D 20: interviewee No. 20/ 22:1 [. . .] The judiciary will investigate and prevent uprising of aggression.. .... (449:828) - D 22: interviewee No. 22/ 22:2 the supreme leader, who is not even elected by the people. [. . .] He sees .... (766:962) - D 22: interviewee No. 22/ 22:4 rom the first days of the revolution, when Khomeini chose several peop .... (1249:1617) - D 22: interviewee No. 22/ 27:4 It appears that the revolutionary courts are under the umbrella of the .... (1575:1658) - D 27: interviewee No. 27/ 27:5 that the Revolutionary courts submits to orders from the security forc .... (1675:1753) - D 27: interviewee No. 27/ 27:8 Whenever the Specials Clerical courts find it appropriate they will tr .... (3163:3346) - D 27: interviewee No. 27/ 27:13 [. . .] Mr Larijani explicitly refers to himself as being the soldier of t .... (4418:4508) - D 27: interviewee No. 27

○ **12- Personal independence of the judges:**
8 Quotations:
11:3 [. . .] the judge also knew that my client was not involved in any drug sm .... (2044:2163) - D 11: interviewee No. 11/ 14:6 And the head of this reformist

party was a Sheikh called Zare-Foomani.. . . . (2884:3139) - D 14: interviewee No. 14/ 16:3 The prosecutor, the judge, and other members of the court violated the . . . . (1421:1677) - D 16: interviewee No. 16/ 19:8 Another important cause of corruption is the selection of judges based . . . . (1601:1779) - D 19: interviewee No. 19/ 22:2 the supreme leader, who is not even elected by the people. [. . .] He sees . . . . (766:962) - D 22: interviewee No. 22/ 22:3 [. . .] There are two main pre requisites for judges, the first is their s . . . . (964:1246) - D 22: interviewee No. 22/ 22:5 The key posts in the past years are in the hands of clerics who has co . . . . (1619:1828) - D 22: interviewee No. 22/ 22:9 These days [after revolution] the position of judges and judicial reme . . . . (2893:3033) - D 22: interviewee No. 22

○ **13-Linkage between judicial corruption and legal culture:**
22 Quotations:
2:3 is filled with old wolves, hence you will have to act promptly otherwi . . . . (1343:1455) - D 2: interviewee No. 2/ 4:3 What was hilarious is that whatever the interrogator ordered the judge . . . . (427:524) - D 4: interviewee No. 4/ 5:2 [. . .] It is so evident that the courts and the Police are all corrupt[. . . . . (333:403) - D 5: interviewee No. 5/ 9:6 in relation to the Integrity and honourability of judges and the lawye . . . . (1912:2187) - D 9: interviewee No. 9/ 11:4 The Revolutionary court is a strange court, not only I was not called . . . . (2165:2401) - D 11: interviewee No. 11/ 11:7 Based on my personal experience, I can say that some lawyers are engag . . . . (2716:3071) - D 11: interviewee No. 11/ 11:9 Hence it is very difficult to differentiate between criminals and non-. . . . (3319:3560) - D 11: interviewee No. 11/ 13:8 Majority of lawyers do not consider their position from a professional . . . . (2986:3071) - D 13: interviewee No. 13/ 14:3 When the prosecutors or inspecting officer sees that the accused will . . . . (1476:1681) - D 14: interviewee No. 14/ 14:7 These powerful political officials always have a few lawyers to repre . . . . (3142:3436) - D 14: interviewee No. 14/ 15:7 [. . .] Judges do not have any shame in using their personal tastes in dea . . . . (4714:4798) - D 15: interviewee No. 15/ 16:4 [. . .] In relation to judicial corruptions I must emphasise that member . . . . (3322:3510) - D 16: interviewee No. 16/ 18:3 There is no real trial [. . .]Trials usually lasts about a few minutes and . . . . (1006:1163) - D 18: interviewee No. 18/ 19:9 I myself saw that judges carried their prayers in such filthy and disg . . . . (1787:1924) - D 19: interviewee No. 19/ 20:3 Some of my colleagues imagine that it is their rights or entitlement t . . . . (463:810) - D 20: interviewee No. 20/ 20:5 I do not wish to justify their wrongful acts of my colleagues [. . .] Men . . . . (1156:1318) - D 20: interviewee No. 20/ 20:6 Judge never considered this illegal demand of money as bribes, instead . . . . (1324:1462) - D 20: interviewee No. 20/ 20:12 Nowadays there are less lawyers acting with proper

and professional co .... (2814:2944) - D 20: interviewee No. 20/ 21:3 Because of this corruption, people try to resolve their differences ou .... (338:560) - D 21: interviewee No. 21/ 22:8 The identity of the judge should be clear, but in Iran, many judges ar .... (2779:2891) - D 22: interviewee No. 22/ 25:2 A lawyer was recommended to us in 2005[. . .] We could claim back a propor .... (972:1435) - D 25: interviewee No. 25/ 27:2 this corrupt act was minimal [. . .] Instead it has become common norm, i .... (1098:1208) - D 27: interviewee No. 27

○ **15-Judicial corruption in Clergy Courts:**
7 **Quotations:**
22:5 The key posts in the past years are in the hands of clerics who has co .... (1619:1828) - D 22: interviewee No. 22/ 26:2 Until the time I was called for an allegation, I was not aware of the .... (160:360) - D 26: interviewee No. 26/ 26:4 In year 1993, sometime after Khamenei was appointed as the supreme lea .... (819:1909) - D 26: interviewee No. 26/ 27:7 The Special Clerical Court was established in 1980 in Qum. It had the .... (2158:3161) - D 27: interviewee No. 27/ 27:9 The functions of this court are as follows: inquisition and suppressio .... (3348:3513) - D 27: interviewee No. 27/ 27:10 For instance suppressing the followers of Ayattolah Shariatmadari or t .... (3514:3970) - D 27: interviewee No. 27/ 28:6 [. . .]They wanted me to defend myself. I was not going to do anything wit .... (1661:2155) - D 28: interviewee No. 28

○ **16-Comparing judicial corruption in Iran before and after the revolution:**
4 Quotations:
19:11 Also, a number of corrupt judges were rare, [. . .] (2195:2243) - D 19: interviewee No. 19/ 21:8 In comparison to the previous judiciary settings during the time of Sh .... (1648:1941) - D 21: interviewee No. 21/ 24:1 [. . .] Regarding the question of paying bribes before the revolution, the .... (44:227) - D 24: interviewee No. 24/ 28:3 If we compare the two judicial systems of the Shah regime and the one .... (761:975) - D 28: interviewee No. 28

○ **17- Judicial corruption before the revolution**
5 Quotations:
19:10 Before the revolution, significant attention was given to judges' stat .... (2030:2192) - D 19: interviewee No. 19/ 19:11 Also, a number of corrupt judges were rare, [. . .] (2195:2243) - D 19: interviewee No. 19/ 21:8 In comparison to the previous judiciary settings during the time of Sh .... (1648:1941) - D 21: interviewee No. 21/ 22:13 It might have been corruption in the judiciary in one particular case,. ... (4780:4977) - D 22: interviewee No. 22/ 28:2 Before the

revolution, there was an independence to the judiciary, the .... (546:674) - D 28: interviewee No. 28

○ 18- Public perception about judges before the revolution:
10 Quotations:
19:10 Before the revolution, significant attention was given to judges' stat .... (2030:2192) - D 19: interviewee No. 19/ 21:9] Under such circumstances, courts were more transparent compared to t .... (1944:2147) - D 21: interviewee No. 21/ 21:10 They used to have more respect and there was a more fair and just syst .... (2152:2586) - D 21: interviewee No. 21/ 21:11 Judges used to earn more salaries compared to other court members [. . .]. ... (2587:2766) - D 21: interviewee No. 21/ 22:12 A number of student officers attended the Law school to obtain relevan .... (3946:4292) - D 22: interviewee No. 22/ 22:14 At that time [Shah era], people looked at judges with special respects .... (4979:5091) - D 22: interviewee No. 22/ 23:1 The existence of corruption in the pre revolutionary period was very s .... (37:148) - D 23: interviewee No. 23/ 23:2. [. . .] Judges had a special status in society and their characters were .... (149:239) - D 23: interviewee No. 23/ 24:2 The training system of judges was very clear with disciplines, hence t .... (229:345) - D 24: interviewee No. 24/ 24:3 Regarding the respect for judges, they used to be admired by people, t .... (347:608) - D 24: interviewee No. 24

○ 19- Independence of the Court before the revolution:
6 Quotations:
21:12 Before the revolution there were still corruptions and the norm of usi .... (2768:2919) - D 21: interviewee No. 21/ 22:11 [In Shah era] After the coup which took place in 1953 and the passage .... (3517:3941) - D 22: interviewee No. 22/ 23:3 With regards to interference of security agencies or powerful organisa .... (241:346) - D 23: interviewee No. 23/ 24:4 . . .]Unless in exceptional circumstances, exercising influence over the j .... (724:840) - D 24: interviewee No. 24/ 27:3 [. . .]I remember what Ahmad Seyed Javadi used to tell me when he was an M .... (1212:1572) - D 27: interviewee No. 27/ 28:2 Before the revolution, there was an independence to the judiciary, the .... (546:674) - D 28: interviewee No. 28

○ 20 - The existence of the Disciplinary Court of Judges before the revolution
4 Quotations:
21:13 The judicial Disciplinary Tribunal existed in the past regime. The nat .... (3110:3358) - D 21: interviewee No. 21/ 22:15 They had opportunities to take

their case further on to high courts if .... (5148:5271) - D 22: interviewee No. 22/ 23:4 [...]. The supervisory body of the judiciary existed, but due to a rare .... (379:580) - D 23: interviewee No. 23/ 24:5 The judiciary disciplinary tribunal was also very prominent at that ti .... (842:1016) - D 24: interviewee No. 24

○ **21- The judge's knowledge (Elme- Ghazi)**
2 Quotations:
13:6 Of course, judge's impartiality is undermined in criminal cases more t .... (1355:1602) - D 13: interviewee No. 13/ 13:7] In civil matters, based on evidence and documentations the judge is .... (1841:2367) - D 13: interviewee No. 13

○ **2-Public perception about Iranian judiciary:**
22 Quotations:
1:1 I had never heard anything about the corruption of the court until I r .... (86:223) - D 1: interviewee No. 1/ 4:1 I was arrested in the Green Movement protest [2009]. I was arrested on .... (67:421) - D 4: interviewee No. 4/ 5:1 [...] It is so evident that the courts and the Police are all corrup (333:399) - D 5: interviewee No. 5/ 6:1 [...] it was the first time I was attending the court. [...] Prior to visit .... (64:284) - D 6: interviewee No. 6/ 7:2] therefore, they would also rely on paying bribes in order to relieve .... (288:502) - D 7: interviewee No. 7/ 7:3 In another instance, a drug smuggler was executed despite paying bribe .... (756:883) - D 7: interviewee No. 7/ 7:5 Some judges play an important role in dividing confiscated properties,. ... (2367:2611) - D 7: interviewee No. 7/ 8:1 [...] I witnessed many cases in both civil and criminal matters indicati .... (280:588) - D 8: interviewee No. 8/ 9:1 [...] I personally see judicial corruption as part of an organised corru .... (40:397) - D 9: interviewee No. 9/ 11:1 Witness No. 11: Ms Shima (Lawyer) [...] Corruption in the judiciary is .... (0:229) - D 11: interviewee No. 11/ 12:2 I had heard before that the court system is based on offering bribes b .... (164:301) - D 12: interviewee No. 12/ 13:1 In relation to judicial corruption, the answer is that yes [...] there .... (42:155) - D 13: interviewee No. 13/ 16:1 I knew from the outset and before I had any encounters to the system t .... (32:163) - D 16: interviewee No. 16/ 17:4 Another crime was the formation of a mafia network by prison officials .... (1879:2307) - D 17: interviewee No. 17/ 19:1 Before I began to work as a lawyer, I found that the justice system in .... (93:198) - D 19: interviewee No. 19/ 19:3 ll segments of society in Iran are somehow involved with the judiciary (490:560) - D 19: interviewee No. 19/ 20:1 [...] I agree that citizens come to court with this background in their .... (46:242) - D 20: interviewee No. 20/ 21:1 The public trust in the

judiciary has completely disappeared. Of cours .... (57:128) - D 21: interviewee No. 21/ 25:1 Before leaving for Iran, everyone had warned me that Iran is a place n .... (827:970) - D 25: interviewee No. 25/ 26:1 I had previously referred to the judiciary as a witness and saw that t .... (60:158) - D 26: interviewee No. 26/ 27:1 I was familiar with its functions and how corrupt it is [. . .] (190:249) - D 27: interviewee No. 27/ 27:12 There is no reputation for the judiciary and the judges [. . .] (4176:4235) - D 27: interviewee No. 27

○ **3-The effects of corruption on the credibility of the judiciary (and trust of citizens):**

25 Quotations:

1:5 Do you not think that the court system is already aware of its employe .... (1414:1508) - D 1: interviewee No. 1/ 3:1 The first time I had to visit the court was for my husband and I witne .... (448:550) - D 3: interviewee No. 3/ 5:6 [. . .] In my opinion, the judge and all employees are like collective ba .... (1267:1342) - D 5: interviewee No. 5/ 6:7 [. . .]Most affairs are run based on bribery in Iran. [. . .]You can even brib .... (2514:2595) - D 6: interviewee No. 6/ 7:1 I have experienced corruption within the judiciary, taking advantage o .... (35:178) - D 7: interviewee No. 7/ 8:7 We see that in such injustice system where there is total lack of publ .... (2069:2249) - D 8: interviewee No. 8/ 8:8 courts that are held for political and social retards, or the Special .... (2590:2710) - D 8: interviewee No. 8/ 9:2 You always wonder in your mind if this case will go through its proper .... (731:1038) - D 9: interviewee No. 9/ 11:1 Witness No. 11: Ms Shima (Lawyer) [. . .] Corruption in the judiciary is .... (0:229) - D 11: interviewee No. 11/ 11:8 When you witness corruption, you would inevitably tell your friends or .... (3074:3318) - D 11: interviewee No. 11/ 12:1 I had never been involved with the judicial system and I hope I will n .... (53:158) - D 12: interviewee No. 12/ 12:2 I had heard before that the court system is based on offering bribes b .... (164:301) - D 12: interviewee No. 12/ 14:8 but after I attended the courts myself this perception of mine got wor .... (3509:3587) - D 14: interviewee No. 14/ 15:1 I had seen judicial corruptions before referring to the judiciary. Due .... (262:483) - D 15: interviewee No. 15/ 15:8 This system of judicial corruption has been a cause for a distribution .... (4804:4931) - D 15: interviewee No. 15/ 17:1 I was arrested on December 2004, and after this illegal arrest, which .... (617:1003) - D 17: interviewee No. 17/ 17:5. [. . .] The law enforcement department of the judiciary is that where co .... (5704:5904) - D 17: interviewee No. 17/ 18:4] I knew of the judicial corruption before I got to experience it fir .... (1252:1420) - D 18: interviewee No. 18/ 19:2 I started studying law in order to become a judge. However, after witn .... (200:319) - D 19: interviewee No. 19/ 20:2 Partially this is caused by my own colleague's wrongdoings [. . .] Of cou .... (246:460) - D 20: interviewee No. 20/ 20:14 it is a shame that this corruption has expanded so much to an extent w .... (3652:3863) - D 20: interviewee No. 20/ 21:2 this corruption is not specific to the judiciary and covers all the pu .... (129:336) - D 21: interviewee No. 21/ 22:6 The lose of hope and faith in the judiciary by ordinary people is more .... (2031:2359) - D 22: interviewee No. 22/ 26:2 Until the time I was called for an allegation, I was not aware of the .... (160:360) - D 26: interviewee No. 26/ 28:1 Until and before I had any dealings with the judiciary, I had a little .... (410:545) - D 28: interviewee No. 28

○ **4-Role of media to combat corruption in Iran(and their Effectiveness): 12 Quotations:**

1:6 Of course the media cannot disclose any corruption running through the .... (1515:1598) - D 1: interviewee No. 1/ 4:5 Even if I reported it to the media they would not be able to publish i .... (735:903) - D 4: interviewee No. 4/ 7:6 Some media are accused of financial and political corruption in Iran [. ... (2615:3041) - D 7: interviewee No. 7/ 9:5 In order to examine the role of the media, it should be noted that cen .... (1570:1911) - D 9: interviewee No. 9/ 11:10 You may rarely find a newspaper who would dare criticise the functioni .... (3562:3652) - D 11: interviewee No. 11/ 12:6 media in Iran would not risk to publish news about corruption in judic .... (2320:2399) - D 12: interviewee No. 12/ 13:5 Except the social media no other official media has been successful in .... (1123:1354) - D 13: interviewee No. 13/ 18:6 The media is not in a position or have the courage to publicize such i .... (1649:1779) - D 18: interviewee No. 18/ 20:9 If any newspaper or media publish a news about judicial corruption, th .... (2085:2355) - D 20: interviewee No. 20/ 21:4 There is no freedom to expose corruption. [. . .] Mr Yashar Salehi is an .... (563:943) - D 21: interviewee No. 21/ 21:5] For example, Mr Bahman Omoue was imprisoned for six years after writ .... (1070:1165) - D 21: interviewee No. 21/ 22:10 Lack of media freedom is a typical example of the current state of cor .... (3034:3516) - D 22: interviewee No. 22

○ **5-Public perception about The Disciplinary Court of Judges: 23 Quotations:**

1:4 It is true that I could complain that a bribe was demanded of me by th .... (1164:1361) - D 1: interviewee No. 1/ 3:6 I would never have gone to complain about the judge. It would be total .... (1877:2064) - D 3: interviewee No. 3/ 4:4 For as long as I am in Iran I would not dare to report such an inciden ....

(582:734) - D 4: interviewee No. 4/ 4:6. I underwent some severe torturing, of course I was unable to complai .... (927:1018) - D 4: interviewee No. 4/ 5:7 For sure there is a regulatory or disciplinary body but do they operat .... (1397:1487) - D 5: interviewee No. 5/ 6:6 I would never dare to make a complaint about the judge's conduct [...] F .... (2081:2403) - D 6: interviewee No. 6/ 7:7 I was aware of the existence of disciplinary court, but I did not go t .... (3232:3563) - D 7: interviewee No. 7/ 8:3 I personally pursued some cases at the disciplinary Court of judges, a .... (895:1134) - D 8: interviewee No. 8/ 8:4 The outcome of my experiences has been that the judge was forced to ex .... (1134:1323) - D 8: interviewee No. 8/ 9:3 I have not been to the disciplinary Tribunal court for the judiciary,. .... (1039:1339) - D 9: interviewee No. 9/ 11:6 I did not report this corruption because complaint against judges and .... (2559:2712) - D 11: interviewee No. 11/ 12:5 then told my attorney that I was going to lodge a complaint against th .... (2174:2319) - D 12: interviewee No. 12/ 14:4 For example, I encountered a situation where the judge of the second b .... (1683:1974) - D 14: interviewee No. 14/ 15:3 I was aware of judge's disciplinary court. When I consult with several .... (774:954) - D 15: interviewee No. 15/ 15:6 There is no point in making a complaint about judicial members who are .... (2019:2398) - D 15: interviewee No. 15/ 18:5 I have never been or intended to associate with judge's disciplinary t .... (1526:1647) - D 18: interviewee No. 18/ 19:5 There has been instances that reporting judges bribe taking has had le .... (1025:1316) - D 19: interviewee No. 19/ 20:7 [...] judges are examined and observed via so many filtering systems. It .... (1463:1719) - D 20: interviewee No. 20/ 21:6 One cannot expect a fair and lawful conduct from the Disciplinary Cour .... (1359:1525) - D 21: interviewee No. 21/ 22:7 [...] The example of ineffectiveness of [current] disciplinary court for .... (2517:2777) - D 22: interviewee No. 22/ 26:3 my tenant and I got into some disagreement, for which he lodged a comp .... (395:686) - D 26: interviewee No. 26/ 27:6 Mr Asghari was the Minister of Justice during the time I was an MP, ye .... (1954:2157) - D 27: interviewee No. 27/ 28:5 [...] Some Mujtaihds as Seyed Hossein Gomi, Seyed Kazim Shariatmadari, S .... (1339:1504) - D 28: interviewee No. 28

○ **6- Abusing judicial power for private gain:**
30 Quotations:
1:3 other party has paid bribes (630:658) - D 1: interviewee No. 1/ 2:2 Because of the threats of imprisonment the manager accepted to sort ou .... (901:1104) - D 2: interviewee No. 2/ 3:4 On one occasion I went to visit the judge so to request for a transfer .... (1047:1613) - D 3: interviewee No. 3/ 5:4 He asked

for five million Tooman to terminate the case. Otherwise the . . . . (871:979) - D 5: interviewee No. 5/ 5:5 He asked for five million Tooman to terminate the case. Otherwise the . . . . (871:1177) - D 5: interviewee No. 5/ 6:4 [. . .] when I won my divorce rights and entitlements, the judge was treat . . . . (1721:1944) - D 6: interviewee No. 6/ 7:4 In relation to my own court case, judge Mortazavi did not act with imp . . . . (1139:1672) - D 7: interviewee No. 7/ 8:2 For example, a judge let his personal views to intervene in the case,. . . . (595:889) - D 8: interviewee No. 8/ 8:9 In one instance, I was representing my client who was facing execution . . . . (2862:3261) - D 8: interviewee No. 8/ 10:2 I was still being tortured for another five months after the $3 millio . . . . (2260:2848) - D 10: interviewee No. 10/ 11:2 within close vicinity to where he used to live. Unfortunately, the int . . . . (742:1767) - D 11: interviewee No. 11/ 11:3 [. . .] the judge also knew that my client was not involved in any drug sm . . . . (2044:2163) - D 11: interviewee No. 11/ 12:3 My attorney also told me that he had paid the court to have the court . . . . (1426:1565) - D 12: interviewee No. 12/ 12:4 In the court trial my client told the judge that you he was literally . . . . (2023:2170) - D 12: interviewee No. 12/ 13:3 I did not encounter bribing the judge in my own caseloads; however, I . . . . (488:594) - D 13: interviewee No. 13/ 14:2 Several corruptions that I had witnessed first-hand was at the office . . . . (736:1175) - D 14: interviewee No. 14/ 14:6 And the head of this reformist party was a Sheikh called Zare-Foomani.. . . . (2884:3139) - D 14: interviewee No. 14/ 15:2 Despite ccumulation of documents and evidence including reports from . . . . (486:773) - D 15: interviewee No. 15/ 15:4 In our own family case, I witnessed corruptive judicial process that w . . . . (955:1566) - D 15: interviewee No. 15/ 15:5 He was charged with drug trafficking at minor level. The judge for tha . . . . (1652:1770) - D 15: interviewee No. 15/ 16:2 I had not committed any crime; however I was arrested [during demonst . . . . (268:1102) - D 16: interviewee No. 16/ 16:3 The prosecutor, the judge, and other members of the court violated the . . . . (1421:1677) - D 16: interviewee No. 16/ 17:2 All this time my case was in the revolutionary prosecutor's office bas . . . . (1004:1389) - D 17: interviewee No. 17/ 17:3 The same judge had issued many unfair and ungrounded summons. Later ce . . . . (1390:1552) - D 17: interviewee No. 17/ 18:1 After a while, they took me to court No 5 of the law enforcements. The . . . . (310:808) - D 18: interviewee No. 18/ 19:4 I witnessed corruption in judiciary, bribe taking and bribery, althoug . . . . (805:910) - D 19: interviewee No. 19/ 20:8 [. . .] We have had cases, that the judge had attended appellant's homes a . . . . (1857:2084) - D 20: interviewee No. 20/ 25:3 After a few months we were called to attend a court hearing. When we e . . . . (1928:2518) - D 25: interviewee No. 25/ 27:11 These courts have the discretionary powers to refer to Sharie law. The .... (3971:4175) - D 27: interviewee No. 27/ 28:4 For instance some of Khalkhali's sentences did not have any written se .... (976:1188) - D 28: interviewee No. 28

○ **7-Justification of judicial corruption by judges or court staff:**
3 Quotations:
20:3 Some of my colleagues imagine that it is their rights or entitlement t .... (463:810) - D 20: interviewee No. 20/ 20:4 The general perception was that judges should have a high moral benchm .... (811:1155) - D 20: interviewee No. 20/ 20:6 Judge never considered this illegal demand of money as bribes, instead .... (1324:1462) - D 20: interviewee No. 20

○ **8-who initiated the bribery process:**
10 Quotations:
1:2 One of the court staff stopped me in the corridor and said I should pa .... (441:529) - D 1: interviewee No. 1/ 3:2 The first impression you would get is that most employees are expectin .... (774:886) - D 3: interviewee No. 3/ 3:3 One of the court personnel even approached me proposing if I had money .... (944:1042) - D 3: interviewee No. 3/ 3:5 On one occasion I went to visit the judge so to request for a transfer .... (1048:1173) - D 3: interviewee No. 3/ 5:3 When I visited the court to follow up my case one of the employees ask .... (479:810) - D 5: interviewee No. 5/ 6:2 [. . .] As soon as I was called to the judge's room he started telling me .... (612:1029) - D 6: interviewee No. 6/ 6:3 asked him what he want? [. . .] he responded that he could ask the judge t .... (1032:1400) - D 6: interviewee No. 6/ 18:2 There are middlemen in Iran whose main job is to receive bribe and pay .... (809:1004) - D 18: interviewee No. 18/ 20:11 People already recognise which judge to go to with appropriate acting .... (2594:2812) - D 20: interviewee No. 20/ 25:2 A lawyer was recommended to us in 2005[. . .] We could claim back a propor .... (972:1435) - D 25: interviewee No. 25

○ **9-Nepotism in the Iranian judiciary:**
2 Quotations:
2:1 Therefore, I discussed it with one of my peer colleagues, he then spok .... (430:899) - D 2: interviewee No. 2/ 14:10 [. . .] After the uprising in 2008 and suppression of people, Mr Ayatollah .... (4142:4638) - D 14: interviewee No. 14

Bibliography

Abdaless, S., Barzi, R., Crowther, D., & Oubrich, M. (2015). *Governance, accountability and sustainable development*. Newcastle upon Tyne, UK: Cambridge Scholars Publishing.

Abouharb, M. R., Moyer, L. P., & Schmidt, M. (2013). De facto judicial independence and physical integrity rights. *Journal of Human Rights, 12*(4), 367–396. doi:10.1080/14754835.2013.812461.

Abraham, A. J. (1999). *Tortured confessions, prisons and public recantations in modern Iran*. University of California Press. Can be retrieved at (partially): https://goo.gl/r7WHVX (Accessed 31-03-2016).

Abtahi, H. (2012). *The relationship between supranational criminal courts and tribunals and transitional justice, Legatum Institute*. Retrieved from www.li.com/docs/default-source/future-of-iran/2012-future-of-iran-by-charles-villa-vicencio-a-south-african-perspective-on-iran.pdf?sfvrsn=2 (Accessed 31-03-2016).

Ades, A., Di Tella, R. (1996). *The causes and consequences of corruption: A review of recent empirical contributions*. University of Sussex, Institute of Development Studies (UK).

Ahmadi, N. (2015, 3 June). *Ghoveh Ghazaei dar gozar tarikh* [History of Iranian judiciary]. Isna. https://bit.ly/35elobh

Al Hussein, Z. (2016, September 13). *Ravand Ghazei dar iran moshkel darad*. [Iranian judiciary has fundamental problems], Retrieved from: http://www.radiofarda.com/a/b5_human_rights_council_open_geneva_zeid_raad_alhussein_iran/27984270.html

Alsheban, A. (2017). *IOSR Journal of Humanities And Social Science* (IOSR-JHSS), *22*(5), Ver. II (May 2017) pp. 37–44 e-ISSN: 2279-0837, p-ISSN: 2279-0845.

Amin, S. (2012). *Moshirodoleh va khanedanesh.* [Moshiro-al-doleh- and his family]. Available at: http://goo.gl/4u2mng

Amin, H. (1992). *Dadresi va nezame ghazeie iran.* [Judicial system in Iran]. Tehran: Daftareh Pazhohesh Publication.

Anand, V., Ashforth, B., & Joshi, M. (2004). Business as usual: The acceptance and perpetuation of corruption in organizations. *Academy of Management Executive, 18*(2), 39–53.

Anand, V., Ashforth, B., & Joshi, M. (2005). Business as usual: The acceptance and perpetuation of corruption within organisations. *Academy of Management Executive, 19*(4), 9–23. http://84.89.132.1/~lemenestrel/IMG/pdf/anand_et_al._ame_2004.pdf

Anckorn, J. (2015). *Judicial conduct investigations office*, Report 2014–15.

Arnaudovska, A. (2018). Understanding and combating judicial corruption. *Journal of Liberty and International Affairs, 4*(1), 115–124.

Arjomand, S. A. (1989). History, structure, and revolution in the Shi'ite tradition in contemporary Iran. *International Political Science Review, 10*(2), 111.

Arjomand, S. A., & Brown, N. J. (2013). *The rule of law, Islam, and constitutional politics in Egypt and Iran.* [electronic resource]. Albany, NY : State University of New York Press.

Arvidsson, A. (2010), *Corruption in the judiciary-balancing accountability and judicial independence.* Oslo: Orebro University.

Ashori, M. (2014). *Keshvar hanoz asar hazfe dadsar ra tahmol mikonad.* [adverse impact of elimination of Prosecutor Office. Isna. http://www.irna.ir/fa/News/81881794/

Asian Development Bank. (1998). *ADB's anticorruption policy.* Can be retrieved at: https://www.adb.org/sites/default/files/institutional-document/32026/anticorruption.pdf

Bahraeini, R., Nayyeri, M., & Sheeran, S. (2014). *Electoral process in Iran: Analysis of political participation and Iran's compliance with international human rights obligations.* University of Essex. https://www.essex.ac.uk/hri/documents/electoral-process-in-iran.pdf

Balogun, M. J. (2003). Causative and enabling factors in public integrity: A focus on leadership, institutions, and character formation. *Public Integrity, 5*(2), 127–147.

Barlowe, S. (2015). What's Islam got to do with it – obstacles in securing fair trial rights under Iran's repressive regime. *Cardozo Journal of International and Comparative Law*, (3), 601.

Basic Principles on the Role of Lawyers. (1999). Adopted by the Eighth United Nations Congress on the Prevention of Crime and the Treatment of Offenders, Havana, Cuba 27 August to 7 September 1990, can be retrieved at: www.ohchr.org/EN/ProfessionalInterest/Pages/RoleOfLawyers.aspx (accessed 31-03-2016).

Becker, G. S., & Stigler, G. J. (1974). Law enforcement, malfeasance, and compensation of enforcers. *Journal of Legal Studies, III*, 1–19.

Begovic, B. (2004). *Corruption in judiciary, Centre for Liberal -Democratic studies*, Belgrade, Retrieved from: pdc.ceu.hu/archive/00002541/01/Corruption_in_judiciary.pdf (Accessed 31-03-2016).

Belton, R. K. (2005). *Competing definitions of the rule of law: Implications for practitioners.* (2005). Carnegie Endowment for International Peace. Carnegie Endowment for International Peace (2005) Stable. https://www.jstor.org/stable/resrep12779

Bergstein, C. F., Gill, B., Lardy, N. R., & Mitchell, D. (2006). *China: The balance sheet, public affairs,* New York, p. 69.

Besley, T., & McLaren, J. (1993). Taxes and bribery: The role of wage incentives. *The Economic Journal, 103*(416), 119–141. https://doi.org/10.2307/2234340.

Bhattacharyya, S., & Hodler, R. (2015). Media freedom and democracy in the fight against corruption. *European Journal of Political Economy*, 3913–24. doi:10.1016/j.ejpoleco.2015.03.004.

Boroumand, L. (2012). *Iranian civil society NGOs and transitional justice what can be done before the transition? Legatum Institute.* Retrieved from: https://goo.gl/uzn8uD (accessed 03/04/2016).

Bracking, S. (2007). *Corruption and development: The anti-corruption campaigns.* Basingstoke: Palgrave Macmillan.

Brooke, R. (2002). *Judicial Independence* — Its History in England and Wales, The Right Honourable Lord Justice Brooke, can be retrieved at: www.judcom.nsw.gov.au/publications/education-monographs-1/monograph1/fbbrook.htm (accessed 31-03-2016).

Brooks, G., Walsh, D., Lewis, C., & Kim, H. (2013). *Preventing corruption: Investigation, enforcement and governance.* Basingstoke: Palgrave Macmillan.

Bryman, A. (2008). *Social research methods.* Oxford and New York: Oxford University Press.

Brytting, T., Minogue, R., & Morino, V. (2011). *The anatomy of fraud and corruption.* [electronic resource]: Organizational causes and remedies. Farnham, Surrey, England; Burlington, VT: Gower.

Burbank, B., & Friedman, B. (2002). *Judicial independence at the crossroads: An interdisciplinary approach.* Thousand Oaks, CA: Sage Publications Inc. Partially can be retrieved at: https://goo.gl/JJbJu3 (accessed 07-11-2016).

Buscaglia, E. (June 2000). An analysis of judicial corruption and its causes: An objective governing-based approach. *International Review of Law and Economics*, Elsevier, vol. 21(2), pages 233–249.

Buscaglia, E. (1999). *Judicial corruption in developing countries: Its causes and economic consequences. Hoover Institution.* Berkeley, CA: University of California.

Buscaglia, E., & Akolias, M. (1999). *An analysis of the causes of corruption in the judiciary.* The World Bank.

Butt, S., & Schütte, S. (2014). Assessing judicial performance in Indonesia: The court for corruption crimes. *Crime, Law & Social Change, 62*(5), 603–619. doi:10.1007/s10611-014-9547-1.

Button, M., & Tunley, M. (2016). *Criminal activity in the financial sector*, The Security Handbook Volume 2. Can be retrieved at: https://goo.gl/NAcFt8

Caiden, G. E., Dwivedi, O. P., & Jabbra, J. G. (2001). *Where corruption lives.* [electronic resource]. Bloomfield, CT: Kumarian Press.

Caiden, G., & Dwivedi, O. (2001). Official ethics and corruption. In G. Caiden, G. Dwivedi, & J. Jabbra (Eds.), *Where corruption lives.* Bloomfield: Kumarian Press.

Cameron, E. (2009). *The need for the independence of the judiciary and the legal profession'.* Ankara, Turkey.

Chang, J., & Liu, C. (2007). The negligence rule in the presence of judicial corruption and social norms. *Atlantic Economic Journal, 35*(2), 203–215.

Chemerinsky, E. (1989). Ideology, judicial selection and judicial ethics. *Georgetown Journal of Legal Ethics, 2*, 643–664. Available at: http://scholarship.law.duke.edu/cgi/viewcontent.cgi?article=2145&context=faculty_scholarship (accessed 31-03-2016).

Choo, K.-K. R. (2011). The cyber threat landscape: Challenges and future research directions. *Computers & Security, 30*(8), 719–731.

CIET international. (1996). *Service delivery survey, corruption in the police, judiciary, revenue.* New York, USA: UN Publishing.

Clarke, R. (1980). Situational crime prevention: Theory and practice. *British Journal of Criminology, 20*, 136–145.

Clarke, R. V. & Mayhew, P. (1989). Crime as opportunity. A note on domestic gas suicide in Britain and the Netherlands. *British Journal of Criminology, 29*(1), 35–46.

Cole, G. F., Frankowski, S., & Gertz, M. G. (1987). *Major criminal justice systems: A comparative survey.* Beverly Hills, CA: Sage.

Combat Corruption: The Role of the World Bank. World bank.

Cooter, R., & Garoupa, N. (2000). *A vicious circle of distrust: A mechanism to deter bribes.*

Council Regulation (EU) No 359/2011 of 12 April 2011, available at: www.eur-lex.europa.eu/legal-content/EN/TXT/PDF/?uri=CELEX:02011R0359-20140412&from=EN

Cress, R., Kent, C., & Nayyeri, M. (2014). *Rule of law in Iran.* University of Essex, retrieved from: https://www.essex.ac.uk/hri/documents/rule-of-law-in-Iran.pdf (accessed 31-03-2016).

Cressey, D. R. (1953). *Other people's money.* Montclair, NJ: Patterson Smith.

Croall, H. (2001). *Understanding white collar crime.* Buckingham: Open University Press.

Cross, F. (2003). Thoughts on goldilocks and judicial independence. *Ohio State Law Journal, 64*, 195.

Cumaraswamy, D. (2000). United Nations Commission on Human Rights, *Report of the Special Rapporteur on the independence of judges and lawyers,* Dato' Param.

Dahlstrom, R., & Nygaard, A. (1999). *Journal of Marketing Research, 36*(2), May 1999, 160–170.

Danilet, C. (2009). *Corruption and anti-corruption in the justice system.* Bucharest: EDITURA C.H. BECK.

De Graaf, G. (2007). Causes of corruption: Towards a contextual theory of corruption. *Public Administration Quarterly*, (1/2), 39.

De Lauri, A. (2013). Corruption, legal modernisation and judicial practice in Afghanistan. *Asian Studies Review, 37*(4), 527–545. doi:10.1080/10357823.2013.832112.

De Soto, H. (1989). *The Other path.* New York: Harper and Row.

Declaration on Independence and Impartiality of the Judiciary, Jurors and Assessors and the Independence of Lawyers, Commission on Human Rights Res. 2004/33 (19 April 2004).

Dobel, J. P. (1978). Corruption of a state. *American Political Science Review, 72*(3), 958–73.

Doeveren, V. (2011). Rethinking good governance. *Public Integrity, 13*, 4. 10.2753/PIN1099-9922130401.

Dorminey, J., Fleming, A. S., Kranacher, M., & Riley Jr., R. A. (2012). The evolution of Fraud theory. *Issues in Accounting Education, 27*(2), 555–579. doi:10.2308/iace-50131.

Dutta, N., & Roy, S. (2016). The interactive impact of press freedom and media reach on corruption. *Economic Modelling*, 58227–236. doi:10.1016/j.econmod.2016.05.008.

ECONOMICREFORM (2004). *Combating corruption: Private sector perspectives and solutions.* Can be retrieved at: web.archive.org/web/20110106181021/http://www.cipe.org/publications/papers/pdf/IP0409.pdf (Accessed 20-0902106).

ECOSOC 2006/23 Strengthening basic principles of judicial conduct, can be retrieved at:https://www.unodc.org/pdf/corruption/corruption_judicial_res_e.pdf (accessed 31-03-2016).

Entessar, N. (1998). Criminal law and the legal system in revolutionary Iran. *Boston College Third World Law Journal, 8,* Article 8.

Enayat, H. (2013). *Law, state, and society in modern Iran.* London: Palgrave Macmillan US.

Eric, C. (2010). The Supreme Court and the making of public policy in contemporary China. *The Michigan Journal of Public Affairs, 7,* Spring 2010. The University of Michigan. Can be retrieved at: http://mjpa.umich.edu/files/2014/06/2010-Ip-ChinaSupremeCourt.pdf

Esfandiari, G. (2012). *Report on Iran.* Freedom House.

European Commission For Democracy Through Law. (2009). *Report on the Rule of Law,* Study No. 512 / 2009, Strasbourg, 4 April 2011, Retrieved from: www.venice.coe.int/webforms/documents/default.aspx?pdffile=CDL-AD(2011)003rev-e (accessed 31-03-2016).

Fallah, H. (1998). Edalatkhaneh Dolati, Vezarat adlieh ya majles? [Judiciary, ministry of Justice, or Parliament?]. *Journal of Alzahrah University.* No 1. Serial 75. 1998.

Fars News (15/08/2013). "*Iranian Parliament Gives Vote of Confidence to Majority of Rouhani's Proposed Ministers*".

Faundez, J. (2012). *Judicial reform: Lessons from Latin America.* London: Legatum Institute.

Fehr, E., & Fischbacher, U. (2005). The economics of strong reciprocity. In H. Gintis, S. Bowles, R. Boyd, & Ernst Fehr (Eds.), *Moral sentiments and material interests. The foundations for cooperation in economic life* (pp. 151–193). Cambridge: MIT Press.

Feld, P., & Voigt, S. (2002). *Economic growth and judicial independence: Cross country evidence using a new set of indicators.* Germany: University of Marburg.

Felson, M., & Santos, R. B. (2010). *Crime and everyday life.* Thousand Oaks, CA: Sage Publications.

Ferrer, A. (2014). *Blind justice: A case for judiciary impartiality in the Philippine Supreme Court.* Can be retrieved at: https://goo.gl/Vq4hNQ (accessed 04/01/2016).

Fierro, M. (2010). The ʿulamāʾ. In *The new Cambridge history of Islam* (Vol. 2, pp. 679–704). Cambridge: Cambridge University Press.

Fijnaut, C. (2002). *Corruption, integrity and law enforcement.* Den Haag: Kluwer Law International.

Finn, J. E. (2004). The rule of law and judicial independence in newly democratic regimes. *The Good Society,* (3), 12.

Friedman, L. M. (1969). Legal culture and social development. *Law & Society Review, 4*(1), 29–44.

Friedman, L. (1994). Is there a modern legal culture?. *Ratio Juris, 7*(2), 117–131, July 1994, can be retired (partially): http://goo.gl/BkubCv (accessed 04/01/2016).

Frisky, L. (2016). Lost in Democracy: "An Analytical Inquest into Africa's Difficulties with Democracy and the Prospects of Finding Alternative Systems of Government That May Work Without Hitches." Bloomington, Indiana.

General Assembly resolutions 40/32, Basic Principles on the Independence of the Judiciary, (29 November 1985). Available from. https://www.ohchr.org/EN/ProfessionalInterest/Pages/IndependenceJudiciary.aspx

Geyh, C. (2008). Methods of judicial selection & their impact on judicial independence. *Daedalus, 137*(4), 86–101.

Geyh, C. (2014). The dimensions of judicial impartiality. *Fla. L. Rev., 65,* 493. Available at: http://scholarship.law.ufl.edu/flr/vol65/iss2/4

Geyh. C. (2014). *The dimensions of judicial impartiality.* Can be retrieved at: scholarship.law.ufl.edu/cgi/viewcontent.cgi?article=1138&context=flr

Ghaemi, H. (2006). *For Iran, the man is the message.* The New Your Times. 29 June 2006. Retrieved from: http://goo.gl/ntweQb (accessed 31-03-2016).

Ghazi, F. (2014). *In favor of Shahroodi: Details of the transaction.* Roozonline, Retrieved from: http://www.roozonline.com/persian/news/newsitem/article/-2d3930d4ee.html (accessed 31-03-2016).

Glenn, P. (2014). *Legal traditions of the world: Sustainable diversity in law.* Oxford University Press. Retrieved from (partially): https://goo.gl/X9TtwC (accessed 3-11-2015).

Gorta, A. (1998). Minimising corruption: Applying lessons from the crime prevention literature. *Crime, Law & Social Change, 30*(1), 67–87.

de Graaf, G. (2007). Causes of corruption: Towards a contextual theory of corruption. *Public Administration Quarterly, 31*(1), 39–86.

Guidelines on the Role of Prosecutors Adopted by the Eighth United Nations Congress on the Prevention of and the Treatment of Offenders, Havana, Cuba, 27 August to 7 September 1990, can be retrieved at: www.ohchr.org/EN/ProfessionalInterest/Pages/RoleOfProsecutors.aspx (accessed 31-03-2016).

Haghdar, A. (2011). *Tajadod hoghoghi dar iran* [Modernity and law in Iran]. Available at: http://cheragheazadi.org/index.php/archives/1782

Haghdar, A. (2016). *Tahvolat siasi in Iran.* [Political change in Iran] Istanbul: Adbiat Publication.

Hague, R., Harrop, M., & Breslin, S. (1998). *Comparative government and politics: An introduction* (4th ed.). Basingstoke: MacMillan.

Hakim, C. (1982). *Secondary analysis in social research: A guide to data sources and methods with examples.* London: Allen and Unwin.

Hancock, M. P., & Bradley, K. (2012), *UK Anti-corruption plan,* London, UK.

Hariri, N. (2000). *Ravesh hay asaasy pashoesh,* [research methods]. Tehran: Azad University Publication.

Heidensohn, F. (2004). Finding new frontiers to cross in criminology. In J. Winterdyk & L. Cao (Eds.), Lessons from international/comparative criminology/criminal justice (pp. 154–69). Willowdale, Canada: De Sitter.

Hill, J. (2010). Corruption in the courts: The Achilles' heel of Nigeria's regulatory framework?. *Third World Quarterly, 31*(7), 1161–1179. doi:10.1080/01436597.2010.518751.

Hirschi, T. (2002). *Causes of delinquency.* New Brunswick, NJ: Transaction Publishers.

Hobbes, T. (1998). *Hobbes: On the citizen.* Cambridge University Press, 20 Aug 1998.

Hoffmann, J. P. (2002). A contextual analysis of differential association, social control, and strain theories of delinquency. *Social Forces, 81*(3), 753–785.

Hough, D. (2013). *Corruption, anti-corruption and governance.* Basingstoke: Palgrave Macmillan.

Hughes, P. (2000). Judicial independence: Contemporary pressures and appropriate responses. *Can. B. Rev., 80,* 181 (2001) https://heinonline.org/HOL/LandingPage?handle=hein.journals/canbarev80&div=12&id=&page=

Human Rights Watch. (2015). *Ministers of murder: Iran's new security cabinet,* can be retrieved at: https://www.hrw.org/legacy/backgrounder/mena/iran1205/iran1205.pdf

Human Rights Watch. (2012) *Codifying repression an assessment of Iran's new penal code*, can be retrieved at: https://www.hrw.org/sites/default/files/reports/iran0812webwcover_0.pdf

Huntington, S. (1989). *Modernization and corruption. In political corruption. A handbook.* Heidenheimer, New Brunswick: Transaction Publishers, can be retrieved at: http://www.brandonkendhammer.com/pols340_winter2012/wp-content/uploads/2011/12/Political-Corruption-pp.-253-264.pdf (accessed 31-03-2016).

International Council on Human Rights Policy. (2007). *Corruption and human rights: Making the connection.* Versoix, Switzerland.

International transparency. (2007). *Global corruption report, corruption in judicial systems* (p. 22). Cambridge, United Kingdom: Cambridge University Press.

Ip, E. C. (2008). Judicial corruption and its threats, to National Governance in China. *JOAAG, 3*(1). joaag.com/uploads/8_IpFinal.pdf

Iran Human Rights Documentation Center. "*Haunted Memories: The Islamic Republic's Executions of Kurds in 1979*", Available at www.iranhrdc.org/english/publications/reports/3508-haunted-memories-the-islamic-republics-executions-of-kurds-in-1979.html?p=12 (accessed 31-03-2016).

Iran Human Rights Documentation Center. (2006). IHRDC Releases Report: *"Impunity in Iran: The Death of Zahra Kazemi"*, available at: www.iranhrdc.org/english/news/press-statements/3103-ihrdc-releases-report%3A-"impunity-in-iran%3A-the-death-of-zahra-kazemi".html (accessed 31-03-2016).

Iranian Parliament Research Centre. (2012). Gozaresh dar mored ghoveh ghazei. [report about judiciary]. Tehran: Parliament publication.

Ismail, A., & Rashid, K. (n.d.). Time series analysis of the nexus among corruption, political instability and judicial inefficiency in Pakistan. *Quality & Quantity, 48*(5), 2757–2771.

Jafaari langarodi, M. (1987). Daireh-al-moraefe eslami [Islamic encyclopedia], Tehran: Jamaran Publication.

Jahanbegloo, R. (2012). *Reflections on forgiveness and transitional justice in Iran.* London: Legatum Institute.

Jain, Arvind K. (2001). Corruption: A review. *Journal of Economic Surveys, 15*(1), 71–121.

James Hyre, *The United Kingdom's Declaration of Judicial Independence: Creating a Supreme Court to Secure Individual Rights Under the Human Rights Act of 1998 (2004).* Available at: http://ir.lawnet.fordham.edu/flr/vol73/iss1/14 (accessed 31-03-2016).

James, H. (2003). *The rule of law: 1603–1660, crowns, courts and judges.* New York: Pearson Education.

Johnson, R. A. (2004). *The struggle against corruption: A comparative study.* New York: Palgrave Macmillan.

Joseph, M., & Phillips, N. (2016). Judicial corruption in Haiti: The need for discipline and civil society participation. *Hastings International & Comparative Law Review, 39*(1), 183.

Juin-jen, C., & Chia-ying, L. (2007). *The negligence rule in the presence of judicial corruption and social norms. Atlantic Economic Journal, 35*(2), 203–215. doi:10.1007/s11293-007-9068-8.

Kaisaer, H. (1995). "*The Media And The Judiciary In The Democratic Process*". Dalhousie University. Can be retrieved from: cjei.org/publications/kaiser.html (accessed 04/01/2016).

Kar, M. (2012). *Who are the judges in the Islamic Republic of Iran.* London: Legatum Institute.

Karimian, R. (2009). Iranian Press Update. *Middle East Research and Information Project.*

Karklins, R. (2012). *Typology of post-communist corruption.* Budapest, Hungary: The Center for Policy Studies at the Central European University.

Kasravi, A. (1945). *Tarikhe-h- mashroteh- Iran.* [History of Persian constitutional revolution]. Tehran: Amirkabir Publication.

Kaufmann, D., Kraay, A., & Mastruzzi, M. (2010). The worldwide governance indicators: Methodology and analytical issues. World Bank.

Kaufmann, D., & Kraay, A. (2008). Governance indicators: Where are we, where should we be going? Oxford University Press. doi:10.1093/wbro/lkm012.

Kaufmann, D., Kraay, A., & Zoido-Lobato'n, P. (1999). "Aggregating Governance Indicators." Policy Research Working Paper 2195. Washington, DC: World Bank.

Kaufmann, D., Aart, K., & Lobatón, P. (1999). *Governance matters.* World Bank, retrieved from: https://goo.gl/h3Fs7V; (accessed 31-03-2016).

Kaufmann, D., Kraay, A., & Mastruzzi, M. (2006). *Measuring corruption: Myths and realities.* Washington, DC: The World Bank.

Kaufmann, D., Kraay, A., & Mastruzzi, M. (2009). *Governance matters VIII.* The World Bank Development Research Group Macroeconomics and Growth Team.

Kaufmann, D., Kraay, A., & Mastruzzi, M. (2010). *The worldwide governance indicators: Methodology and analytical issues.* World Bank Policy Research Working Paper No. 5430

Khandan, R. (2015, May 20).Soltani ra azad konid [Fee soltani]. Facebook. Retrieved from https://goo.gl/YVP0da

Khosravi, M. (2011). Hakemiat ghanon chist [Rule of Law, law as a norm]. Can be retrieved at: http://yasharparsa.com/?p=1670

King, R. D., & Wincup, E. (2008). *Doing research on crime and justice.* Oxford: Oxford University Press.

Klitgarrd, R. (2008). *A holistic approach to the fight against corruption.* The Second Session of the Conference of State Parties to the United Nations Convention against Anti-Corruption, can be retrieved at: www.cgu.edu/PDFFiles/Presidents%20Office/Holistic_Approach_1-08.pdf

Klerman, D., & Mahoney, P. (2005). The value of judicial independence: Evidence from eighteenth century England. *American Law and Economics Review, 7*(1), 1–37.

Klitgaard, R. (1988). *Controlling corruption.* Berkeley, CA: University of California Press.

Klitgaard, R. (1998). Combating corruption. *UN Chronicle, 35*(1), 90.

Klitgaard, R. (2006). Introduction: Subverting corruption. *Global Crime, 7*(3/4), 299–307. doi:10.1080/17440570601063724.

Knaul, G. (2012). Report from *The United Nations special Rapporteur on the independence of judges and lawyers,* Retrieved from: available at: http://www.ohchr.org/EN/NewsEvents/Pages/DisplayNews.aspx?NewsID=12692&LangID=E#sthash.198TkyID.dpuf (accessed 31-03-2016).

Kőhalmi, L., & Tóth, D. (2014). Judicial corruption - Quis custodiet costodes?. *Journal of Eastern European Criminal Law,* (2), 55–62.

Kohlbacher, F. (2005). The use of qualitative content analysis in case study research [89 paragraphs]. *Forum Qualitative Sozialforschung / Forum: Qualitative Social Research, 7*(1), Art. 21, http://nbn-resolving.de/urn:nbn:de:0114-fqs0601211.

Krippendorff, K. (1980). *Content analysis. An introduction to its methodology*. London: Sage Publications.

Kurkchiyan, M. (2007). *Judicial corruption in the context of legal culture*. In D. Rodriguez, & L. Ehrich (Eds.), *Global corruption report 2007*. Cambridge: Cambridge University Press.

Kurkchiyan, M. (2007). *Judicial corruption in the context of legal culture*. Berlin: Cambridge University Press.

La Porta, R., De Silanes, L., Eleches, C., & Sheleifer, A. (2004). Judicial checks and balances. *Journal of Political Economy, 112*(2), 445–470. https://doi.org/10.1086/381480.

La Porta, R., Florencio Lopez-de-Silanes, Shleifer, A., & Vishny, R. (1997). Trust in large organizations. *The American Economic Review, 87*(2), 333–338. Retrieved from http://www.jstor.org/stable/2950941

La Porta, R., Florencio, L., Shleifer, A., & Vishny, R. (1999). The quality of government. *Journal of Law, Economics, & Organization*, (1), 222.

Lahidji, K. (2012). *The history of the judiciary in Iran*. London: Legatum Institute.

Lambsdorff, J. (2002). Making corrupt deals- contracting in the shadow of the law. *Journal of Economic Behavior & Organization, 48* (2002), 222–241.

Lambsdorff, J. (2005). Consequences and causes of corruption: What do we know from a cross-section of countries? Passauer Diskussionspapiere - Volkswirtschaftliche Reihe, No. V-34-05 available at: http://hdl.handle.net/10419/55031

Lambsdorff, J., & Nell, M. (2007). *Fighting corruption with asymmetric penalties and leniency*. Discussion Papers, No. 59. Göttingen: University of Göttingen, Center for European, Governance and Economic Development Research (cege).

Lambsdorff, J. G. (2007). *The institutional economics of corruption and reform: Theory, evidence and policy*. Cambridge: Cambridge University Press.

Larijani, A. (2003). *Tasvieh mashroote peymane mobarezeb ba fesad* [Conditional approve of international convention about countering corruption]. Available at: rc.majlis.ir/fa/law/show/134837

Lawyers Committee For Human Rights (LCHR), The Justice System of the Islamic Republic of Iran. 1991 Retrieved from: iranrights.org/library/document/93/the-justice-system-of-the-islamic-republic-of-iran (accessed 31-03-2016).

Leiken, R. S. (1996–97). Controlling the global corruption epidemic. *Foreign Policy*, Winter 1996–97.

Le Seuer, A. (2012). *The Chief Justice of Malaysia addressing Commonwealth Lawyers Association* 'Judicial Accountability Workshop' in April 2002, cited by Andrew Le Seuer (n 75) 52.

Lessig, L. (2013). Foreword: "*Institutional corruption*" defined. *Journal of Law, Medicine and Ethics, 41*(3), 553–555. doi:10.1111/jlme.12063.

Levenstein, R. H., & Sisco, M. (2016). Crisis of knowledge: The importance of educating the public about the role of fair and impartial courts in our system of government. *Florida Bar Journal, 90*(5), 34–37.

Levi, M. (2003). The Roskill Fraud Commission revisited: An assessment. *Journal of Financial Crime, 1*, 38.

Li, L. (2012). The 'Production' of corruption in China's courts: Judicial politics and decision making in a one-party state. *Law & Social Inquiry, 37*(4), 848–877. doi:10.1111/j.1747-4469.2012.01285.x.

Lindstedt, C., & Naurin, D. (2010). Transparency is not Enough: Making Transparency Effective in Reducing Corruption (La transparence ne suffit pas: rendre la transparence efficace dans la lutte contre la corruption) (La transparencia no basta: Cómo crear una transparencia efectiva para reducir la corrupción). *International Political Science Review / Revue internationale de science politique*, (3), 301.

Locke, J., & Laslett, P. (2003). *Two treatises of government* (Student ed., Cambridge texts in the history of political thought). Cambridge: Cambridge University Press.

Lynch, T. D., & Lynch, C. E. (2003). Corruption, reform, and virtue ethics. *Public Administration Review, 63*(3), 370–371.

Macaulay, b. (1889). *The history of England from the accession of James the second.* Popular Edition in Two Volumes I. London: Longmans.

Macaulay, M. (2012). *Corruption in the UK.* London, UK: Teesside University and TI-UK.

Madani, J. (1980). *Zamaneh Journal.* Number 7 and 8.

Madison, J. (1788, February 1). *These departments should not be so far separated as to have no constitutional control over each other.* Retrieved from https://www.congress.gov/resources/display/content/The+Federalist+Papers#TheFederalistPapers-48

Manion, M. (2015). The challenge of corruption. In J. DeLisle & A. Goldstein (Eds.), *China's challenges* (pp. 125–138). University of Pennsylvania Press. Retrieved from http://www.jstor.org/stable/j.ctt9qh43f.9

Mashhadi, A. (2010). *Motaleh Tatbighi dar hoghoghe Iran* [Comparative study about jury role in Iran and other countries). Tehran: Research Center for citizen's right Publication.

Masoumi (P). (2015). *Killing history,* Retrieved from: https://en.iranwire.com/features/6353/ (accessed 31-03-2016).

Matsueda, R. L. (1982). Testing control theory and differential association: A causal modeling approach. *American Sociological Review*, 47(4), 489–504.

May, O. (2016). *Fighting Fraud and corruption in the humanitarian and global development sector.* Milton Park, Abingdon, Oxon: Routledge.

Mayne, G. (2007). Judicial integrity: The accountability gap and the Bangalore Principles. In D. Rodriguez & L. Ehrich (Eds.), *Global corruption report 2007.* Cambridge: Cambridge University Press.

Mayring, P. (2000). Qualitative content analysis. *Forum: Qualitative Social Research, 1*(2), 105–114. Retrieved from: http://www.qualitative-research.net/index.php/fqs/article/view/1089/2386 (accessed 31-03-2016).

Mayring, P. (2007). '*Qualitative Inhaltsanalyse*' [Qualitative Content Analysis] in Flick, Uwe; Kardorff, Ernst von; Steinke, Ines (Eds.), *Qualitative Forschung – Ein Handbuch.* Reinbek: Rowohlt Taschenbuch Verlag GmbH (Quoted from another research).

Mayring, P.(2014). *Qualitative content analysis: Theoretical foundation, basic procedures and software solution.* Klagenfurt, 2014. Retrieved from: https://goo.gl/Ll428y (accessed 31-03-2016).

McCormick, J., & Paterson, N. (2006). The threat posed by transnational political corruption to global commercial and development banking. *Journal of Financial Crime, 13*(2), 183–194.

Mcilwain, H. (1913). The tenure of English judges. *PoL. Sci. REV. 217, 218* (1913). Retrieved from: https://archive.org/details/jstor-1944895 (accessed 31-03-2016).

Medema, G., & Zerba, R. (1999). *The Coase theorem*, Retrieved from: encyclo.findlaw.com/0730book.pdf (accessed 28/03/2016).

Melton, J., & Ginsburg, T. (2014). *Does De Jure judicial independence really matter? A reevaluation of explanations for judicial.* (Coase-Sandor Institute for Law & Economics Working Paper No. 612, 2014).

Miller, W., Gradeland, T., & Koshechkina, Y. (2001). *A culture of corruption: Coping with government in post-communist Europe.* Budapest: Central European University Press. Can be retrieved partially at: https://goo.gl/XDdRWE (accessed 28/06/2016).

Modona, G. (2012). *External and internal aspects of the independence of the judiciary.* OECD: Proceedings of the Regional Seminar.

Mohseni, M. (2010, 2 August). *Ijade herasat.* [creating intelligence service] Mardomsalari newspaper. Can be retrieved at: http://goo.gl/omMyYb

Montesquieu, C. (1949). *The spirit of the laws* (Hafner library of classics; 9). New York: Hafner.

Morgan Shuster, W. (2013). *The strangling of Persia.* Redditch: Read Books Ltd.

Montinola, G., & Jackman, R. W. (2002). Sources of corruption: A cross country study. *British Journal of Political Science, 32*, 147–70.

Moschtaghi, R. (2010). *Rule of law in Iran, Freie university* (Berlin), retrieved from: www.wikis.fu-berlin.de/display/SBprojectrol/Iran (accessed 31-03-2016).

Musembi, C. (2007). *Gender and corruption in the administration of justice.* London: Cambridge University Press.

Nassiri, M. (1995). *Iran's judicial system after the revolution.* London: Legatum Institute.

Nelken, D. (2010). *Comparative criminal justice: Making sense of difference.* London: SAGE Publications Ltd.

Nelken, D. (2014). Thinking about legal culture. *Asian Journal of Law and Society, 1*(2), 255–274.

Newburn, T. (2002). Atlantic crossings: 'Policy transfer' and crime control in the USA and Britain. *Punishment & Society, 4*(2), 165–194. doi:10.1177/14624740222228536.

Newburn, T. (2013). *Criminology.* London : Routledge.

Nohlen, D. (2001). *"Iran": A data handbook.* I. Oxford: Oxford University Press.

Nyamu-Musembi, C. (2007). *Gender and corruption in the administration of justice.* In D. Rodriguez, & L. Ehrich (Eds.), *Global corruption report 2007.* Cambridge: Cambridge University Press.

O'Donnell, M. (2006). Post-conflict corruption: A rule of law agenda? *Official Journal of the European Union*, retrieved from: justice4iran.org/persian/wp-content/uploads/2014/08/First.EUSank1DL.pdf (accessed 31-03-2016).

Ohen, L. E., & Felson, M. (1979). Social change and crime rate trends: A routine activity approach. *American Sociological Review, 44*(4), 588–608.

Paldam, M. (2001). Corruption and religion add to the economic model. *Kyklos. 54.* (2/3), 383.

Pasquino, P. (2003). *Prolegomena to a theory of judicial power: The concept of judicial independence in theory and history.* Can be retrieved at: http://www.heinonline.org/HOL/Page?handle=hein.journals/lpict2&div=8 (accessed 07-11-2016)

Patton, M. Q. (2015). *Qualitative research & evaluation methods: Integrating theory and practice* (4th ed.). Los Angeles : SAGE.

Patton, Q. (2002). *Qualitative research and evaluation methods* (3rd ed.). Thousand Oaks, CA: Sage Publications.

Pimentel, D. (2014). Culture and the rule of law: Cautions for constitution-making. *Fordham Int. Law Journal, 37,* 101, retrieved from: www.fordhamilj.org/files/2014/04/Pimentel_FILJOnline.pdf (accessed 04/01/2016).

Popova, M. (2012). Why doesn't the Bulgarian judiciary prosecute corruption?. *Problems of Post-Communism, 59*(5), 35–49.

Powell, R. R. (2006). Evaluation research: An overview. *Library Trends, 55*(1), 102–120.

Punch, M. (2000). Police corruption and its prevention. *European Journal on Criminal Policy and Research, 8,* 301–324.

Rashmi, G., & Goodmark, L. (2015). *Comparative perspectives on gender violence.* Oxford University Press.

Rawls, J. (1971). *A theory of justice.* Oxford: Oxford University Press.

Rider, B. K. (1997). *Corruption: The enemy within.* London: Kluwer Law International.

Rios-Figueroa, J. (2012). Justice system institutions and corruption control: Evidence from Latin America. *Justice System Journal, 33*(2), 195–214.

Rizvi, M. A. (2012). Velayat-e-Faqih (Supreme Leader) and Iranian foreign policy: An historical analysis. *Strategic Analysis, 36*(1), 112. doi:10.1080/09700161.2012.628471.

Robertson, G. (2006). *Crimes against humanity: The struggle for global justice* (3rd ed.). London: Penguin.

Robertson, G. (2007). The media and judicial corruption. In D. Rodriguez & L. Ehrich (Eds.), *Global corruption report 2007.* Cambridge: Cambridge University Press.

Robertson, G. (2014). *Judicial independence: Some recent problems.* International Bar Association's Human Rights Institute (Ibahri); Thematic Papers No 4.

Rose-Ackerman, A. (2007). Judicial independence and corruption. In D. Rodriguez, & L. Ehrich (Eds.), *Global corruption report 2007.* Cambridge: Cambridge University Press.

Rose-Ackerman, S. (1999). *Corruption and government: Causes, consequences and reform.* Cambridge, United Kingdom: Cambridge University Press.

Rose-Ackerman, S. (1999). *Corruption and government: Causes, consequences, and reform.* Cambridge: Cambridge University Press.

Rose-Ackerman, S. (2001). *Political corruption and democratic structures.* In A. K. Jain (Ed.), *The political economy of corruption* (pp. 111–141). New York: Routledge.

Rose-Ackerman, S. (2004). *The challenge of poor governance and corruption.* Cambridge University Press.

Rose-Ackerman, S. (n.d). The pursuit of absolute integrity: How corruption control makes government ineffective – Anechiarico, F, Jacobs, J. B. *Journal of Policy Analysis and Management, 16*(4), 661–664.

Ross, I. (2016). *Exposing Fraud: Skills, process and practicalities.* Chichester: Wiley.

Rothstein, B. (2013). *Corruption and social trust: Why the fish rots from the head down. Social Research, 80*(4), 1009–1032.

Sabi, H. (2012). *Is there a future for Iran's judiciary?* London: Legatum Institute.

Sadjadpour, K. (2010). *The supreme leader. United States Institute of Peace the Iran Primer.* Retrieved from: iranprimer.usip.org/resource/supreme-leader

Saham, N. (2015, August 22). *Bazdasht moaven ghoveh ghazeio for rape* [Deputy of Iranian judiciary was arrested for rape]. AlArabia. Dubai. Retrieved from http://goo.gl/PpUuVo

Salehi, Z. (1993). Ertegha dar dastgah-e- ghaza [Promotion in the judiciary]. *Criminal Law Journal,* (1), 65–79.

Santiago Basabe-Serrano. (2013). Explaining judicial corruption in the courts of Chile, Peru and Ecuador. *Perfiles Latinoamericanos, 21*(42), 79–108.

Scott, R. (1995). *Institutions and organizations.* Thousand Oaks: SAGE.

Seligson, M. (2001). Corruption and democratization: What is to be done? *Public Integrity, 3*(3), 221–241. https://doi.org/10.1080/15580989.2001.11770873.

Sen, A. (2000). '*What Is the Role of Legal And Judicial Reform In The Development Process?*' Speech delivered at the World Bank Conference on Legal and Judicial Reform. http://www1.worldbank.org/publicsector/legal/legalandjudicail.pdf (accessed 04/01/2016).

Senior, I. (2006). *Corruption: The world's big C: Cases, causes, consequences, cures.* London: Institute of Economic Affairs.

Shah, A. (2006). *Corruption and Decentralized Public Governance. World Bank Policy Research Working Paper No. 3824.* Retrieved from: http://ssrn.com/abstract=877331 (accessed 31-03-2016).

Shah. A. (2007). *Tailoring the fight against corruption to country circumstances.* Washington: The World Bank.

Shahroodi, M. (no date). *Elme- ghazi* [Judge's knowledge]. Tehran: Adlieh publication. Available at: https://goo.gl/WN9D6M

Shahrooz, K. (2007). With revolutionary rage and rancor: A preliminary report on the 1988 Massacre of Iran's political prisoners. *Harvard Human Rights Journal,* 20227–261.

Shea, N. (2009). *"Insulting Islam": One Way Street in the Wrong Direction.* http://www.hudsonny.org/2009/01/insulting-islam-one-way-street-in-the-wrong-direction.php

Shepherd, R., Barnett, J., Cooper, H., Coyle, A., Moran-Ellis, J., Senior, V., & Walton, C. (2007). Towards an understanding of British public attitudes concerning human cloning. *Social Science & Medicine, 65*(2), 337, (Accessed 31-03-2016). doi:10.1016/j.socscimed.2007.03.018.

Sherrill, C. W. (2011). After Khamenei: Who will succeed Iran's supreme leader? *Orbis,* 55631–647. doi:10.1016/j.orbis.2011.07.002.

Shihatam, I. (1997). Corruption-A general review with an emphasis on the role of the World Bank. *Penn State International Law Review, 15*(3), Article 2. Available at: http://elibrary.law.psu.edu/psilr/vol15/iss3/2

Siegel, L. J., & McCormick, C. (2006). *Criminology in Canada: Theories, patterns, and typologies* (3rd ed.). Toronto: Thompson.

Silverman, D. (2006). *Interpreting qualitative data: Methods for analyzing talk, text and interaction.* London: SAGE.

Silverman, D. (2014). *Interpreting qualitative data.* Los Angeles: SAGE.

Situngkir, H. (2011). *The structural dynamics of corruption-artificial society approach.* Bandung Fe Institute. retrieved from: https://arxiv.org/ftp/nlin/papers/0403/0403042.pdf

Slapper, G. (2015). *Judicial delinquency. Journal of Criminal Law, 79*(2), 73–75. doi:10.1177/0022018315573104.

Smith, G. (2011). *Studying fraud as white collar crime.* Basingstoke : Palgrave Macmillan.

Stephen, B., & Friedman, (B) (2002). *Judicial independence at the crossroads: An interdisciplinary approach.* California: Sage Publications.

Stolpe, O. (2000). *Strengthening judicial integrity against corruption.* NY, USA: UN Publication.

Strauss, A., & Corbin, J. (1990). *Basics of qualitative research: Grounded theory procedures and techniques.* Newbury Park, London, New Delhi: Sage Publications, Inc.

Sullivan, J. D., & Shkolnikov, A. (2004). *Combating corruption: Private sector perspectives and solutions.* Washington, DC: CIPE. Retrieved 26/11/2016, from: https://goo.gl/kvASCm

Sutherland, E. (1939). *Principles of criminology.* Philadelphia: Lippincott.

Sutherland, E. (1940). White-collar criminality. *American Sociological Review, 5*, 1–12.

Swamy, A., Knack, S., Lee, Y., & Azfar, O. (2001). Gender and corruption. *Journal of Development Economics*, 6425–55. doi:10.1016/S0304-3878(00)00123-1.

Tanzi, V. (1998). Corruption around the world: Causes, consequences, scope, and cures. *IMF Staff Papers, 45*(4), 559–594. International Monetary Fund.

Tavasolian, N. (2016). *Fasedtarin bakhsheh ghoveh ghazei* [Most corrupt part of the Iranian judiciary]. IranWire, available at: https://iranwire.com/fa/features/4020

Tavassolian, N. (2012). *Reform within the judiciary of Iran.* London: Legatum Institute.

Teorell, J. (2007). *Corruption as an institution: Rethinking the nature and origins of the grabbing hand.* Göteborg University. Retrieved from: www.qog.pol.gu.se/digitalAssets/1350/1350653_2007_5_teorell.pdf (accessed 04/01/2016).

The Abdorrahman Boroumand Foundation. (1993). *Independence of judges and lawyers.* Retrieved from: https://iranrights.org/library/document/93/the-justice-system-of-the-islamic-republic-of-iran (accessed 31-03-2016).

The International Covenant on Civil and Political Rights (ICCPR), adopted by the United Nations General Assembly on 16 December 1966, can be retrieved at: https://treaties.un.org/doc/Publication/UNTS/Volume%20999/volume-999-I-14668-English.pdf (accessed 31-03-2016).

The World Bank. (1997*). Helping countries combat corruption the role of the World Bank.* Retrieved from: www1.worldbank.org/publicsector/anticorrupt/corruptn/corrptn.pdf (accessed 31-03-2016).

The World Justice Project. (2015). WJP Rule of Law Index 2015.

Thomas, P. (2011). Different responses to judicial corruption: The South African common law. *Fundamina*, (2), 139.

Thompson, D. (1995). *Ethics in congress: From individual to institutional corruption.* Washington, DC: Brookings Institutions.

Thompson, S. (2013). *Two Concepts of Corruption* (August 1, 2013). Edmond J. Safra Working Papers, No. 16. Available at SSRN: https://ssrn.com/abstract=2304419 or http://dx.doi.org/10.2139/ssrn.2304419

Thoumi, F. E. (1987). Some implications of the growth of the underground economy in Colombia. *Journal of Interamerican Studies and World Affairs*, (2), 35.

Transparency International. (2014). *Corruption Perceptions Index 2014*. Retrieved March 1, 2017, from https://www.transparency.org/cpi2014/results

Transparency International. (2007). Executive summary: key judicial corruption problems. In D. Rodriguez, & L. Ehrich (Eds.), *Global corruption report 2007*. Cambridge: Cambridge University Press.

Transparency International. (2007). *Global corruption report 2007*. Berlin: Cambridge University Press.

Transparency International. Toolkit. (2007). *Combating corruption in judicial systems advocacy toolkit*, transparency international. Berlin: Cambridge University Press.

Treisman, D. (2000). The causes of corruption: A cross-national study. *Journal of Public Economics*, 76399–457. doi:10.1016/S0047-2727(99)00092-4.

Trochev, A. (2010). Meddling with justice. *Demokratizatsiya*, *18*(2), 122–147.

Tsunga, A., & Deya, D. (2007). *Lawyers and corruption: A view from East and Southern Africa*. In D. Rodriguez, & L. Ehrich (Eds.), *Global corruption report 2007*. Cambridge: Cambridge University Press.

Tsunga, R., & Deya, D. (2007). *Lawyers and corruption: A view from East and Southern Africa*. Cambridge: Cambridge University Press.

U.S Agency for International Development. (2009). *Reducing corruption in the judiciary office of democracy and governance usaid program brief*. Washington, USA.

UN Secretary General. (2004). *Report on the Rule of Law and Transitional Justice in Conflict and Post-conflict Societies*. Retrieved from: http://www.ipu.org/splz-e/unga07/law.pdf (accessed 31-03-2016).

United Nations Convention Against Corruption. (2003). Can be retrieved at: https://www.unodc.org/documents/treaties/UNCAC/Publications/Convention/08-50026_E.pdf (accessed 31-03-2016).

United Nations Office on Drugs and Crime. (2004). The Global Program Against Corruption, Un Anti-Corruption Toolkit, 2004. The Netherlands, available from https://www.unodc.org/documents/corruption/Toolkit_ed2.pdf (Accessed 31-03-2016).

van Koppen, M. V., de Poot, C. J., & Blokland, A. A. J. (2010). Comparing criminal careers of organized crime offenders and general offenders. *European Journal of Criminology*, *7*(5), 356–374. doi:10.1177/1477370810373730.

Vanderbilt, A. (1954). *Challenge of law reform*. New Jersey: Princeton University Press.

Vijayan, K. (2007). "*Payout Fight Over 'Biased Judiciary' Rejected: Firm's Final Bid to Canada's Highest Court Fails, so S'pore Court Judgment Stands*", The Straits Times (27 January 2007).

Vile, M. J. C. (1998). '*Constitutionalism and the separation of powers*', Liberty Fund Indianapolis.

Voigt, S. (2008). The economic effects of judicial accountability: Cross-country evidence. *European Journal of Law & Economics, 25*(2), 95. doi:10.1007/s10657-007-9035-5.

Voigt, S., & Gutmann, J. (2015). On the wrong side of the law – Causes and consequences of a corrupt judiciary. International Review Of Law & Economics, 43156–166. doi:10.1016/j.irle.2014.04.005.

Voigt, S., & Gutmann, J. (2015). On the wrong side of the law – Causes and consequences of a corrupt judiciary. *International Review of Law and Economics*, 156.

Wang, Y. (2013). Court funding and judicial corruption in China. *The China Journal*, *69*(1), 43–63.

Webster, R. (2002). *Sectoral perspectives on corruption. Corruption and the private sector.* Retrieved 26/11/2016, from: https://goo.gl/lB2KOc

Wendel, W. B. (2011). The behavioral psychology of judicial corruption: A response to judge Irwin and Daniel Real. *Mcgeorge Law Review, 42*(1), 35–46.

Wilfrie, B. (2000). *Who rules Iran?: The structure of power in the Islamic Republic.* Washington, DC: The Washington Inst. for Near East Policy ISBN 0-944029-39-6.

Wilson, J. Q., & Kelling, G. L. (1982). Broken windows: The police and neighborhood safety. *Atlantic Monthly, 211*, 29–38.

Wilson, J. (1968). *Corruption is not always scandalous.* New York Times Magazine, April 28,

Wolfe, D. T., & Hermanson, D. R. (2004). The Fraud diamond: Considering the four elements of Fraud. *CPA Journal, 74*(12), 38–42.

World Bank. (1997). *Combat corruption.* Poverty Reduction and Economic Management, Helping Countries.

World Justice Project. (2016). Rule of Law Index 2016. Available at: https://worldjusticeproject.org/sites/default/files/documents/RoLI_Final-Digital_0.pdf

Yar, M. (2005). The novelty of 'Cybercrime': An assessment in light of routine activity theory. *European Journal of Criminology, 2*(4), 407–427.

Zamiran, M., & Ebadi, Sh. (1996). *Sonnat and tajadod dar hoghogh-e-iran.* [traditions and modernity in Iranian law]. Tenran: Ganj Publication.

Zedner, L. (1995). *Comparative research in criminal justice.* In L. Noaks, M. Levi, & M. Maguire (Eds.), *Contemporary issues in criminology* (pp. 8–25). Cardiff: University of Wales Press.

Zhilla, F. (2011). Organised crime and judicial corruption in the Western Balkans: Are customary norms playing any role?. *Journal of Financial Crime, 18*(4), 387–404. doi:10.1108/13590791111173713.

Zhong, N. (2010). *The causes, consequences, and cures of corruption: A review of issues.* Department of Finance, Hong Kong University of Science and Technology.

Zimberlman, F. M., Albrecht, C. C., Albrecht, S. W., & Albrecht, O. C. (2012). *Forensic accounting* (4th ed.). South Western: Cengage Learning.

Zyglidopoulos, S. C., Fleming, P. J., & Rothenberg. (2009). Rationalization, overcompensation and the escalation of corruption in organizations. *Journal of Business Ethics January 2009*, 84(Supplement 1), 65–73. doi:10.1007/s10551-008-9685-4.

www.ingramcontent.com/pod-product-compliance
Ingram Content Group UK Ltd.
Pitfield, Milton Keynes, MK11 3LW, UK
UKHW021827100926
8556IPUK00003B/201